Creating Business Agility

HOW CONVERGENCE OF CLOUD, SOCIAL, MOBILE, VIDEO, AND BIG DATA ENABLES COMPETITIVE ADVANTAGE

Rodney Heisterberg

Alakh Verma

WILEY

Cover Design: C. Wallace
Cover Photograph: Sparkling Network Connection
© iStockphoto/Jamie Farrant

Published by John Wiley & Sons, Inc., Hoboken, New Jersey.
Published simultaneously in Canada.

Limit of Liability/Disclaimer of Warranty: While the publisher and author have used their best efforts in preparing this book, they make no representations or warranties with respect to the accuracy or completeness of the contents of this book and specifically disclaim any implied warranties of merchantability or fitness for a particular purpose. No warranty may be created or extended by sales representatives or written sales materials. The advice and strategies contained herein may not be suitable for your situation. You should consult with a professional where appropriate. Neither the publisher nor author shall be liable for any loss of profit or any other commercial damages, including but not limited to special, incidental, consequential, or other damages.

For general information on our other products and services or for technical support, please contact our Customer Care Department within the United States at (800) 762-2974, outside the United States at (317) 572-3993 or fax (317) 572-4002.

Wiley publishes in a variety of print and electronic formats and by print-on-demand. Some material included with standard print versions of this book may not be included in e-books or in print-on-demand. If this book refers to media such as a CD or DVD that is not included in the version you purchased, you may download this material at http://booksupport.wiley.com. For more information about Wiley products, visit www.wiley.com.

Library of Congress Cataloging-in-Publication Data

Heisterberg, Rodney J.
  Creating business agility : how convergence of cloud, social, mobile, video, and big data enables competitive advantage / Rodney Heisterberg, Alakh Verma.
        1 online resource.
    Includes index.
      Description based on print version record and CIP data provided by publisher; resource not viewed.
ISBN 978-1-118-72456-9 (hardback); ISBN 978-1-118-86931-4 (ebk); ISBN 978-1-118-86945-1 (ebk)
1. Technological innovations–Management. 2.   Information technology–Management.
3. Organizational effectiveness. 4. Strategic planning. I. Verma, Alakh,
1963- II. Title.
  HD45
  004.68–dc23   2014018188

Printed in the United States of America

10 9 8 7 6 5 4 3 2 1

I humbly dedicate this book to my parents, without their blessings I could not have reached this stage; to my lovely wife, Kavita, who constantly motivated and supported me; and to my children, Akshay and Akshita, who always encouraged me in all my endeavors.

In addition, I also dedicate this book to my academic mentors and colleagues at Oracle who have helped and nurtured throughout its lifecycle of ideas to completion.

—Alakh Verma

To Claire: my partner, my best friend, and my love of all the years. Your patience and passion makes the world fun!

—Rodney Heisterberg

Contents

x   Contents

Foreword: How to Survive in the Jungle

During the dot-com era, analysts and executives worried constantly about being "Amazoned": the swift and effective way incumbents were being eliminated by Amazon.com's massive inventory, low pricing, and great service every time the e-commerce pioneer entered a new market.

Fifteen years later: No industry is safe. Every sector has comfortable market leaders that have been attacked by a new tech-driven competitor. Witness Tesla in the auto space, Salesforce.com in the software world, and even Amazon's own Redshift in data storage.

Indeed, today's business world is a jungle. Incumbents must adapt to survive in this ecosystem. Only the smartest, most nimble players will stay alive.

We are entering yet another new paradigm for business computing. The challenge is to embrace and leverage the massive technological convergence that is taking place **right now**. Consider the combined impact of these developments:

1. **Cloud computing:** In November 2013, more than 100,000 people attended Salesforce.com's Dreamforce conference. That's equivalent to the attendance of enterprise software's two established shows: Oracle's Open World and SAP's Sapphire. Beyond being a testament to Salesforce's *current* popularity, Dreamforce attendance points to where businesses want to be in the *future*—and that's in the cloud.

2. **Mobile:** Be it a smart phone, tablet, or laptop, corporate citizens must be able to access all company information wherever they are, from whichever device they chose. This mobile power presents productivity opportunities—and security threats.

3. **Social media:** There's no doubt savvy companies know the power of Facebook, Twitter, Pinterest, and the countless other social media platforms on which customers and competitors are active—but do they know what to do about it? The integration of social media into corporate computing is critical to reach consumers in the next era.

4. **Video:** The preference of video content has expanded far beyond the boundaries of YouTube. Where social media is responsible for the proliferation of video communication, businesses are now leveraging video in all types of corporate applications making it an increasingly important part of the enterprise IT landscape.

5. **Big data:** Enterprises now capture terabytes-worth of data about customers, prospects, products, vendors, and competitors. But today, most of this intelligence sits unused in silos. Very soon, all of the data from internal and external systems will combine to form a business intelligence engine that will deliver a competitive advantage to the companies who use it best.

These five technological developments are converging to change the engines of modern business. Consider the "Internet of Things" (IoT) taking shape now. Gartner predicts the IoT will connect 26 billion everyday objects by 2020. While manufacturing and healthcare are leading the way, all industries are working rapidly to deploy ways to communicate with their products in order to understand and optimize their usage.

To stay alive, companies must fundamentally change how they operate. It is critical that executives manage in a way that takes advantage of these amazing technological advances by changing business processes, offering new products and solutions—in essence, operating in a completely different way than ever before.

The bottom line? Surviving in today's business jungle takes agility.

In this book, *Creating Business Agility*, Rodney Heisterberg and Alakh Verma provide real-world cases that illustrate how today's companies can avoid getting Amazoned by incorporating next-generation technology in their strategic plans—and learn to thrive in the jungle.

—M.R. Rangaswami
Founder, Sand Hill Group
Publisher SandHill.com

Preface

Problem: The key problem is that our business environment is changing—changing at an ever-faster pace. Now the only thing constant is change; with a higher frequency since the Internet as disruptive innovation became a fundamental of the business world. Yet human behavioral changes always happen more slowly than the technological changes that spawn them.

In order to see ahead, it's useful to look back 20 years across five stages of the first generation of revolutionary business practices:

1. E-commerce along the information superhighway
2. E-business in the dot-com era
3. Collaborative commerce by virtual enterprises at the turn of the twenty-first century
4. Social business evolution of Web 2.0 over the past decade
5. Business ecosystems as a twenty-first-century business model of a digital business

A *digital business* consists of a set of digital stakeholder relationships. They empower employees and engage trading partners to form a *virtual enterprise.* The digital businesses operate separately along with social business practices and processes. Today, a customer-focused digital business model leverages stakeholder relationships using digital collaboration channels in their virtual enterprise to deliver a great customer experience that will produce a market leader. Yet the only way to sustain their competitive advantage is for digital businesses to sense changes in their *business ecosystem,* and then adapt their plans based on predictions of how these insights will produce customer delight and advocacy. A discussion of these agile business practices in Chapter 1 provides a context for this new way of doing business—digitally.

Even as these stages have progressed rapidly over the past 20 years, the enabling technologies have changed more quickly. Information technology (IT) evolution is now measured in terms of "Internet time" as fourth-generation hardware, software, and network system technologies are deployed. Ubiquitous access to information at any time, in any place, and in any way is expected as a routine practice that provides a state of presence that drives personal experience delivery as the new normal of customer service.

The basis of business competition evolved from product-centered financial assets to customer-centered information assets. This business model paradigm shift has moved away from "past is prelude" thinking characterized by business-as-usual planning. With this traditional practice, extrapolation of strategy plans is based on assumptions that the future will continue like the past, with historical time-series sales forecasting and static regression analysis models. Now best practices lead to outside-the-box thinking. This is reflected by scenario-based planning that anticipates change via adaptive sense-and-respond business intelligence processes, real-time customer-facing decision support, and dynamic simulation analytic models.

Business agility produces a sustainable competitive advantage and is the goal for next-generation digital businesses. We define business agility as *innovation via collaboration to be able to anticipate challenges and opportunities before they occur.* This definition is made actionable as a business practice by incorporating a holistic performance management system using a balanced scorecard for the business ecosystem as a whole. This is enhancing the balance sheet with the balanced scorecard. In Chapter 1 we elaborate on this approach in terms of how the concept of a business ecosystem provides a model for sustainable competitive advantage. This ecosystem approach works by leveraging collaborative commerce synergy with "coopetition."

Such actionable use cases and scenarios, when combined with proven conceptual frameworks and including insightful research, create a forum to understand the ways of putting these ideas into practice. This research draws from both our own primary sources as well as secondary sources via key thought leaders. From our IT outpost here in Silicon Valley, we'll bring you what's happening with the "next big thing"—utilizing the convergence of a decade's worth of technological advancement in low-cost, efficient computing power to extract action-able information from large data sets.

Challenges and Opportunities: The challenges and opportunities resulting from these evolving digital business models have generated a "perfect storm" for *creating business agility*. The convergence of cloud, social, mobile, and big data is synergistic—where the power of the whole is greater than the sum of the parts. The transformative nature of a digital environment has not only caused the nature of business competition to change, but it has also changed the fundamental business value-creation processes and measures of performance. We explore this convergence in more detail in Chapter 2 and add video as a fifth force of the perfect storm that is powerfully transforming the way businesses relate to and engage their customers via technology.

Throughout this book we take a use-case approach via a technology–industry–applications framework reflected in this three-dimensioned collection of practical examples.

1. Technology—how the Force 5 Tornado spawned by a perfect storm creates a rainbow that leads to a pot of gold.

The convergence of cloud, social, mobile, video, and big data provides synergy for determining what the vision, mission, and strategy of the next generation of digital businesses is using in collaboration internally to align functional resources and externally to leverage trading partner capabilities with compatible core compe-tencies. In this manner we can use the digital business value chain to develop a market-leading ecosystem where the power of the whole is greater than the sum of the parts.

2. Industry—travel and sports scenario planning examples.

People are familiar with the global travel industry and interna-tional sports events from their personal experience, so these exam-ples provide an entertaining way to tell compelling stories about creating business agility. Travel generated over one billion tourist experiences last year, according to Elizabeth Becker, author of *Over-booked* (Simon & Schuster, 2013). It is the number one economic development engine of the biggest business sector in the world economy. The nature of sports as a universal human activity provides the team metaphor for collaboration enabling agility for competitive advantage.

The story of how the Kauai Marriott Resort and Beach Club formed a business ecosystem to enable the success of its new hospitality venture provides an insider's look at building a virtual enterprise. Such insights demonstrate how digital business teams may leverage their understanding of these converging technologies to share their intellectual capital in order to fulfill the expectations of their trading partner community.

With the "Selling Sonoma County Wine Country" use case scenario, we feature an integrated case study of Sonoma County Tourism's Sneakaway marketing campaign to illustrate key concepts of business agility readiness described in each chapter. These insights focus on how CXO teams (the chiefs of business functions and units) may leverage their understanding of these converging technologies to create business agility in terms of innovation via a collaborative culture that mitigates risk by celebrating failures as lessons learned in order to drive future success.

Use cases from the world of sports are led by the latest competition for the oldest trophy in international sports. The story of how ORACLE TEAM USA harnessed the perfect storm of this Force 5 Tornado to propel the greatest comeback in sports history illustrates the business value of IT in creating the agility to produce a sustainable competitive advantage.

3. Applications—CIO and CMO business value using big data.

Featured along the applications dimension is the marketing function in general, with a specific focus of the framework on the relationship between the chief marketing officer (CMO) and the chief information officer (CIO) in delivering the business value of IT. The best practices for both the CIO and the CMO in terms of digital business management are viewed through the lens of business agility readiness.

Use cases presented are in conjunction with the "CMO-CIO Partnership for Collaborative Marketing Agility" scenario. This business value theme is developed using a strategy of innovation for CMO-CIO alignment around big data analytics based on collaborative marketing best practices. A Business Agility Readiness Roadmap is presented using a balanced scorecard to describe and measure the alignment gap. Such a tool may be used to assess how to best vet the internal/external collaboration activities associated with management of big data for driving predictive analytics. This is a critical success factor in managing the digital business for competitive advantage of the business ecosystem as a whole.

Solution: The solution to build a next-gen digital business is business ecosystem integration. Our approach was created by utilizing the two fundamental elements of virtual enterprise information systems engineering:

1. Ecosystem Hub architecture that employs the Force 5 Tornado technologies using collaborative commerce concepts
2. Ecosystem implementation roadmap that is a model for digital business evolution using business agility readiness gap analysis concepts

The collaborative commerce architecture is described throughout the book with use case scenarios from the ubiquitous global multi-trillion-dollar travel industry to provide clear examples to demonstrate the "what-why-how" story. Such familiar scenarios use a virtual enterprise integration methodology that is illustrated by a virtual Visitor Information Center platform as an ecosystem hub that is developed using an iterative incremental implementation roadmap.

Lessons Learned: What are the lessons learned from this accelerating pace of information technology disruption that has created a climate of innovation further multiplied by the convergence of those same technologies? The global consumerization of IT and the resulting "bring your own device" (BYOD) phenomenon in the business world are driving the winds of change—generating the perfect storm of technology convergence with cloud, social, mobile, video, and big data acting like a Force 5 Tornado disrupting the business playing field.

In the context of the disruptive technology metaphor, enterprises that are forward-looking can harness this disruptive power to their advantage via big data with predictive analytics in order to:

- Produce early warnings to strengthen infrastructure via the cloud.
- Collaborate for real-time problem solving in their communities via social networks.
- Communicate vital decision-making information to the right people, places, and times via mobility solutions.
- Provide interactive messages for alerts and instructional information via videos.

By developing readiness for creating business agility and harnessing the five technological forces that have converged in our present business environment, market leaders will transform the Force 5 Tornado spawned by this perfect storm into a coherent pattern of light, creating a rainbow that leads to a pot of gold—achieving success.

Innovators will change the way they do business as they develop customer-centric business models to compete as a collaborative ecosystem. Such digital businesses will use this technological tornado to reengineer their decision-making processes with embedded predictive big data analytics to create valuable customer insights that deliver compelling customer experiences. This strategy will enable a new generation of market share leaders to produce a sustainable competitive advantage.

In the spirit of putting the data back into data processing, we have created a business agility data model that describes how this convergence enables building next-generation digital businesses. In doing so we have extended the conventional cloud, social, mobile technology conversation to reflect predictive big data analytics and include video as shared content for internal/external collaboration with customer co-creation. This data model provides the context for the content in the following chapters in order to describe an actionable Business Agility Readiness Roadmap in terms of people, processes, and technology that is integrated by data.

Next Steps: Taking the next steps on the journey to create business agility requires the understanding of how sense-and-respond information management strategies facilitate executing adaptive business strategies, as well as the courage to lead the change management initiatives necessary to transform internal processes and external relationships. Fundamental to this transformation is to reengineer the decision-making processes in order to make better resource allocation decisions. This requires the capability to sense business ecosystem signals that are key performance indicators, and respond with customer insights using predictive analytics. This creates business agility and when paired with a culture of customer experience management produces a sustainable competitive advantage.

The purpose of this book is to facilitate the translation of technical issues to business people and business issues to technical people so that they can collaborate to improve the competitive advantage of their business ecosystems, as well as contribute to the quality of life in our global marketplace. The target audience is the CXO team and their direct reports and staff in general, with special focus on establishing and strengthening the CMO-CIO partnership as an example of game-changing collaboration.

The strategic themes of the book focus on how the convergence of cloud, social, mobile, and video technologies with predictive big data analytics can produce sustainable business value. Chapters are organized to curate a compelling story about how this perfect storm of technology is creating business agility for market leaders. They are developing a competitive advantage via enabling the next generation of digital businesses to build sustainable ecosystems around the cultivation and harvesting of big data as a "whole product" solution. These themes explain how this convergence works in terms of the classic input-process-output model of a data processing system expressed as data-driven discovery processes feeding predictive analytics engines to produce insightful fact-based decisions while being mindful of garbage in, garbage out traps.

In writing this book, we take a business ecosystem point of view for developing digital business architecture. And we frame the twenty-first-century business value of IT in terms of business agility while relying on other sources as references for the construction details in the hands-on processes of doing the building itself. Many books have already been written about the cloud, business analytics, and social, mobile, and video technologies as separate topics in great detail. This book is written to satisfy the market need to integrate key concepts for digital business as a 360-degree transformation in terms of customer-centric strategy, customer-focused processes, and customer-facing apps.

This architectural view of a business ecosystem is reflected by the following list of the book's contents, which provides a preview of the technology convergence impact as highlights of a roadmap for business agility readiness:

Chapter 1 Bridging the Digital Divide

Chapter 2 Disruptive and Evolving Business Model

Chapter 3 Hyperconnectivity Drives Innovation

Chapter 4 Breaking the Barrier of Physical Infrastructure

Chapter 5 Power of Collaborative Management

Chapter 6 Mobility Drives Agility

Chapter 7 Listening to the Voices

Each chapter is structured to first feature a deep discussion of the key concepts and is illustrated by use cases to provide a broad view of their general applicability. The collection of use cases in each chapter features examples of best practices from industries such as travel, health care, education, and financial services, as well as expert insights in context with the technology–industry–applications framework.

At the end of the book, the Epilogue describes a use scenario about *Selling Sonoma County Wine Country*. It features an illustrative example of how a digital business can employ these concepts to create business agility. This travel destination and event industry scenario of a collaborative marketing campaign provides the context for an Ecosystem Hub implementation story that shows how to make it all work at the virtual enterprise level within the business ecosystem. This Business Agility Readiness roadmap is expressed in terms of people, processes, and technology that are integrated by data. The roadmap is keyed to the respective business, applications, and technology levels of the Ecosystem Hub architecture.

We intend to evolve this book with a clear, concise, and compelling story of "ecosystemism" as the driver of business agility for a game-changing strategy. We hope that your reading experience provides the understanding to be able to ask the right questions, as well as to provide some important answers.

CHAPTER 1

Bridging the Digital Divide

The world of business is changing more broadly, deeply, and rapidly than ever before. As the global marketplace has been flattened by the Internet, the leading industrialized nations are being challenged by the developing economies led by the BRIC countries of Brazil, Russia, India, and China. Today there is no company that is big enough, strong enough, rich enough, or smart enough to lead any market without partners.

As a result of this tectonic shift in their competitive space, market leaders have digitized their business relationships with trading partners to keep up with their ever-changing world in the increasing pace of Internet time. In this manner, these customer-centric digital businesses, which vary in size and scale, product type, as well as market reach, have created digital value chains as virtual enterprises with compatible core competencies in order to compete in their business ecosystems. The foundation of these thoughts has been long established. Marshall McLuhan observed when writing his 1967 classic *The Medium Is the Message* that "Any technology gradually creates a totally new human environment."

Business Agility Concepts

Business agility is defined here as *innovation via collaboration to be able to anticipate challenges and opportunities before they occur.* Accordingly, a gap analysis methodology can be used to evaluate the business agility readiness (BAR) needed to implement successfully an information management system of customer engagement for creating the business agility that produces the culture needed to enable a sustainable competitive advantage.

1

The recognition of the business value of business agility is not new. It was articulated several decades ago as "management productivity"—timelier decisions with greater insight and impact on business performance. This was as a result of implementing corporate management information systems with an integrated database enabling real-time decision support systems (Heisterberg 1985). Such a computer data-driven "silicon crystal ball" capability creates a culture of adaptive decision-making processes. With the advent of commercial Internet technology, this internal agility evolved as a competitive advantage with ubiquitous corporate intranet deployments.

In order to see the future of business agility that lies ahead, it's useful to look back 20 years across the previous generation of revolutionary business practices, in which innovation has resulted in continuous decision process reengineering (Heisterberg 2001):

- Electronic commerce (e-commerce) along the "information superhighway"
- E-business in the dot-com era
- Collaborative commerce (c-commerce) by virtual enterprises as value chains at the turn of the twenty-first century
- Social business evolution of Web 2.0 over the past decade
- Business ecosystems as the twenty-first-century business model for competition within and between industry markets

Even as these stages have progressed for more than two decades, the enabling technologies have changed more quickly. Information technology (IT) evolution has been measured in terms of Internet time as a set of next-generation hardware, software, and network system technologies that are continually deployed in faster enterprise implementation cycles.

This technology evolution has produced the ability to monetize innovative ideas. During the same period strategic business management theories, principles, and practices have evolved with the development of "customer value" as a framework for organizing resource allocation decision making. The associated abstract concept of Intellectual Capital for measuring the creation and delivery of customer value expressed as intangible assets has become a core element of today's customer-centric business models. As illustrated in Figure 1.1, this new rule of competitive advantage has become the driver for digital business in a knowledge-based marketspace.

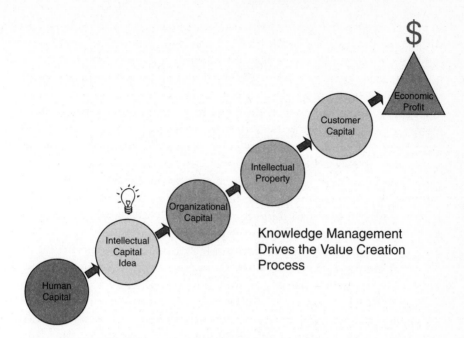

Figure 1.1   **Intellectual Capital Business Model of Innovation Monetization**

Digital Business Organization

Ubiquitous Internet connectivity has created a data-rich business environment. Access to information at any time, in any place, and in any way is now expected as a routine practice that provides a digital "state of presence" that drives personal experience delivery as the new normal of customer relationships. As their customers become increasingly connected to their suppliers and distributors via the Internet, businesses need to develop strategies and organizational structures that reflect this dependency on their digital ecosystems of trading partners. Such a new digital business has both physical and virtual relationships that must be managed for successful execution of that strategy.

    Businesses today are now reliant on these trading partners to be able to deliver a whole product with an experience that matches their customer expectations. This expression of the customer-centric value proposition in terms of the bundle of tangible goods and intangible services as a whole product provides insights into the necessary structure of a market-leading organization. A winning digital business strategy requires collaboration with trading partners that have compatible core competencies for developing and delivering a whole product. The organizational structure that is formed by a set of digital businesses around a whole product value chain is called a virtual enterprise. Likewise, coevolution of the collection of virtual enterprises collaborating to grow a rich business environment for their mutual benefit while competing to lead their market space is known as a business ecosystem. For example, Apple and Google as digital businesses with their respective virtual enterprises of iOS and Android whole products compete to lead their tablet business ecosystem while collaborating in order to build it more strongly as a vibrant competitor against the personal computer business ecosystem.

The basis of business competition has also evolved from product-centered financial assets to customer-centered information assets. This business model paradigm shift has moved away from "past is prelude" thinking characterized by business-as-usual planning. With this traditional practice, extrapolation of strategy plans was based on assumptions that the future will continue like the past using historical time-series sales forecasting and static regression analysis models. Now best practices lead to outside-the-box thinking. This is reflected by scenario-based planning that anticipates change via adaptive sense-and-respond business intelligence processes, real-time customer-facing decision support, and dynamic prescriptive analytic models. The growing criticality of digital customer relationship channels that augment conventional physical customer relationships and the inexorable progression of digital relationship management as a core competency are now fundamental enablers of agility for digital business success.

Business Ecosystem Strategic Concepts

This approach builds on the work of James F. Moore in *The Death of Competition: Leadership and Strategy in the Age of Business Ecosystems* by identifying and defining the business ecosystem as a strategic inter-enterprise organizational paradigm (Moore 1996). He describes the linking of synergistic core competencies in terms of four stages of strategic business coevolution. This process dynamically strengthens the ecosystem as a whole through an iterative cycle of collaboration and competition. These concepts of coevolution will be explored and elaborated throughout this book.

Collaborative commerce strategic concepts provide the foundation for digital business practices that enable business ecosystem trading partners to create, manage, and use data in a shared environment to design, build, and support their whole product throughout its life cycle, working separately to leverage their core competencies together in a value chain that forms a virtual enterprise (Heisterberg 2003). Sustainable competitive advantage has been realized by creating a culture for adoption of digital business strategies and customer-centric business models. This definition of digital business is made actionable by blending the elements of operations management, performance management, and information management in order to realize virtual enterprise integration within business ecosystems. It is important to understand that a precondition for success of this integration is creating an ecosystem culture that rewards innovation as a strategic customer value proposition based on mutual trust. (See Figure 1.2.)

These concepts for business ecosystem success are predicated on collaboration, as the Internet "killer app" and cloud technologies enable the IT agility that drives the sense-and-respond processes that create business agility. Taking a systems approach to business

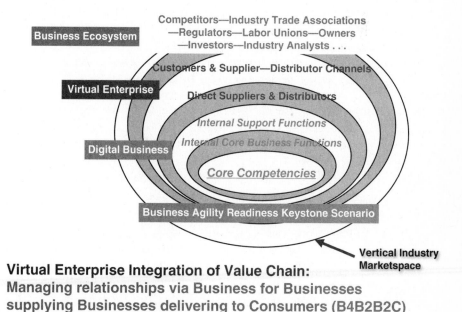

Virtual Enterprise Integration of Value Chain:
Managing relationships via Business for Businesses
supplying Businesses delivering to Consumers (B4B2B2C)

Figure 1.2   Business Ecosystem

ecosystems, referred to as "ecosystemism," fosters business agility thinking with twenty-first-century strategic goals: grow revenue, reduce cost, and manage risk. This provides the organizing principles for development of customer-centric business models. As such an approach to articulating a contemporary vision of creating business value, ecosystemism is based on systems theory in general, and specifically the fundamental first two laws.

The first law is known as "synergy" or commonly referred to as "the whole is greater than the sum of its parts." It has been adopted as the mainstream business practice of collaboration and often implemented using "crowdsourcing" processes. The second law is known as "sub-optimization." This concept may be understood as simply "a chain is as strong as its weakest link." It is best reflected by the business practice of innovation utilizing core competencies.

An ecosystemism digital divide is defined by the ecosystems that are characterized by their associated enterprise system scale:

- Digital business intranet → Developing a partnership between the chief marketing officer (CMO) and the chief information officer (CIO) that leverages the business value of IT
- Virtual enterprise extranet → Enabling competitive parity of small and medium-sized enterprises (SMEs) versus big enterprises by executing c-commerce strategies
- Business ecosystem Internet → Creating global market spaces in a flat world driven by social business models

As a matter of fact, just as e-business concepts have been subsumed into twenty-first-century standard practice for the management of business, c-commerce concepts are now simply expressed in the context of collaboration. Clearly, the business world has recognized they are all strong at something, yet not everything, and have concluded that two or more heads are better than one. This is evidenced by how ubiquitous the term *collaborate* is in everyday business conversation, as well as its widespread use in the trade press and in advertising copy of all media.

The expression of digital business management in terms of c-commerce principles and practices is both broad and deep. A complete treatment of this subject is worthy of several books covering strategies, tactics, and operations across the full spectrum of business value chain functions. Furthermore, coverage needs to include virtual enterprise integration issues such as the formation and management of virtual organizations at various levels from the enterprise to the project team. Then there is also the articulation of the critical success factors associated with a collaborative culture, as well as the critical role of trust in building an effective business ecosystem. Obviously, such a treatment is beyond the scope of this book. In order to make the definition of digital business actionable, we will focus on introducing experienced business managers to ecosystem-level strategic concepts of business agility.

Stages of Business Ecosystem Coevolution

In today's business management climate, the four stages of strategic business coevolution of business ecosystems may be viewed as intense innovation leadership challenges that can be enabled by the strategic business value of IT. The role of innovation as a critical success factor has been growing rapidly because of the climate change due to technology advancement, globalization of markets, and the diffusion of knowledge expressed in terms of intellectual capital as well as financial capital. Innovation as cultural imperative is a hallmark of leading digital businesses. They work collaboratively and competitively with the trading partners in their virtual enterprise to develop new core and whole products, satisfy customer demands, and integrate the next cycle of innovation.

Moore (1996) describes this climate of innovation in terms of the "opportunity environment." This is the "space of business characterized by unmet customer needs, unharnessed technologies, potential regulatory openings, prominent investors, and many other untapped resources . . . shaping cohesive strategy in the new order starts by defining the opportunity environment . . . strategy making revolves around devising novel ways to seize opportunities and create viable networks with other business ecosystems."

According to Moore, business ecosystems develop over four stages of strategic business coevolution:

Stage I: Pioneering an ecosystem. Link capabilities to create core offers on which to build; create value that is much superior to the status quo.

Stage II: Expansion of an ecosystem. Start with a core set of synergistic relationships and invest in increasing their scale and scope to establish critical mass within whatever market boundaries you wish to respect and exploit.

Stage III: Authority in an established ecosystem. Concentrate on embedding your contributions within the heart of the ecological community to maintain your authority within the business ecosystem.

Stage IV: Renewal or death. Find ways to insert new ideas into the order; stay competitive with other alternatives.

The following example describes how business ecosystems develop over these four stages of ecosystem maturity, viability, and growth. This coevolution is analyzed using the story found in the following Marriott Kauai ecosystem case study published by The Center for Corporate Citizenship at Boston College in 2002. It deals with the problem of creating and sustaining food and beverage customer experience management as a core competency. These business ecosystem insights are amplified by Brad Snyder, General Manager, Kauai Marriott Resort and Beach Club. His experiences provide a context for how virtual enterprises may leverage their understanding of these converging technologies to share their intellectual capital in order to fulfill the expectations of their trading partner community. The resort management used a balanced scorecard approach to building their business ecosystem strategy based on a customer-centric business model.

Stage I: Pioneering an Ecosystem

Fine cuisine plays a prominent role at the Kauai Marriott Resort and Beach Club, which has five restaurants and lounges. Its chefs favor locally grown produce for its freshness and its appeal to guests, who are eager to sample the island's offerings. When Marriott International opened its resort on Kauai, it hoped to differentiate itself and attract guests by featuring on its menu native cuisine prepared with locally grown produce. But Hawaii's northernmost island lacked a strong, diversified farming infrastructure, and this was matched with a struggling local economy. Without a reliable source of quality fruits and vegetables, the Kauai Marriott Resort and Beach Club was forced to turn to offshore sources. Ironically, the chefs found themselves preparing native cuisine with food shipped from the continental United States (IN PRACTICE, 2002).

This required establishing a system of synergistic relationships that resulted in a differentiated value to the customer. The new value proposition was developed in collaboration with key suppliers and customers. The resort management also worked to create a business model for delivering offerings in a way that was significantly superior to previously available food and beverage customer services, while protecting proprietary intellectual property.

Stage II: Expansion of an Ecosystem

The resort found a solution to its produce needs when it partnered with the Kauai Food Bank to support a broad-based community development program through which local residents were taught to grow high-quality produce on a small farm owned by the Food Bank. Over a two-year period, this program evolved into the Hui Meai'ai, training local independent growers in producing high-quality fruits and vegetables on their own land. The Hui Meai'ai then began functioning as a wholesale purchaser, buying the growers' produce for resale to local grocers, hotels, resorts, and restaurants. The words *Hui Meai'ai* translate from Hawaiian into "the club of things to eat" (IN PRACTICE, 2002).

This required establishing a critical mass of ecosystem trading partners, including suppliers, distributors, as well as customers in order to be able to coevolve the Kauai food and beverage ecosystem. The new food production capabilities expanded the supply to support a viable hospitality market. The resulting business model became a procurement best practice and the basis of the standard adopted by the leading suppliers and their key customers for delivering food services.

Stage III: Authority in an Established Ecosystem

The resort's ultimate goal in partnering with the Kauai Food Bank was to form strong working relationships with local growers. Such relationships generate competitive advantage by allowing the resort's chefs a reliable low-cost, high-quality source of local produce that would support the development of attractive, seasonal menus that offer guests fresh, native-grown fruits and vegetables. The partnership has benefited both Marriott and the Kauai Food Bank (IN PRACTICE, 2002).

This provided the Kauai Marriott Resort and Beach Club with the opportunity to lead the innovation that drives the coevolution of the

Kauai food and beverage ecosystem. The strategy reflected in the balanced scorecard has created the hospitality "spirit of aloha" that is embraced by stakeholders throughout the island.

Stage IV: Renewal or Death

The Kauai Marriott Resort and Beach Club continues to purchase a significant supply of its produce from the Hui Meai'ai. The Hui now has over 50 growers and supplies over 25 island customers, providing a self-sustaining local agricultural economy. The for-profit business model of the Kauai Food Bank with its continuous performance improvement practices has enabled the nonprofit Hui Meai'ai to realize its goal of becoming an economically viable virtual enterprise.

Digital Business Stakeholders

A digital business consists of a set of digital stakeholder relationships. They empower employees and engage trading partners to form a virtual enterprise. The digital businesses operate separately with social business principles, practices, and processes. Today, a customer-focused digital business model leverages stakeholder relationships using digital collaboration channels in their virtual enterprise to deliver a great customer experience that will produce a market leader. Yet the only way to sustain their competitive advantage is for digital businesses to sense changes in their business ecosystem, and then adapt their plans based on predictions of how these insights will produce customer delight and advocacy. A discussion of these agile business practices here provides a context for this new way of doing business—digitally.

Today, forward-looking enterprises are seeking to achieve the benefits of c-commerce by leveraging the Internet as an enabling technology in order to transform their core business management decision-making practices. These real-time enterprise value propositions for decision making are based on managing information rather than inventory. The business case for digital businesses is predicated on IT investments to facilitate collaborative business practices with shared demand/supply data and virtual enterprise visibility information in real time that will reduce uncertainty to improve decision effectiveness. Here is where digital businesses develop and execute a customer experience management strategy enabled by social business technology to drive a customer-centric value chain as a virtual enterprise.

The collaborative commerce architecture is described throughout the book with use case scenarios from the ubiquitous global multitrillion-dollar travel, tourism, and hospitality industry to provide clear examples to demonstrate the "what-why-how" story. Such familiar scenarios utilize a virtual enterprise integration methodology that is illustrated by a virtual Visitor Information Center (vVIC) platform as an Ecosystem Hub that is developed using an iterative incremental implementation road map (Heisterberg 2009).

The key for building next-generation digital businesses is integrating the business ecosystem with customer engagement solutions. Our approach was created by utilizing the two fundamental elements of enterprise information systems engineering. These methodologies have evolved over the past 25+ years of virtual enterprise integration research and development:

- Ecosystem Hub architecture that employs the *Force 5 Tornado* technologies using collaborative commerce principles
- Ecosystem Hub implementation road map that is an extensible, robust, scalable model for digital business transformation in accordance with business agility readiness gap analysis concepts.

Both of these subjects are introduced in this chapter in order to provide an overview of our strategic framework for creating business agility. Ecosystem Hub architecture concepts will be further elaborated in the next chapter, while the Ecosystem Hub implementation roadmap will be illustrated by use case scenarios throughout the remainder of the book.

Ecosystem Hub Concepts

What are the lessons learned from this accelerating pace of information technology disruption that has created a climate of innovation further multiplied by the convergence of those same technologies? The global consumerization of IT and the resulting "bring your own devices" (BYOD) phenomenon in the business world are driving the winds of change—generating the "perfect storm" of technology convergence with cloud, social, mobile, video, and big data acting like a "Force 5 Tornado" disrupting the business playing field.

Note that we have created this metaphor as a "conceptual shorthand." The use of the term "Force 5" refers to both the five technology trends as well as the highest strength level of the winds in such a storm. The "Tornado" terminology is based on Geoffrey Moore's technology adoption model associated with disruptive innovations described in *Crossing the Chasm,* and in *Inside the Tornado* where he refers to technologies evolving from niche markets into the business mainstream.

In the context of the disruptive technology metaphor, enterprises that are forward-looking can harness this disruptive power to their advantage via big data with prescriptive analytics in order to:

- Produce early warnings to strengthen infrastructure via the cloud
- Collaborate for real-time problem solving in their communities via social networks
- Communicate vital decision-making information to the right people, place, and time via mobility solutions
- Provide interactive messages for alerts and instructional information via videos

By developing readiness for creating business agility, and harnessing the five technological forces that have converged in our present business environment, market leaders will transform the Force 5 Tornado spawned by this perfect storm into a coherent pattern of light, creating a rainbow that leads to a pot of gold—achieving success.

This book describes the Ecosystem Hub architecture as an enterprise information management system (EIMS) in terms of three integrated layers consisting of business, applications, and technology. We leverage the top five information technology trends in the context of building collaborative commerce business architectures and putting the "data" back into "data processing" by incorporating master data management principles and practices into a big data strategy for building a digital business. It is a strategy for the next stage of digital business evolution. Collaborative commerce business practices enable trading partners to create, manage, and use data-driven processes in a shared environment to design, build, and support products throughout their life cycles, working separately to leverage their core competencies together in a value chain that forms a virtual enterprise.

Traditionally, technology has been utilized within the four walls of the enterprise to facilitate improvements in business processes. With the advent of the Internet, enterprises have extended their use of information technologies to include external transactions based on digital touch points with trading partners termed electronic commerce (e-commerce). The emerging digital business models provide the enterprise with a collaboration capability across suppliers and customers that facilitates ease of information sharing and improved decision making. This in turn requires the development of virtual enterprise management principles with new business practices for the formation and operation of alliances with collaborative partners having a mutual interest in their shared value. This is a proven approach and has been accomplished in accordance with the evolution of business information management best practices over the past 20 years. An Ecosystem Hub is a standards-based, secure, shared data platform:

- Developed as the proprietary Integration Hub for Lockheed during the 1990s to create, manage, and use shared program/project/product data in the aerospace industry in accordance with a standard for providing contractor integrated technical information management software as a service via the Internet.
- Evolved as commercially sourced independent enterprise information portal (EIP) software packaged products.
- Now available as an integrated turnkey EIP software suite via the cloud as software-as-a-service (SaaS) packages.

As previously stated, Business Ecosystem Hubs provide the environment that facilitates digital business web services for applications such as inventory visibility, business process management, and performance metrics displayed in real-time dashboards. Application software developed using a service-oriented architecture (SOA) and deployed as web services has provided the technology base for the concept of the next-generation Internet—Web 2.0.

The customer relationship management (CRM) application software product that led the demand chain integration movement was Salesforce.com, a sales force automation package that was delivered as an online service for an affordable monthly subscription fee. This spawned establishment of a new sector of the software industry now referred to as the cloud and software as a service (SaaS) applications. The widespread adoption of SaaS products that support collaboration within and between small, medium-sized, and large corporations around the world has enabled Enterprise 2.0.

Social network SaaS applications are enabling Enterprise 2.0–driven business cases in terms of virtual enterprise collaboration. Note that the cloud and SaaS sector has its early roots in the computer time-share industry with the deployment of corporate accounting and payroll services, and then later with the aerospace industry delivery of contractor integrated technical information services (CITIS) on U.S. Department of Defense (DoD) programs via an extranet using EIP technologies. The Digital Business Ecosystem (DBE) Initiative launched by the European Union introduced the concept of "extended dynamic clusters" for deployment of c-commerce solutions via SaaS applications targeted for small and medium-sized enterprises (SMEs) to enable their participation in global value chains (Nachira, Nicolai, Dini, Leon, and Le Louarn 2007).

The DBE project provided an opportunity for innovative software application development by software producer SMEs and for the achievement of greater information and communication technology adoption by SMEs in general. SaaS changes the way SMEs navigate their ecosystems by dynamically linking internal and external resources and associated value networks for allocation according to their business goals in order to achieve virtual enterprise integration (Dini and Nicolai 2003).

Thought leaders such as McKinsey, Gartner, Forrester Research, *Harvard Business Review*, and the MIT Center for Digital Business agree that companies that adopt digital information asset-based policies and processes generate significantly higher growth, market share, and profits. Industry leaders are building new data-driven customer-centric businesses leveraging information-based assets with agility derived from big data analytics (BDA) to create innovative revenue streams. This is now becoming a mainstream business model across many industries, with big data technology challenging conventional information infrastructures using innovation to provide opportunities for collaborative customer-facing applications enabled by predictive customer insights. Information management is becoming a critical success factor for business leaders around the globe.

This concept was articulated by Regis McKenna at the dawn of the Internet era in his seminal book *Real Time: Preparing for the Age of the Never Satisfied Customer* (McKenna 1997). He observed that for Silicon Valley companies, "Growth forecasts, such as five- and ten-year projections for product sales, are routinely ignored because they are seen as mere extrapolations from history. Instead, people are in constant touch with the technological and competitive environment of the moment. Change is treated as an opportunity that, if spotted ahead of competitors and acted on as fast as possible, can transform the ranking of companies in an industry virtually overnight."

These "perfect storm" technologies have emerged separately over the past decade and been widely written about in much detail. Several thought leaders have come forward recently to address the symbiotic character of this set of technologies that are trending together, such as Geoffrey Moore in terms of the "chasm" decision making for enterprise information technology adoption, Malcolm Frank of Cognizant with the "SMAC Stack" concept (social, mobile, analytics, and cloud), as well as the Gartner "Nexus of Forces" (social, mobile, cloud, and information). We will take a "whole product" approach to digital business strategy for virtual enterprise formation and operation with digitization of customer-focused business practices, processes, and protocols. We will explore this convergence in more detail in Chapter 2 and add video as a fifth force of the perfect storm, which has strong implications for transforming the way businesses relate to and engage their customers via technology.

Ecosystem Hub Implementation Concepts

The Ecosystem Hub implementation roadmap that is a model for digital business transformation has also been developed in accordance with the corresponding business performance management best practices over the past 25+ years:

1. Developed as proprietary advanced manufacturing technology system integration methodology by the Computer Aided Manufacturing–International research consortium and deployed for consortium members, such as General Motors and General Electric, to provide interoperability for factory management planning, execution, and shop floor control systems.
2. Augmented with the Department of Defense contractor-integrated technical information service business case methodology project in accordance with Military-Standard 974 for CITIS.
3. Deployed integrally to Gartner IT balanced scorecard projects, as well as numerous c-commerce IT management consulting engagements worldwide.

Collaborative business practices require the sharing of business and technical data that are often proprietary or at least competition-sensitive information. It is important to emphasize that relationship management is a fundamental core competency for digital businesses and trust is the associated critical success factor. A relationship portfolio approach provides a framework to facilitate intelligent partnering. Trust as the foundation of the business ecosystem culture is realized by means of:

- Developing a capability-based strategy
- Building a portfolio of relationships
- Managing the relationship portfolio

Trust is the key to relationship management by increasing the velocity of the value chain. In the real-time virtual enterprise, trust is an economic driver and not trusting is a bigger risk (Covey 2008).

Trust as well as information integration and business process management standards are imperatives for effective digital businesses management. This decision making necessitates establishing business rules that are driven by value chain needs in formation and operation of the virtual enterprise. This is based on the trading partners' risk/reward contributions and value-added core competencies. A set of digital business critical success factors includes:

- Leveraging Internet technologies for first internal and then external data sharing
- Providing loosely coupled application interoperability via Ecosystem Hubs across the virtual enterprise's value chain
- Focusing on core competencies associated with the established collaborative business practices for the demand chain and the supply chain
- Building virtual enterprises on trusted value chains in one or more business ecosystems to redefine competitive advantage
- Generating real-time visibility, event notification, and performance measurement throughout the value chain
- Reengineering value chain management decision-making processes using a knowledge management approach

We will further elaborate on the role of trust as a critical success factor for virtual enterprise formation and operation, as well as business ecosystem optimization of the delivery of customer value in Chapter 2. Our approach to multidimensional scoring (MDS) for balanced scorecard initiatives can become an actionable methodology for measuring business agility readiness (BAR).

The business transformation that is being realized via digital business can be described in terms of management decision-making processes utilizing feedback to leverage real-time virtual enterprise information. The fundamental elements of digital business are business processes that facilitate collaboration that are enabled by Internet technology. Originally, c-commerce focused on the supply chain back end of the value chain. Now, using Web 2.0 technologies, this scope has been expanded to embrace the demand chain activities incorporating social networking functionality, which will ultimately enable optimizing the holistic virtual enterprise value chain from beginning to end.

There are two key adaptive strategic planning processes for virtual enterprise integration in a business ecosystem:

1. Building virtual enterprise infrastructures using the Ecosystem Hub architecture
2. Making decisions to optimize business performance of the virtual enterprise value chain

They both play a role in our strategic framework for creating business agility and are explored in the following section and further in Chapter 2.

Ecosystem Hub Implementation Roadmap for BAR

Enterprises may employ a business agility strategic planning methodology to build a roadmap for the design, development, and deployment of a virtual enterprise enabled by an Ecosystem Hub based on the perfect storm of technology convergence with cloud, social, mobile, video, and big data acting like a Force 5 Tornado, disrupting the business playing field to create a competitive advantage.

Step 1: Visioning via the Strategic Framework

During this step, the enterprise must establish a corporate business agility vision, and therefore, a resulting high-level digital business strategic direction for the enterprise's "to be" state in the envisioned future. A top-down and bottom-up approach is adopted in Step 1 to ensure that the entire organization has input into establishing the corporate business agility vision for the system of engagement (SOE) and buys into it with CEO leadership.

Strategic virtual enterprise scenarios using an Ecosystem Hub reflect the different applications of value chain management under four main categories:

1. Demand chain management
2. Customer/partner relationship management
3. Supply chain management
4. Supplier relationship management

Any c-commerce initiative can be positioned according to one of these four headings. Using the iterative incremental implementation model for pilot project development, enterprises can develop business agility competencies by investing in a portfolio of IT initiatives that may include the following examples:

- Ecosystem Hub infrastructure development via SOE technologies
- Intranet integration via Ecosystem Hub
- Virtual enterprise extranet integration via Ecosystem Hub
- Business ecosystem membership for virtual enterprise integration

Having identified the four ways in which virtual enterprises can be applied, strategic scenarios are ranked through a robust evaluation process in terms of both the value of opportunity each scenario represents to the enterprise as well as the ability to deploy it. The resultant ideal target zone can be represented diagrammatically as illustrated in Figure 1.3.

Enterprises must formally evaluate each of the candidate scenarios against a number of business factors. These business factors relate to either opportunity or capability and are scored under each heading, which generally consists of from eight to 12 metrics that correspond to the enterprise balanced scorecard.

The business agility visioning process requires three perspectives. The *enterprise perspective* provides insight into a company's current capabilities, culture, and vision. The *marketplace perspective* provides a view of realities and changes in industry practice, barriers to entry, competition, constituent behavior, and offerings. The *technology perspective*, with its associated policy impacts on the enterprise and

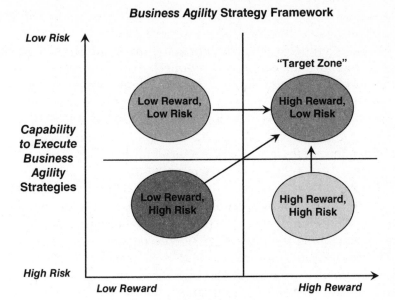

Figure 1.3   Strategic Visioning

marketplace, extends strategic thinking outside of the box by discounting commonly held beliefs about markets, products, and competition. This forces enterprises to address new methods of doing business, new product offerings, and new competitive paradigms within the business ecosystem.

Development of the business agility vision and digital business strategy is not a one-time process. Because of the evolving nature of best practices, state-of-the-art product offerings, quality expectations, and cultural changes, strategy development is iterative. Virtual enterprise business models and their associated digital business strategies must be dynamically updated on a continuous basis.

Step 2: Business Agility Readiness Assessment

In Step 2, existing enterprise processes and infrastructure of the system of record (SOR) are formally evaluated in order to establish a baseline of enterprise digital business capabilities "as is." The existing processes will indicate the need for and the ability of the organization to adapt to change. The infrastructure assessment will provide an understanding of the level of investment needed to implement a c-commerce initiative. The combination of these metrics will provide a score that will allow the aforementioned virtual enterprise scenarios to be positioned in the business agility strategic framework.

Virtual enterprises need to assess the maturity of their business, technology, and organization domains for evaluating BAR. They must assimilate the information gained through a due-diligence process for assessment of their core competencies and develop a mapping of pertinent IT capabilities to virtual enterprise business practices. This process should include a review of enabling technology and business model trends in their industry as a benchmark. Solidifying the understanding of the enterprise's technology and business challenges, as well as developing the knowledge of core competencies concerning technology, business processes, and organizational capabilities, is fundamental to crafting a digital business strategy. The digital business can then build a trading partner value proposition that can be leveraged in forming or joining virtual enterprises in a way that make strategic business sense.

Enterprises should look at three technology categories to assess their readiness to support a virtual enterprise business model: application portfolio, systems infrastructure, and network infrastructure. They should compare their collaborative business vision to benchmarks pertaining to business-to-business (B2B) and business-to-consumer (B2C) digital business models, as well as industry trends for virtual enterprise value chain scenarios. It is critical for enterprises to also evaluate their business process infrastructure, as well as organizational structure with respect to their ability to support customer-centric value chains. Again it is essential for digital businesses to understand their core competencies from a product life cycle perspective, in terms of product development through product support, including customer and supplier relationship management capabilities in the context of customer-focused business processes.

Step 3: Business Agility Gap Analysis

Although the preliminary digital business strategies and c-commerce initiatives were identified in light of both virtual enterprise opportunities and capabilities, there is still a need to subject the enterprise digital business strategic architecture to a formal gap analysis. In this step of the business agility strategic planning methodology, the magnitude of the difference between the current "as is" SOR environment as assessed in Step 2 and the future SOE in the "to be" state of the enterprise as envisioned in Step 1 is formally evaluated.

A complete business agility gap analysis, at a corporate level and in relation to each line of business, must cover the following four headings:

1. Digital business drivers
2. Virtual enterprise business processes
3. Force 5 Tornado enabling technologies
4. Business ecosystem organization and culture

The business agility gap analysis must precede the next step of the project, which is to make recommendations on the implementation of the system of engagement (SOE) in the digital business strategy. Performing this gap analysis allows for the identification of specific management approaches or activities required to ensure that the lines of business can execute their strategies as planned in support of the corporate business model.

Step 4: Strategic System of Engagement Architecture

Virtual enterprise integration is conducted in Step 4. This is where the vision, strategies, and initiatives generated during Step 1 are synthesized into an enterprise SOE strategic architecture. This top-level enterprise scenario can then be executed by the operational lines of business and integrated into their c-commerce strategy process with their resulting balanced scorecard performance management system at the line of business level.

The enterprise SOE strategic architecture integrates the total of all the initiatives developed within the corporate-level visioning and the line-level initiatives and collectively represents the associated corporate and lines of business strategic plans. The SOE strategic architecture for virtual enterprise integration is comprised of:

- The business agility vision for digital business strategies
- The core strategies applicable at a corporate level and a business line level, and their prioritization based on the attractiveness blend of the opportunity values and capabilities risks

- The c-commerce initiatives that will realize the strategies at a corporate level and a business line level, as well as their relative prioritization

Note that this concept of virtual enterprise integration utilizes a three-architecture approach as a model for c-commerce initiatives that provide real-time decision making for virtual enterprise value chain management:

1. *Technology architecture.* Force 5 Tornado technology architecture for Ecosystem Hub platforms via EIP products and web services provides semantic interoperability for value chain visibility.
2. *Application architecture.* SOE application architecture for value chain management integration of demand chain management, customer/partner relationship management, supplier relationship management, and supply chain management processes provides real-time business process management for event notification.
3. *Business architecture.* Business agility decision architecture for virtual enterprise scenarios provides adaptive performance measurement.

The technology, application, and business architectures comprise an architectural framework for a business ecosystem that is fundamental to leveraging the enterprise's core digital business strategy and driving development of a collaborative business management environment. This in turn enables the implementation of adaptive strategic planning and operations management processes in order to execute the virtual enterprise integration strategy guided by real-time feedback from virtual enterprise results.

Step 5: Ecosystem Hub Implementation via System of Engagement Value Chain Analysis

The results of the SOR gap analysis and SOE strategic architecture development must be sequenced, and the interproject dependencies must be taken into consideration in order to develop a roadmap for how to resolve the identified gaps. The implementation recommendations will also provide inputs into the business agility strategic planning process that exists at a line of business level because each of the business lines may need to adopt specific enterprise recommendations for implementation of their specific initiatives and projects.

It is important for business leaders to understand that pilot testing of emerging collaborative SOE business practices, in a representative management decision-making environment that has been instrumented for business case analysis, is the only rational way to mitigate the change management risks associated with the execution of a comprehensive enterprise strategy. An implementation roadmap must be orchestrated to identify and evaluate potential business process and enabling technology gaps by use of such a shared data environment capable of supporting the intranet, extranet, and Internet value chain scenarios, as well as to deliver incremental benefits in a self-funding or pay-as-you-go manner.

The pilot test and evaluation results will also provide implementation requirements for recommended Force 5 Tornado information technology investments. The pilot testing will further enhance the enterprise business agility strategic planning process that exists at a business line level (e.g., value chains for key commodities or customer/trading partner initiatives within the business ecosystem).

Iterative incremental implementation of the SOE pilot projects is a required tactic for successful execution of a comprehensive enterprise digital business strategy that necessitates deploying value chain initiatives according to their related Ecosystem Hub implementation roadmap. The following series of tasks serves as a guideline for navigating the incremental roadmap to implement the SOE pilot projects. This methodology reflects a model of business agility readiness achieved in terms of the following eight milestones using the iterative incremental Ecosystem Hub implementation roadmap:

1. Decide business ecosystem agility goals.
2. Design social graph as EIMS architecture.
3. Plan keystone scenario concept of operations.
4. Acquire enabling Force 5 Tornado technologies.
5. Build virtual enterprise using agile work plan.
6. Evaluate business case via balanced scorecard.
7. Deliver business ecosystem agility solution.
8. Transform with sustainable competitive advantage.

This Ecosystem Hub iterative incremental implementation roadmap is a framework for creating and deploying value chain management scenarios. It is further defined in terms of representative EIP service-oriented architecture products that may be used to source a scalable and extensible Ecosystem Hub platform. Key to an effective EIP product selection is a solid understanding of virtual enterprise requirements and identification of the audiences for which the portal will be targeted. Different audiences (employees vs. suppliers vs. trading partners vs. customers) will have very different needs, tastes, demographics, and requirements. Multiple portals in any large enterprise are quite likely and even desirable, since the EIP product selected must meet the needs of each intended community of interest for their intranet, extranet, or Internet-based value chain management scenarios. Choosing a product requires sound research and expert advice. Enterprises should leverage all available technology resources, perform due diligence on comparable reference implementations, and perform pilot tests with the EIP product vendors before finalizing the selection of the best source for each Ecosystem Hub platform. Using this implementation model as a framework for a pilot project roadmap, enterprises can develop business agility competencies by investing in a portfolio of IT initiatives, which may include the spectrum of digital business, virtual enterprise, and business ecosystem scenarios.

Strategic planning for creating business agility can incorporate a balanced scorecard utilizing a real-time performance management system to facilitate an adaptive strategic planning process for value chain optimization. An individual business case for each c-commerce initiative must be orchestrated in a manner that is logically consistent with the respective enterprise and lines of business balanced score-cards. This business agility strategic planning methodology cultivates a culture that blends a compelling customer experience value proposition with virtual enterprise capabilities in value chain scenarios to realize SOE benefits for a sustainable competitive advantage.

The integrated IT investment portfolio of c-commerce initiatives consists of strategic value chain pilot projects. The pilot projects may build on recommendations that enterprises employ a technology approach that transforms business agility competencies to improve overall enterprise readiness and integrates key technology and application architecture components in a customer-centric manner via virtual enterprise scenarios. The projects may produce pilot value chain solutions that can realize immediate competitive advantage and bottom-line payoff. For example, Cisco believes that collaboration—from its TelePresence videoconferencing system at the top to its products, services, and collaborative business practices for seamless, effortless, constant interaction throughout the business ecosystem—will drive the next wave of productivity gains (Martin 2008). The portfolio of virtual enterprise pilots may then serve as a critical business agility transformation model for SOE change management, as well as provide the fundamental incremental investments for self-funding of c-commerce initiatives.

Balanced Scorecard Delivering Business Value

A challenge in the new twenty-first-century economy is to adapt quickly to new business opportunities or threats by realigning enterprise strategy to efficiently and effectively create value. An adaptive strategic planning solution for enterprise business management decision making can provide a holistic approach to strategy management, business planning, target setting, rolling and event-driven forecasting, and business performance management based on financial and leading nonfinancial key performance indicators (KPIs). Big data analytics (BDA) applications can be used to support these activities in executing c-commerce strategies across a virtual enterprise that consists of multiple value chains with diverse organizational structures and management decision-making processes.

Identifying and analyzing value chain performance trends enables enterprises to adapt their strategic plans, redesign virtual enterprise configurations, and reallocate resources for their core competencies in order to optimize profitability in response to customer and market dynamics. The benefits of digital business can then be realized via leveraging the Internet as an enabling technology in order to transform virtual enterprise core business management decision-making practices.

This trend has amplified business interest in the balanced scorecard as part of a strategic business planning methodology that is being used to communicate the enterprise business strategy throughout the value chain. Kaplan and Norton, the creators of the balanced scorecard, describe adaptive strategic planning in the context of "making strategy a continual process." Accordingly, there are three key e-business drivers for including the balanced scorecard as a fundamental model for the solution to the digital business strategy management problem (Kaplan and Norton 2001):

1. *Linking strategy and budgeting.* Strategic initiatives and performance targets on the balanced scorecard link the enterprise strategy to the specific resource allocations for operating each value chain using rolling forecasts in a manner that reflects operating in continuously changing environments.
2. *Closing the strategy loop.* Digital business messaging applications, including systems displaying performance metrics in real-time dashboards, can be linked to the balanced scorecard, providing a new framework for exception reporting and adaptive business management practices, as well as a focus on intangibles with leading indicators, such as intellectual and social capital, management talent, core competencies, and customer loyalty assets that are neglected by traditional lagging financial measurement.
3. *Testing, learning, and adapting.* Virtual enterprise management can be more proactive by testing and evaluating strategic value chain hypotheses with the information from the c-commerce messaging applications. Strategies for each value chain can evolve in real time in response to market dynamics.

An adaptive strategic planning system enables value chain management teams to make strategy a continual process by: monitoring performance against enterprise and line-of-business strategies, updating the performance measures on the balanced scorecards using actual operations data in real time, collaborating as virtual teams with an executive dashboard to interpret the performance metrics, developing strategic insights with knowledge management tools in order to formulate new competitive directions, and then reallocating enterprise resource allocations to continuously reflect the dynamics of the business environment.

Such a digital business planning and control application, implemented using a big data analytics (BDA) model, can be based on an enterprise and line-of-business balanced scorecard as well as real-time customer relationship management/supply chain management (CRM/SCM) performance analytics. It enables progress in executing the strategy to be monitored, as well as supporting corrective actions to be performed in a timely manner. This adaptive strategic planning system serves as an enabler of a digital business strategy improvement process that links the real-time value chain performance as feedback for the business operations control process via BDA with the business ecosystem–level strategy.

It is important to understand that collaborative strategies emphasizing demand chain optimization need to be focused on customer relationships, which require interactive and individualized communications. Trading partners must have bidirectional communication in a cooperative manner in order to recognize and respond to their mutual needs, not simply broadcast information without knowing that it is both received and understood. Also note that CRM systems are most successful when delivered as a community environment enabled by trust as a critical success factor.

Change Management Imperatives

Change management initiatives need to cultivate competitive information asset value. This means developing capabilities and competencies for business agility asset management. Such a stewardship of enterprise data requires roles and responsibilities for handling the transition from tangible SOR product data transactions to intangible SOE customer data relations. Thus, relationship management must become a core competency of any enterprise that aspires to be a leader in its business ecosystem.

The true value comes from an integrated view of analytics and technology that connects marketing operations with multichannel campaigns. This is where CMOs and CIOs can jointly calibrate the financial, operational, and customer impacts of every single marketing activity. The result is that businesses not only create better customer experiences, but do so more efficiently and cost-effectively. This capability reflects the evolutionary stages of the Gartner Business Analytics Maturity Model in order to answer the questions:

- Descriptive → what?
- Diagnostic → why?
- Predictive → when?
- Prescriptive → how?

Customer-Centric Business Strategy

The CMO Council and SAS have conducted a study titled "Big Data's Biggest Role Aligning the CMO & CIO: Greater Partnership Drives

Enterprise-Wide Customer Centricity" that provides insights that can help the CMO and CIO align around the following four imperatives to achieving customer centricity:

1. *Enable a single customer viewpoint.* Successful customer-centric organizations tend to have a more centralized data and information management system for a single view of the customer. Marketing and IT must enable the different parts of the organization to gather customer interaction data from all internal and external customer channels in a consistent way.
2. *Develop actionable insight by automated, predictive analysis of the data.* The next challenge for marketing and IT will be for the analytics team to create actionable insights that support specific customer-centered outcomes. These customer analytics will need to run in real time for an ever-increasing number of customer segments and more elaborate microsegments by audience attitude, location, channel, and more.
3. *Distribute contextualized customer insight to support specific marketing actions.* BAR also helps marketing and IT to create output from the customer data that targets the employees and other partners who have the potential to interact with customers. More than just information, they need to agree on the answers and actions that are most relevant at a specific touch point and design interactions that are adaptable to different skill levels.
4. *Deliver an outstanding customer experience based on insight, not only data.* Like their partners in marketing, CIOs are recognizing the importance of the external customer as the primary driver of technology strategy. BAR strategies provide marketing analytics and customer analytics technologies to help redirect IT's traditional focus on delivering value to the internal IT customer to align with marketing in its external customer centricity.

That change in IT focus from SOR to SOE puts the customer at the locus of IT planning, deployment, and support. In addition, frontline agents and customer-facing systems can now consistently deliver answers to a specific customer need at a specific touch point to create a compelling and customized brand experience.

Business Agility Alignment Issues

Business ecosystem insights focus on how digital business teams may leverage their understanding of these converging technologies to share their intellectual capital in order to fulfill the expectations of their trading partner community. Digital business insights focus on how CXO teams (the chiefs of business functions and units) may leverage their understanding of these converging technologies to create business agility in terms of innovation via a collaborative culture that mitigates risk by celebrating failure as lessons learned in order to drive future success.

The chief information officer (CIO) insights focus on how CIOs may leverage their understanding of these converging technologies to use the top 10 characteristics for CIO success to deliver the business value of IT for digital businesses. Featured on the applications dimension is marketing in general, with a specific focus of the framework on the chief marketing officer (CMO) insights that leverage the CMO use case studies created in conjunction with development of the "CMO-CIO Partnership for Collaborative Marketing Agility" theme by enhancing the balance sheet with a balanced scorecard. We have been developing a strategy for collaboration with the CMO Council for CMO-CIO alignment around big data analytics based on collaborative marketing best practices. A digital business practice can be created for using a balanced scorecard to describe and measure how to best vet the internal/external collaboration activities associated with management of big data for driving predictive analytics as a critical success factor in managing the business ecosystem. These insights focus on how CMOs may leverage their understanding of these converging technologies to better communicate with their customers through the media they prefer, to engage prospective customers through common interests, and to utilize information to build stronger, more personal, and more lasting relationships.

Business Agility Readiness Roadmap

Business agility, defined as *innovation via collaboration to be able to anticipate challenges and opportunities before they occur,* produces a sustainable competitive advantage. The business value of IT is realized by creating business agility using a strategy of innovation for CIO-CMO alignment around big data analytics based on collaborative marketing best practices. This is made actionable as a decision framework by incorporating a holistic customer-centric performance management system using an IT balanced scorecard as the basis for a Business Agility Readiness (BAR) Roadmap.

The BAR Roadmap is defined in terms of an enterprise architecture that consists of the following three elements, integrated by data:

- People → Business architecture
- Process → Application architecture
- Tools → Technology architecture

BAR is actionable by means of using a gap analysis methodology to measure the change in business value associated with each of the four elements as scored in terms of a customer-centric model of business agility. The model is defined by four customer moments of engagement dimensions: profile, engagement, life cycle, and conscience. As the enterprise architecture evolves from the "as-is" state of the current system of record (SOR) to the "to-be" state of the envisioned system of engagement (SOE) supported with multidimensional scoring (MDS), the business is transformed in terms of its competitive position in the business ecosystem.

The basis of the gap analysis is documented in the form of two social graphs reflecting both the current and the future states of the enterprise architecture. The social graph for the SOR is articulated by a concept of operation that describes how the product data is created, managed, and used by internal/external stakeholders in the context of their roles in the keystone use scenario. A corresponding social graph for the SOE depicts the concept of engagement for the shared customer data environment expressed as one of the following four levels of relationship:

1. From the initial state of *Communication* → exchange of information in a relationship,
2. Through *Coordination* → communicating status while working separately,
3. Then *Cooperation* → working separately together,
4. To fully realize *Collaboration* → working separately together using intellectual capital for sharing risk and reward.

Note that each higher level inherits the properties of the lower levels.

The change management rationale for evolving the enterprise IT systems is to transform the corresponding business model and its fundamental strategy from product-centered to customer-centered. This transformation drives data management practices that enable reengineering decision-making processes.

The roadmap is presented using a balanced scorecard to describe and measure the CIO-CMO partnership alignment gap in the context of the moments of engagement that drive the transformation from a system of record to a system of engagement. Such a tool is used to assess how to best vet the internal/external collaboration activities associated with management of big data for driving advanced business analytics initiatives. This is accomplished by measuring the strategic readiness of the intangible assets associated with human capital, information capital, and organizational capital, which describe the knowledge perspective of the balanced scorecard. Illustration of how the Business Agility Readiness Roadmap works is shown in terms of a gap analysis for a travel industry scenario based on a "Selling Sonoma County Wine Country" case study contained in the Epilogue.

Sonoma County Tourism Sneakaway Marketing Campaign Leverages Hybrid Cloud Deployment as Platform for Ecosystem Hub

Operation of a central Ecosystem Hub as a hybrid cloud with integrated private and community cloud platforms by a DMO will facilitate a SOA-based infrastructure for the virtual enterprise enabled as a network of Ecosystem Hubs providing collaborative marketing campaign management services for their business ecosystem. Such an information system architecture is both robust and scalable, as well as extensible to a wide variety of travel industry scenarios (Heisterberg, 2010).

In an endeavor to build virtual Visitors Information Center (vVIC) Sonoma County Tourism (SCT) evaluated various cloud deployment models. They finally chose a hybrid approach to deploy various business applications such as ecosystem social media applications on public clouds hosted and managed by third parties. While back-end applications such as Financials, as well as customer-facing CRM, are on a Private cloud.

The travel life cycle is intended to provide the foundation of a vVIC architectural concept for building a collaborative travel planning community as a social media network. This system architecture may be described in terms of the hardware, software, and Internet resources needed for implementing the distributed multiplatform portal as an Ecosystem Hub for a DMO ecosystem. Development is recommended to be performed in accordance with a DMO technology plan describing an iterative incremental implementation strategy expressed as a multiyear vVIC roadmap documenting the business ecosystem keystone scenarios (Heisterberg, 2008).

SCT launched the winter/spring 2013 promotional campaign, called "Sonoma Sneakaway," to encourage overnight visitation to Sonoma County during the slower months from January to May.

The "Sonoma Sneakaway" campaign, hosted on a public cloud with a stakeholders and visitors engagement portal, allows tourism-related businesses to promote themselves, for free, to the millions of potential travelers they reach globally. Thus breaking all geolocation boundaries with access to pervasive devices.

Tourism businesses who are interested in participating in the Sneakaway campaign submit their specials to Sonoma County Tourism through the partners section of their website, www.sonomacounty. com/partners. The campaign, which is free for tourism-related businesses in Sonoma County, was centered on the website, www.SonomaSneakaway.com, which held all the offers.

Refer to the Epilogue for the full story on business agility readiness at SCT for the Sneakaway campaign. This overview of the concept of operation for the Ecosystem Hub via the cloud-based Simpleview platform further describes the SCT Ecosystem. The bottom-line is that successful execution of this Sneakaway keystone scenario strategy is enabled by CIO-CMO alignment as a critical success factor. This case study will continue to evolve in order to provide a rich and real-time story of how to leverage the Force 5 Tornado technologies to create the business agility needed to gain and sustain your competitive advantage. It may be accessed via the Creating Business Agility blog. Stay tuned for more . . . !

References

CMO Council. 2013. "Big Data's Biggest Role Aligning the CMO & CIO: Greater Partnership Drives Enterprise-Wide Customer Centricity."

Covey, S. 2008, July 29. "The SPEED of Trust." Keynote Presentation at 94th Annual Convention, Las Vegas, NV: Destination Marketing Association International.

Dini, P., and A. Nicolai. 2003, November 1. "The Digital Business Ecosystem: FP6 IST e-Business Integrated Project." European Commission.

DMAIF. 2008. "The Future of Destination Marketing: Tradition, Transition, and Transformation." Destination Marketing Association International Foundation.

Heisterberg, R. 1985. "DSS for Shop Floor Control." Research Note. Pennsauken, NJ: Auerbach Publications.

Heisterberg, R. 2001, February 22. "Data Ownership Extends Outside the Enterprise." Research Note. Stamford, CT: Gartner Group.

Heisterberg, R. 2003. "Collaborative Commerce (C-Commerce)." *The Internet Encyclopedia*, vol. 1. Hoboken, NJ: John Wiley & Sons.

Heisterberg, R. 2008, August 6. "Creating a Collaborative Travel Planning Community: Lessons Learned in Migrating to a Web 2.0 Experience." Strategy White Paper. Mountain View, CA: Rod Heisterberg Associates.

Heisterberg, R. 2009, November 22. "Strategic Architecture for a Virtual Visitor Information Center." Strategy White Paper. Mountain View, CA: Rod Heisterberg Associates.

Heisterberg, R. 2010. "Collaborative Commerce." *The Handbook of Technology Management*, vol. III, Chapter 33. Hoboken, NJ: John Wiley & Sons.

IN PRACTICE. 2002. "A Productive Partnership: The Kauai Marriott Resort and Beach Club and the Kauai Food Bank." The Center for Corporate Citizenship at Boston College.

Kaplan, R., and D. Norton. 2001. *Strategy-Focused Organization: How Balanced Scorecard Companies Thrive in the New Business Environment.* Boston: Harvard Business School Press.

Martin, R. 2008, January 28. "Collaboration Cisco Style." *Information Week:* 30–37.

McLuhan, M. 1964. *Understanding Media: The Extensions of Man.* New York: McGraw-Hill.

McKenna, R. 1997. *Real Time: Preparing for the Age of the Never Satisfied Customer.* Boston: Harvard Business School Press.

Moore, J. 1996. *The Death of Competition: Leadership and Strategy in the Age of Business Ecosystems.* New York: HarperBusiness.

Nachira, F., A. Nicolai, P. Dini, L. Leon, and M. Le Louarn. 2007. "Digital Business Ecosystems." Bruxelles: European Commission–Information Society and Media.

CHAPTER 2

Disruptive Innovation and Evolving Business Model

We walk into a store to buy some products, and the moment we like something we are tempted to scan the bar code with our handheld smartphones to compare the price at Amazon. We are motivated to place an order instantly if it is cheaper at the online store and to claim the incentive offer. Sometimes we go to the mall with family and while those folks are busy shopping for their stuff, we receive text alerts about discounts or instant offers by business merchants or service providers near us in the mall with the help of location-based services offered by Foursquare, Google, and others. We are experiencing these changes in the products and services offered, marketed, and served with the help of disruptive innovation and a changing business model.

Disruptive Innovation Creates Business Dilemma

In a rapidly changing technology and business environment, companies across industries such as information technology (IT), airlines, retailers, media, and banking are experiencing major disruptions by new and disruptive technologies and business models. The success of recent companies such as Dell, Facebook, Google, Best Buy, eBay, Salesforce.com, Virgin Blue, easyJet, Netflix, and ING Direct in capturing market share is a classic example of disruptive technologies and business models. The term *disruptive innovation* first gained popularity in 1997, coined by Harvard Business School professor Clayton Christensen in his book *The Innovator's Dilemma*. Christensen focused on how to embrace disruptive innovation to advantage and for survival. A sustaining innovation hardly results in the downfall of established companies, because it improves the performance of existing products along the dimensions that mainstream customers value. Disruptive innovations create new user excitement and acceptance along with the dumping of existing products and services. Apple's iPhone and iPad are clear examples of disruptive innovations that users accepted unequivocally.

Disruptive Innovation Introduces New Paradigm

Disruptive business models focus on creating, refining, reengineering, or optimizing a product/service, role/function/practice, category, market, sector, or industry. The most successful companies incorporate disruptive thinking into all of their business and management practices to gain distinctive competitive value propositions. Despite that, many established and often well-managed companies struggle with disruptive innovation. This is mostly because companies have been doing the same things with a regular source of sustained revenue and are not willing to cannibalize and change. We have seen many companies across every sector that have failed to embrace disruptive technologies or business models. They remained focused on making incremental gains through process improvements, were satisfied with their business models, and didn't recognize the threat of disruption until the last moment. Companies that haven't seen these innovative models as an opportunity have lost their edge and gone out of business.

To stay ahead in today's rapidly changing business environment, organizations need agile business processes that allow them to adapt quickly to evolving markets, customer needs, policies, regulations, and business models. The convergence of these emerging technologies and business practices—cloud, social, mobile, video, and big data–driven analytics, along with business process management (BPM)—is opening up interesting avenues for businesses.

Service-Oriented Architecture and Business Process Management Drive Systems of Engagement

Social and mobile business models have already contributed important new frameworks for collaboration and information sharing in the enterprise. While these technologies are still in a nascent state, BPM and service-oriented architecture (SOA) solutions are well established, providing a history of clear and complementary benefits. This is not surprising, given that BPM and SOA have arisen as the natural result of business and information technology (IT) users striving to work together more efficiently and effectively.

Learning from customers' past experiences, interactions, and social conversations provides valuable insight that can be used to improve products, enhance customer-facing processes, and ultimately improve the overall customer experience. As stated in Chapter 1, although the five "Perfect Storm" technologies (cloud, social, mobile, video, and big data) have developed separately, their convergence at this time has been recognized as the "Tornado" phenomenon described by Geoffrey Moore. This "chasm" decision making is driving enterprise information technology adoption strategies for IT that is creating business value in terms of agility. Since we are taking a "whole product" approach to digital business strategy for virtual enterprises, utilizing the digitization of customer-focused business practices, processes, and protocols will produce superior customer experience management solutions.

Clearly how this convergence is transforming customer value propositions throughout the business world is the theme of this book. So we want to illustrate how the converging actions of the Force 5 Tornado may be harnessed to enable competitive advantage by defining their synergistic interrelationships as shown in Figure 2.1

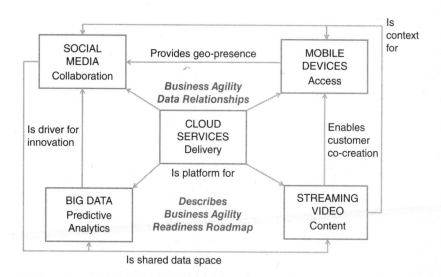

Figure 2.1   Force 5 Tornado Data Model

as the Force 5 Tornado Data Model. The common element of the Force 5 Tornado technologies of cloud, social, mobile, video, and big data–driven analytics is the value of information to anticipate the future. The interrelated five Forces of the Tornado are disrupting product-focused businesses as laggards and replacing them with more valuable customer-centric business ecosystems.

As the technologies and business practices surrounding cloud, social, mobile, video, and big data–driven analytics as well as SOA and BPM mature, IT and business stakeholders are discovering new ways to work together and engage customers via dynamic business processes that address several important business imperatives.

Contemplating further, we find that fragmented data, disjointed systems, and multichannel interactions make it difficult to deliver a consistent customer experience. Such inconsistent experiences result in lower customer satisfaction and a loss of business in the longer term. There are multiple opportunities to up-sell and cross-sell products that impact the bottom line. If companies can't identify such opportunities, bring a product to market quickly, or offer the right product to the right customer at the right time, significant loss of revenue may occur. Furthermore, it is paramount for businesses to embrace regulations such as know your customer (KYC), export/import laws, payment card industry/data security standards (PCI/DSS), and taxation policies. They must also comply with the service-level agreements (SLAs) that they have committed to their customers. If they don't meet these requirements, they can face serious fines, penalties, and losses of business.

Business processes are at the heart of what makes or breaks a business, as well as what differentiates it from the competition. Business processes that deliver operational efficiency, business visibility, and agility give an enterprise an edge by enabling it to conduct business in a cost-effective, dynamic way. As organizations strive for greater efficiency and effectiveness, they create or adapt technology to fill their needs. Force 5 Tornado technologies of cloud, social, mobile, video, and big data–driven analytics are driving a fundamental business transformation with agility. Astute organizations are implementing these technologies to respond to today's multifaceted business challenges and to take advantage of new opportunities.

In order to take advantage of the convergence of cloud, social, mobile, video, and big data–driven analytics to become more innovative, nimble, and adaptive to change, we must first understand how these technology-based solutions work independently of one another.

We will explore this convergence in more detail later in Chapter 2 with the focus on video as a fifth force of the perfect storm. Video has strong implications for transforming the way businesses relate to and engage their customers via technology. The fact that we include video reflects our convictions that it is another important technology enabler that recently has changed consumers' behavior in many ways. Smart devices with built-in cameras that record good quality video offer consumers the power to capture events on film at the time of happening and report them to the world via social media. Real-time news streaming is relying on crowdsourcing for real-time news and videos from social feeds. These videos have not only challenged and transformed news agencies and media reporting, but also have helped in capturing consumers' feedback and support across all industries around the globe.

The recently emerging cloud-based technologies and cloud operating environment (discussed in detail in Chapter 3) based on a scalable elastic model have supported a new services deployment model that can be consumed globally from anywhere on any device. The cloud platform has enabled enterprise solutions to fit into Christensen's framework for disruptive innovation. This new technology platform for computing offers cheaper, simpler, and often wider alternatives compared to legacy models of enterprise computing.

These models have encouraged established corporations to respond by adopting the new business models alongside their established ones. According to Michael Porter and other strategy theorists, managing two different business models in the same industry at the same time is challenging because the two models and their underlying value chains can conflict with each other. For example, airlines selling tickets through the Internet to fight back against their low-cost competitors risk alienating their existing travel agents.

Social computing concerns the intersection of social behavior and computational systems. It encompasses various technologies and tools for social engagement, social media monitoring, and analytics. As consumers share experiences on social networking sites such as Twitter, Facebook, LinkedIn, and Google+, astute organizations are tapping into the dialogue to better understand their customers and prospects. Analyzing the data generated from social interactions can reveal insights into what customers want, need, and prefer, a body of knowledge commonly called customer sentiment. Social computing tools help organizations identify key trends and develop ideas for new products and services. Within the workplace, companies use similar social technologies for collaboration, brainstorming, and innovation. Wikis, chats, discussion threads, content ratings, gamification, and crowdsourcing are commonplace.

Mobile computing implies more than just doing familiar tasks from new devices and locations. Today's mobile applications infuse device-centric features such as GPS-driven geolocation services, contextual search results, gamification, and the ability to interact easily with social media sites for group validation. Smartphones and tablets support these new modes of interaction while integrating traditional work-related tasks, drawing on information from enterprise information systems. The mobile technology landscape is driven by consumer apps that utilize a variety of operating systems, tools, languages, and platforms. Innovative organizations are taking advantage of mobile computing advancements to help employees, partners, and customers connect and collaborate, regardless of location.

Big data is a major revolution of current times and will have a larger impact in advanced analytics in the coming years (discussed in detail in Chapter 8). Big data is becoming relevant in all business cases and will help in gaining competitive advantage. As the technology platform is maturing rapidly, organizations need to give strategic importance to big data sources to gain insights and to offer their products and services based on customer needs. Analytics and business intelligence based on new big data sources will help business decision makers with greater predictability.

Business process management (BPM) represents a strategy of managing and improving business performance by continuously optimizing business processes in a closed-loop cycle of modeling, execution, and measurement. Everything companies do to attain their business goals involves a process, structured or unstructured. BPM technology helps organizations to create, document, and modify business processes quickly and drive process changes in a nontechnical, business-friendly manner, along with technology for implementing, executing, and monitoring end-to-end processes. BPM systems often span numerous departments and IT systems in an organization. By merging technologies and functions into a seamlessly integrated environment, BPM gives technologists and business specialists a common language for achieving their shared and separate goals.

Service-oriented architecture (SOA) has become a popular method for linking disparate applications across many different business lines and functions, thereby centralizing and improving process efficiency. It facilitates the creation of loosely coupled, interoperable business services that are easily shared within and among enterprises. Companies utilize this architecture for its reuse and agility. When properly constructed and interfaced, SOA applications can last for decades in the form of virtualized enterprise applications. SOA interoperates with all parts of the IT architecture to integrate business applications, moving them onto a common service bus and a common work flow engine.

Having understood these key technologies concepts at a very high level, we need to analyze further how the convergence of these technologies and business models would help in driving business agility.

Effective collaboration is often fueled by information that is created and managed both within the business and through external sources. To complete an assigned task, knowledge workers must access and discover many pieces of information. For many organizational processes, this has increased the number of people who are involved in a completely unscripted and undefined chain of events. Without a defined process, the time required to complete an activity increases.

In addition to discovering information and people who can aid decision making, employees continually create new information using a variety of tools and resources, both within and outside the company. The use of these tools is typically not well coordinated in the context of what these people are working on. Even more troubling, many knowledge workers can't access them. The term *social BPM* is sometimes used to describe the use of social tools and techniques in business process improvement efforts. Social BPM helps eliminate barriers between decision makers and the people affected by their decisions. These tools facilitate communication that companies can leverage to improve business processes. Social BPM enables collaboration in the context of BPM and adds the richness of modern social communication tools.

In conjunction with SOA, social BPM increases business value by extracting information from enterprise systems and using it within social networks. Meanwhile, social technologies permit employees to utilize feedback from social networks to improve business processes.

Let's look at some examples of how the convergence of BPM, SOA, and social technologies can improve internal efficiency for employees and create better experiences for customers.

With the advent of social networks and mobile technology, companies need to focus not only on process efficiency but also on customer engagement. Customers demand to interact with companies via new types of social and mobile channels. They want to place their orders using mobile phones and tweet about their issues. Companies need to gear up to meet these expectations according to the customers' demands. Most companies are organized into departments such as marketing, sales, and service. They might maintain prospect data in a salesforce automation system, order information in an enterprise resource planning (ERP) system, and customer issues in a customer relationship management (CRM) system. In order to best serve the customers, organizations must pull information scattered across systems, include information from social networks, and create a unified customer view. No matter what channel customers use and no matter what departments they contact, they get a consistent response from the company. BPM helps deliver these experiences and design customer experiences that integrate the underlining channels, systems, and applications to make sure that accurate, consistent information is delivered to the right people at the right time across any channel of interaction.

In addition to orchestrating systems and channels for consistency, BPM also enhances decision making. By using data from both current and historical transactions, sales and service professionals can determine customer preferences, customer value, and churn propensity. When infused into the process and presented in the right context, this insight can enable knowledge workers to make timely suggestions, such as presenting a targeted offer, giving a discount, or offering a troubleshooting tip based on experiences with similar customers. BPM in conjunction with complex event processing (CEP) capabilities can "listen" for event patterns and identify customer issues as they arise (credit card stolen, baggage lost, or change of address). Powered with this insight, systems can trigger alerts or invoke corrective processes immediately. Such abilities let customer service reps take action before routine issues snowball into disasters.

In order to succeed in the most competitive business environment, an IT organization needs to understand the business requirements for new information and how it can affect measurable business outcomes and help drive innovation. The increasing volume, variety, and velocity means data will need different infrastructures for accessing, storing, managing, analyzing, governing, presenting, and collaborating on, and sharing information.

CIO-CMO Alignment via Business Process Management and Balanced Scorecard

The need for developing a system of engagement (SOE) using cloud SOA products, including platform as a service (PaaS) middleware for BPM services, is a fundamental core of the Ecosystem Hub architecture. This will also support adaptive strategic planning processes, described in Chapter 1, as well as adaptive real-time operational planning processes with big data analytics (BDA) collaboration services. See Figure 2.2 for an illustration of the key elements of BDA services delivered by the Ecosystem Hub architecture.

As previously stated, Ecosystem Hubs provide the environment that facilitates digital business web services for applications such as inventory visibility, BPM, and performance metrics displayed in

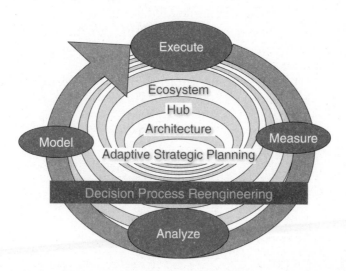

Figure 2.2 Adaptive Strategic Planning and Operational Planning Processes with BDA

real-time dashboards. Application software developed using an SOA and deployed as web services has provided the technology base for the concept of the next-generation Internet—Web 2.0.

Systems of engagement (SOEs) are emerging as a new paradigm for both consumer and business applications. Users are tempted to access multiple channels such as mobile, social, locations, and maps in the context of their transactional applications to make effective decisions. These sources render various data types (mostly unstructured or semi-structured) that need to be captured, processed, and analyzed in real or near real time to provide information that users are seeking from their systems.

In a 2011 white paper, management and IT leader Geoffrey Moore introduced the term *systems of engagement* to describe systems that focus on "empowering the middle of the enterprise to communicate and collaborate across business boundaries, global time zones, and language and culture barriers, using next-generation IT applications and infrastructure adapted from the consumer space" (Castiglioni and Crudele 2013).

Adaptive Strategic Planning Framework

Enterprises need a framework that facilitates adaptive strategic planning for value chain management. A suite of BDA applications provides the functionality needed to implement c-commerce business models. A continuous c-commerce strategic planning process approach, which adapts to the real-time execution of the business plans, is essential to value chain management success.

The four key BDA framework elements deployed in a service-oriented architecture as a network of Ecosystem Hub platforms are defined as follows:

1. Execute via balanced scorecard.
2. Measure via business activity monitoring.
3. Analyze via knowledge management.
4. Model via dynamic simulation.

Execute via Balanced Scorecard

The execute function allows an enterprise to continuously translate c-commerce strategy into action within day-to-day business activities and by constantly adapting strategy with real-time feedback based on the actual operational performance of each value chain. Adaptive ability can be expressed in terms of three types of actions resulting from the management decision-making process: predictive, pro-active, and reactive. Predictive controls involve anticipating a problem and deploying a solution in time to avoid the adversity. Proactive responses are associated with smooth recovery from a problem before it escalates. Reactive capabilities are limited by supply chain uncertainties to just-in-case deployments of inventory safety stock, as well as excessive resource allocation for production and distribution capacity in order to maintain contractual service-level agreements.

Measure via Business Activity Monitoring

The most important feature of the adaptive strategic planning process is the ability to provide feedback by means of real-time performance measurement. As the enterprise executes its c-commerce strategy for each value chain, the world around it changes and that strategy must adapt accordingly. As a strategic management practice, adaptive strategic planning must be a learning process. The BDA should facilitate a dialogue throughout the value chain so that performance can be interpreted, knowledge can be transferred, and improvements can be made. Real-time measurement is crucial because the longer the BPM latency, the more management is limited to reactive rather than proactive decision making. Leading enterprises are using IT solutions for SCM to speed relevant performance information to the appropriate managers and to display these key performance indicators (KPIs) in a desktop dashboard as exception reporting to focus decision-making attention. Critical success factors involve not only the determination of the correct KPIs, but also the refresh frequency for each KPI on each manager's dashboard.

Analyze via Knowledge Management

Key enabling technology trends in knowledge discovery and business intelligence are making management decision-making break-throughs possible. Data-mining techniques permit extracting and transforming data from multiple sources. Data mining can be classi-fied as either descriptive or predictive, where descriptive mining tasks characterize the general properties of the data whereas predictive mining tasks perform inferences on the source data. These knowl-edge discovery techniques can be used to explore trends and relationships across a value chain. Knowledge management enabled by a BDA with these tools and databases can support analytic approaches used to test and evaluate value chain design and operational policy hypotheses, explain the higher-level trends associated with the dynamics of supply and demand as part of the value chain management system, or generate new insights that update and refine the c-commerce strategy.

Model via Dynamic Simulation

The use of dynamic simulation of value chain business models will dramatically increase the effective execution of c-commerce strategies. Simulation allows the balanced scorecard cause-and-effect linkages of the strategy to be described mathematically and used for testing scenarios. This capability will help companies evaluate what-if scenarios. It will allow the entire management team to participate in interactive sessions for the real-time development of strategy. Dynamic simulation software will have the same impact on strategic planning that spreadsheet software has had on financial planning.

The BDA for adaptive strategic planning can be applied to a range of business process modeling applications and work with live operational data to dynamically model processes. Although such functionality provides a tool that allows users distributed across a virtual enterprise to collaborate in examining the potential opportunities or threats to planned business operations, it is important to note that virtual enterprise integration (VEI) is a precursor for success. The result of such collaboration is a clear understanding of the options, the risks, and the impacts across each value chain. Such predictive analyses can be shared across the value chain for joint decision making on the optimal alternatives that facilitate collaborative planning and forecasting activities.

BDA technology is emerging to enable the design and management of complex value chains for strategic, as well as tactical and eventually operational decision making. For example, Intel uses a BDA at the strategic level to design a value chain based on validated SCM models that ensure that the right product is placed in the right location in the right amount at the right time based on service-level agreement performance objectives (SCOR, 2002). Then the tool can be used tactically to determine if these inventory management decisions are still valid based on the demand dynamics of the marketplace or on daily replenishment priorities, such as adaptive supply chain execution decisions in terms of which distribution center should fulfill an order.

The result is a new type of management tool that helps enterprises to quickly identify the impact of changing market conditions on value chain performance and to access the best course of action to minimize risk and maximize revenue based on specified KPIs. It also provides rapid what-if analysis to make decisions quickly, and then can facilitate effective communication of that predicted performance information throughout the virtual enterprise using a service-level agreement framework.

Deploying Big Data Analytics: Adaptive Strategic Planning

An incremental implementation roadmap for BDA leverages the practical application of various enabling technologies for an adaptive strategic planning framework discussed in the previous section. The fundamental concept is to generate and/or evaluate a strategic plan that adapts to the tactical and operational-level performance changes based on the feedback from KPIs.

Such a roadmap for developing an adaptive strategic planning infrastructure is navigated in accordance with the following six tasks:

1. Develop c-commerce business models by value chain. Craft a set of integrated intranet, extranet, and Internet value chain scenarios that represent value chain optimization opportunities using the leverage of the business ecosystem models as a benchmark.
2. Focus on the Ecosystem Hub SOA to evaluate enterprise information portal (EIP) product functionality for providing content management, enterprise application integration, and semantic interoperability services to support a BDA. Such a supply chain integration framework includes a value chain model repository featuring analysis and reporting tools with data mining capabilities to evaluate Ecosystem Hub functionality for providing knowledge management capabilities.
3. Identify specific value chain operating scenarios and supply chain management issues within key enterprise initiatives, and model the core processes using the dynamic simulation tools. The value chain models are populated with balanced scorecard

KPIs. These models are then used to identify supply chain bottlenecks and analyze areas for process improvement, evaluate the business case associated with c-commerce initiatives, and design optimal value chains for specific target customer or market initiatives.

4. Focus on developing and testing the feedback mechanisms for balanced scorecard KPIs reporting of real-time business activity monitoring visibility data and event-based notifications captured from operational transactions that are facilitated by Ecosystem Hubs. This is a key element of the adaptive decision-making process that links supply chain performance management and business operations budgeting with enterprise-level c-commerce strategy.

5. Deployment of this initial adaptive strategic planning BDA completes the initial effort. The BDA facilitates changes to the alternative supply chain systems design and experimentation with potential outcomes as a result of these scenario changes, thereby evolving the strategic plan. The BDA provides a knowledge base for investment portfolio management of the c-commerce initiative information needed for the strategic and business planning effort, as well as facilitating the development of business cases supporting these initiatives.

6. For the adaptive strategic planning decision-making process reengineering to be fully realized, the successful BDA pilot system implementation must be extended and rehosted on an enterprise-class server. This provides the scalable Ecosystem Hub platform needed to support a fully operational competency center for real-time value chain management as part of a multiphase iterative implementation effort to realize incremental benefits. The strategic balanced scorecard KPIs are then deployed using a distributed network of Ecosystem Hubs, thereby instrumenting each of the various c-commerce value chain scenarios with the appropriate dashboards. Each dashboard reflects actual KPIs as the performance metrics associated with the individual decision maker's point of view for the virtual enterprise operations in an actionable way.

The combination of a BDA for strategic planning with an operational value chain management system competency center provides the feedback system to optimize value chain investment, as well as assure virtual enterprise agility. Thus, the benefits of VEI are achieved by implementing an orchestrated choreography of collaborative value chain scenarios executed in accordance with the appropriate intranet, extranet, and Internet business case analysis.

Once again there is an imperative need for the IT organization to work with key business leaders to develop an iterative information management strategy to support effective decision making. Bottom line: The value of CIO-CMO alignment goes way beyond surviving. It promotes a dominant digital business leading a strong virtual enterprise in a thriving business ecosystem.

Business Agility Readiness Transformation

The disruptive technologies such as delivery platforms (cloud, social, mobile), communication and collaboration channels (web, mobile, social), and big data (structured and unstructured) are influencing major business transformations almost at the same time. As written by Geoffrey Moore, systems of records such as enterprise resource planning (ERP), supply chain management (SCM), customer relationship management (CRM), and human capital management (HCM) have delivered great transactional and operational efficiencies to business. These systems need to undergo major transformation and be complemented with systems of engagement, and finally need to be supported with multidimensional scoring (MDS) to create business agility.

Business Agility Circle of Influence

The biggest technology influences of the next half decade include cloud computing, social media (or more specifically social business), next-generation mobility, big data, and predictive analytics. These will not only help the current businesses to survive and thrive but also help build digital businesses with greater agility. Systems of records (SORs) of the past helped business with transactional data, providing facts, numbers, charts, and reports to run business operations successfully. Systems of engagement (SOEs) with the evolution of social media influence relationships and trust in the context of records.

Now in the current business environment, multidimensional scoring is the big idea to explore, evaluate, and deploy to measure business agility in a much more tangible way.

What Is Multidimensional Scoring (MDS)?

Grading, rating, scoring, and return on investment (ROI) have been talked about in many business contexts. We have discussed use of the balanced scorecard to evaluate the success of business parameters. Lead scoring has been extensively used in the context of customer relationship management, but Lauren Littlefield explains three-dimensional scoring as the next big thing in measuring success in business quantitatively. This concept is illustrated in Figure 2.3.

Systems of records (SORs) render facts and figures about businesses while systems of engagement (SOEs) drive relationships, and, in turn, relationships drive revenue. Three-dimensional scoring ultimately turns engaged relationships into revenue-driving streams that can be measured.

We tend to measure the effectiveness of everything in our lives, and that holds true for businesses as well. Business entities such as products, services, customers, suppliers, employees, and their profiles, life cycles, and engagement must be measured for agility that provides sustainable competitive advantage.

Customers are the most valuable assets of any business, and they are directly responsible for the success of business; therefore it is extremely important to profile them (company, contacts, etc.) and score them individually as to their likes and dislikes, behavioral patterns, buying decisions, recommendations, connections, favorites,

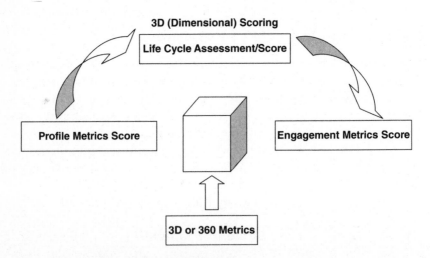

Figure 2.3 The Concept of 3-D Scoring

and so on. The profile score enables direct communication and engagement strategies, helping achieve a higher conversion rate of closure.

Scoring and profiling all business entities such as customers, employees, partners, and suppliers will directly provide metrics to measure the time and resources that need to be deployed based on the score.

Measuring Relationship in Systems of Engagement

We have assessed the significance of relationship in business. We know that business entity relationship plays an important role in business process optimization and effectiveness. But new behavioral and social inputs in the process add the third dimension in the 3-D metrics that will play a highly significant role in the next generation of business agility.

Recall the discussion in Chapter 1 of the role of trust in the culture of a digital business as the key to virtual enterprise relationship management as a core competency for business ecosystem success. Therefore, we add trust expressed in terms of "listening to own conscience" as the fourth dimension in the multidimensional scoring (MDS), as shown is Figure 2.4 that would further enhance innovation in driving business agility.

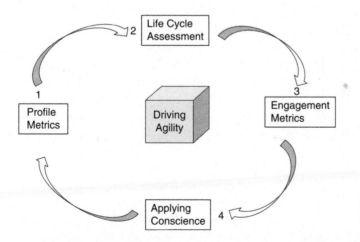

Figure 2.4   Trust Cycle Drives MDS

Listening to Own Conscience: Fourth Dimension in Driving Agility

Listening to our own inner conscience offers the voice that will add the fourth dimension in the multidimensional metrics to provide business agility.

In his book *Self Power* (Ebury Publishing, 2012), Deepak Chopra, MD, highlights the power within every individual and the spiritual awakening coming from divine power to create something new or to solve the greatest challenges. He describes the three levels of emotions in awareness:

1. Contracted
2. Expanded
3. Pure

This concept is both logical and spiritual, and has higher levels of consciousness relationship to self-power. He further describes how consciousness is linked to the spiritual solution that must be scored and graded in the multidimensional metrics.

Stephen R. Covey in his book *The 8th Habit: From Effectiveness to Greatness* (Free Press, 2004) also emphasizes the necessity to find your own inner voice and express your voice with vision, discipline, and passion, and as coming from divine power and conscience. He then advocates inspiring others to find their voices to inculcate leadership.

In the book *Behind the Cloud* (John Wiley & Sons, 2009), Marc Benioff, founder and CEO of Salesforce.com, outlines his initial awakening to leverage the disruptive innovation offered by the Internet. He made several trips to Hawaii over several months in quest of his inner voice and conscience. Benioff decided it was time to think more deeply about the technological landscape—and his own career—so he took a sabbatical that started with a trip to India, where he met a diverse variety of people, including a spiritual leader and humanitarian, Mata Amritanandamayi. Despite all the technological resources available to him, he listened to his inner conscience and executed what he found there with passion to create Salesforce.com as one of the most innovative business corporations of recent times.

In accepting Hall of Fame induction by the San Francisco Bay Area Council, Larry Ellison, founder and CEO of Oracle, chose to praise Steve Jobs for his creative genius in our generation. He characterized Jobs as a philosopher, an artist, and an inventor who always listened to his inner voice and conscience and applied what he found there with tireless diligence and meticulous precision until his last breath to put the most sophisticated Apple devices in our hands and to converge major technologies. According to Ellison, Jobs was our Edison and our Picasso who was singularly focused on turning ideas into things that worked.

These references to inventions and innovations support the notion that people should listen to their own inner consciences, surrounding them with all other dimensions of information. It is paramount to allocate a grading pattern to this fourth dimension.

Oracle Fusion Applications: Great Innovation as Cloud SaaS Offerings

Realizing this disruptive innovation in technology and business model, Oracle has already committed huge development resources to build the next generation of Fusion Applications to meet the growing need for new applications to offer various choices of on-premises, on-cloud, or on-hybrid deployment, and has recently begun unveiling the next generation of business applications. By setting the standard for application architecture, design, and deployment, Oracle enables customers to extend the value of their applications environment by using Oracle Fusion Applications components side by side with their existing applications portfolio. Delivered as a complete suite of modular applications, Oracle Fusion Applications coexist with existing Oracle Applications. As one module, a product family, or the entire suite, customers can choose to leverage the advances pioneered by Oracle at a pace that matches business needs for a new level of performance.

Designed from the ground up, leveraging the latest technology advances, and incorporating best practices gathered from Oracle's thousands of customers, Oracle Fusion Applications are 100 percent open standards–based business applications that set a new standard for users to innovate, work, and adopt technology. Oracle Fusion Applications provide rich functional capabilities with more than 100 modules in seven different product families providing functionality for many industries and geographies—financial management, procurement and sourcing, project and portfolio management, human capital management, customer relationship management, supply chain management, and governance risk and compliance.

Built on an SOA foundation, Oracle Fusion Applications give users the ability to uniquely manage functions across a heterogeneous environment, such as distributed order orchestration and shared services procurement. Oracle Fusion Applications offer a revolutionary new role-based user experience, uniting exception-based processing, business intelligence, transactions, and collaboration in the context of the work being performed.

Oracle Fusion Applications offer a complete set of deployment options—from on premises to private clouds, public clouds, and business process outsourcing or hybrid combinations of these. The ability to implement in a modular fashion and to coexist with existing applications from either Oracle or third parties provides customers with the broadest choice in adopting Oracle Fusion Applications without having to necessarily rip out and replace existing investments.

Continuing with an aggressive cloud strategy, Oracle recently acquired Taleo for $1.9 billion, a cloud-based talent management software provider with 5,000 customers and 1,400 employees. It provides recruiting and on-boarding, performance management and goal setting, compensation, succession, and learning and development. This complete suite tied to reporting and analytics is designed to streamline human resources operations and employee career management across retail and hospitality, travel, health care, media and entertainment, financial services, technology, and energy and mining.

In its continued drive to address the disruptive innovation and customers' demand for solutions in the public cloud space, Oracle also acquired RightNow for $1.43 billion on October 24, 2011, to address its gaps in its customer service solutions. The Taleo purchase addresses a gap in talent management solutions that rival SAP plugged with its recent acquisition of Success Factors for $3.4 billion.

Oracle hopes to gain massive cloud scale through Taleo's 74 million transactions per day and 240 million candidates on Taleo Talent Exchange. In order to fill a gap and address disruptive innovation in the area of the cloud business model, on February 8, 2013, Oracle completed the acquisition of Eloqua for $871 million. The combination of companies will accelerate the pace of the Modern Marketing revolution and enable Oracle and Eloqua customers to offer exceptional customer experiences.

With consumerization of IT (CoIT) and with major disruptive innovation in technology and its business model, Oracle has taken a major leap to stay as a forerunner in this emerging cloud computing space.

The automobile industry is not an exception to this disruptive innovation in technologies. U.S. automakers lost their competitive edge in the face of Japanese automakers' innovative cost and fuel efficiency. Recently, Tata Motors announced its Nano, which will retail for 1 lakh, or about $2,500, in the Indian market. It is a fully functional, four-door vehicle that aims to replace motorbikes. Small Brazilian company Obvio is set to release its first hybrid car, the 828, at a price of $14,000, less than half the cost of a Toyota Prius. By radically redesigning the traditional automotive production and distribution processes, Tata is positioned to grow sales of cars across the developing world and perhaps ultimately in low-end segments of the developed world. This is an example of disruptive innovation where competitors will have to create entirely new processes to produce a similar product, and it will not be easy to make a profit at this price by stripping down a conventional car. Tata Motors is targeting not only scooter and motorcycle buyers who pay around $1,250 today but also customers who need cars for commuting in busy traffic. Tata Motors introduced new automobile design and production processes to create a new market for the Nano. The company is also planning an innovative distribution model of shipping semifinished parts to rural entrepreneurs who can assemble and service these cars and customize them to suit customer needs. This innovative and disruptive model of distribution and being able to make to order on demand would help facilitate greater customization in the auto industry.

These emerging technologies such as social and collaborative power of software (discussed in Chapters 4 and 5) have also started disrupting the conventional business model by encouraging the carrying out of business from anywhere, not necessarily needing to have physical infrastructure. It is much easier to start business operations remotely, assemble the team globally, and build the global virtual team with the help of collaborative technologies.

Dell's Direct Sales

Dell Computer established a niche in the direct sales model that bypassed the dealer in the supply chain and delivered computers directly to customers on a build-to-order model. Unlike other major vendors such as Hewlett-Packard (HP) and IBM, Dell does not manufacture the components; it merely assembles computers based on the best available ones in the market. It uses the latest e-business and e-commerce platform based on a robust web technology to support virtual integration among suppliers, manufacturers, and consumers. Dell treats suppliers and service providers as though they are inside the company, and its systems are linked in real time with theirs; they collaborate with Dell employees in all activities: design, sales, and support.

Dell implemented a zero inventory and just-in-time delivery model that helped the company to lower warehouse costs and manage inventory costs, and also to reduce staff, making the company smart and efficient. Its virtual integration allowed Dell to meet customers' needs faster and more efficiently than others; at the same time it became more efficient and responsive to change. The exceptional performance of Dell Computer in recent years illustrates an innovative response to a fundamental competitive factor in the personal computer industry—the value of time. Dell's strategies of direct sales and build-to-order production have proven successful in minimizing inventory and bringing new products to market quickly, enabling it to increase market share and achieve high returns on investment.

The Dell case illustrates how one business model may have inherent advantages under particular market conditions, but it also shows the importance of execution in exploiting those advantages. This competitive advantage has not been sustainable in recent years, because the strategy for a build-to-order business model was copied due to the low barrier to entry by competitors and is now a best practice in the PC industry.

Note that Dell's use of emerging information technology (IT) has been vital to executing both elements of its business model—direct sales and build-to-order. This case study provides valuable insights into how emerging technologies can be applied to achieve speed in an industry in which time to market is critical, as well as the need for developing a digital business culture of innovation to create the business agility necessary to sustain the competitive advantage.

The changing need to access the right information and to collaborate with the virtual team at the right time has led the corporate groups to build a next-generation workplace leveraging with emerging Enterprise 2.0 technologies that tie together people, ideas, content, processes, systems, and enterprise applications. Next generation organization may effectively manage their global team in virtual environment by effective use and deployment of technologies for collaboration with document, conferencing, chat, and bulletin board.

We have witnessed the failure of electronic retailer Circuit City, which was focused on low prices, while competitor Best Buy rapidly moved to greater value for customers, not just a focus on price. Circuit City, the consumer electronics giant, went bust and closed down its large number of retail stores due to the lack of innovation in its business model while Best Buy offered value-added services and an innovative approach to business that helped it to survive, thrive, and prosper.

Besides many other factors, Circuit City was slow to adopt the latest technology and remained in Web 1.0 with its website not being easy to navigate. In contrast, Best Buy kept enhancing the customer experience with the latest technology on the Oracle Web Experience platform and with online strategies that had the customer at the center of the company's efforts. Similarly, leading bookseller Barnes & Noble, video rental store Blockbuster, and Circuit City were all faced with a dilemma and unable to recognize the leading technology innovation of Internet-based delivery that gave rise to Amazon, Netflix, and Best Buy. It's the same thing that has been happening to the newspaper and publishing industries: New and more efficient business models have emerged, making previous models increasingly obsolete.

Netflix's rental-by-mail model and Redbox's $1 DVD kiosks are the clear winners over Blockbuster's business model, but the online video distribution models that Netflix, Hulu, YouTube, and others have pioneered are also disrupting the DVD market.

Video: New Disruptive Technology for Digital Content

The amount of video has rapidly increased in recent years. Creating video content and dissemination has been easier than ever before using smart devices with powerful cameras. Recently, YouTube reported more than 4.5 billion hours watched per month. Netflix reported 1.5 billion hours of video consumption. People post their videos on YouTube, look for some entertainment, and send videos to friends on social media.

The share of total video plays by mobile and tablet platforms continues to take away playing time from other devices, as reported by Ooyala as part of its Global Video Index for the fourth quarter of 2013. Ooyala, the software as a service (SaaS) video management and analytics company, releases the aggregated numbers developed from its client base that serves 200 million viewers globally. The mobile plus tablet share of video plays reached almost 18 percent—an increase of more than 10 percentage points over the 7 percent reported a year earlier. The report predicts that mobile video "could make up to half of all online video consumption by 2016" (Seave 2014, March 31).

Long-form content dominates all device viewing. Long-form content is considered content that runs 10 minutes or longer, and even longer-form content is 30 minutes or longer (Seave 2014, April 1):

- Watching content for longer than 10 minutes is at 61 percent for desktop video viewing, 60 percent for tablets, 75 percent for mobile devices, and 81 percent for connected TVs.
- Watching content for longer than 30 minutes is at 34 percent for desktop video viewing, 36 percent for tablets, 53 percent for mobile devices, and 63 percent for connected TVs.

We live in an increasingly digital age. More than a third of the world's population uses the Internet today; by 2017, nearly half will. In developed economies, these numbers are far higher: In the United States, for example, the share of the population using the Internet will increase from 83 percent today to 87 percent by 2017 (Webster and Perry 2013).

Reaching the connected audience effectively requires the ability to create highly engaging experiences, and digital video has quickly become a critical component of these experiences. About half of worldwide Internet users watch video online today; by 2017, almost two-thirds of worldwide Internet users will be watching video online (i.e., some 2.2 billion people). In the United States, 76 percent of Internet users watch video over the Internet today; by 2017, 85 percent of Internet users will watch video over the Internet.

Let's explore some of the use cases for digital video. Broadly, there are two camps that publish digital video, and their goals are somewhat different.

Digital Video in Marketing

Marketers are using digital video to tell their brand story, increase sales, and turn customers into fans. They use digital video to help sell or deliver products and services, and their digital video publishing costs typically become line items in the marketing budget. They measure ROI from video in terms of increased conversions and revenue, reduced customer churn, and increased customer loyalty and advocacy.

The marketing use case isn't just about brands, of course. Enterprises use video to communicate with shareholders, educate buyers, train sales teams and channel partners, and improve customer support. Schools, faith-based organizations, and other nonprofits use video to teach, build community, and inspire support. In federal, state, and local governments, elected officials use video to communicate with their constituents.

All of these organizations and individuals need to be able to analyze consumption and correlate video analytics with website analytics, shopping cart data, and other consumer information to target relevant content and optimize their marketing mix.

Digital Video in Media and Entertainment

For media and entertainment (M&E) companies, by contrast, digital video is the product; they need the ability to monetize it—whether through advertising, subscription, pay per view, or a mix of the three—and costs related to digital video publishing and delivery represent the cost of goods sold (COGS). M&E companies typically measure their ROI from video in terms of increased viewer engagement with the content itself (video starts and minutes consumed) and the increased advertising and paid content revenues that result.

Companies from every segment of the media and entertainment industry publish digital video today. Traditional newspaper publishers are equipping journalists with digital video cameras, bringing storytelling to a whole new level. Mainstream television broadcasters are putting recent shows online for catch-up viewing and making current episodes available via multichannel video programming distributor (MVPD) authentication together with added-value backstory content. Sports networks are streaming games and providing highlights to new audiences around the globe. Cable and satellite providers are extending the reach of their proprietary networks to over-the-top (OTT) devices via TV Everywhere (TVE) initiatives. Major studios are putting content online to expand their fan bases, and new programmers are being born on the Internet. All of these organizations need to be able to monetize their content—either by authenticating users or by injecting advertisements (or both); they must also analyze consumption and optimize placement, as well as optimize the experience through search and recommendations.

Overlapping Use Cases

The distinction between these two groups is not quite as cut-and-dried as it might appear, however. Companies that sell online training courses share many of the same concerns as media and entertainment companies regarding content protection and monetization, and athletic departments in large universities are often major broadcasters. Conversely, news organizations that make most of their digital video content freely available over the web are monetizing their websites more than the video itself. And media and entertainment companies are marketers, too: They need to promote their content—whether it's a new film, a TV series, or a championship sporting event—and what better way to do that than by using clips? So, despite some differences in the way different video publishers may think about their use of digital video and the particular features they need, it turns out that they share common requirements. This is why we've continued to see digital video solutions target and serve both market segments.

Another use case is Mobile Video Collaboration. It is the poster child for the Force 5 Tornado technology convergence model driven by three megatrends (Levitas, Berlinsky, Ellison et al. 2012):

- The consumerization of IT driven by the use of consumer-oriented devices and applications crossing over into the small and medium-sized businesses (SMB) and enterprise markets
- The increased adoption and usage of videoconferencing across the consumer, SMB, and enterprise markets
- Technology advances in the underlying foundation of mobile video driven by rapidly growing network broadband capacity and compounded by the growth of video-capable mobile devices such as smartphones and tablets

Blue Jeans Network and FuzeBox are two leading vendors in this market space. Both of these companies are disrupting the voice teleconferencing industry by leveraging the BYOD trend with support for all popular consumer devices as well as commercial video and data conferencing systems based on international networking standards. The following are key considerations with regard to widespread adoption of mobile video collaboration (Levitas, Berlinsky, Ellison et al. 2012):

- *Interoperability.* Creating a secure, seamless handoff to multiple networks and enabling integration with solutions in the areas of instant messaging/presence, telephony, web conferencing, mobile, and social media is key to tying remote video collaboration into the enterprise. Among the most important considerations is the ability to launch video collaboration sessions easily and intuitively from within familiar interfaces and normal work flows, enabling seamless dial plan integration to connect end points and devices from different vendors and consolidating multiple dial-in codes into one.

- *Scalability.* The growing number of desktop and mobile video users will present increasing scalability challenges for enterprise networks. The requirement for easy setup and management is critical in order to manage and secure a fast-growing volume of end points. Statistically, when more users are registered with the server, more calls are placed. If the number of calls per second exceeds the maximum supported by the server's architecture, the server slows down and starts rejecting or dropping calls.
- *Security.* When organizations are considering a bring your own device (BYOD) corporate policy, security is usually the first consideration for IT managers. Usage of embedded media encryption available for videoconferencing, such as H.235 security using 128-bit AES encryption, is among the technological advances that will provide a secure environment for the support of remote video collaboration tools.
- *Ease of use.* An easy-to-use video collaboration environment is perhaps the most important feature and affects the user and IT manager in different ways. The user wants ease of use, but simplicity on the surface depends on a number of hidden capabilities at work in the background, including effective firewall traversal, a centralized directory, straightforward authentication, and seamless encryption. The IT manager needs to control access and security and ensure enterprise-class management and redundancy.

There are numerous websites offering video content streaming services exploiting the capabilities of the cloud challenging conventional TV media. A few examples that follow illustrate the significance of video that has come by storm combined with convergence of cloud, social, mobile, and big data to enable business agility.

Current TV is a website that acts also as a TV channel, but is unlike other TV sites that post their content from TV on their video sites. Current TV does the reverse: It plays the content from its website on TV. People post their videos or podcasts on the site, and these are voted on by the community; the highest-ranking ones get shown on the television channel.

TED is extraordinary at streaming video—its whole concept is to spread ideas by enlisting some of the most brilliant minds in the world to create talks about many topics.

Following a style very similar to TED, Big Think takes an interview approach to its video instead of a prepared talk. It is based on prepared questions and answers that provoke some interesting facts about issues.

Blip.tv has mimicked what network television channels offer but uses independent producers. It currently has about 48,000 independently produced web shows and approximately 22 million viewers. It shares the revenue from ads with the producers, which allows them to make some income from their shows and keep producing them; in exchange, Blip.tv gets a constant supply of episodes for the video site.

Hulu carries content from many TV channels at very high streaming quality. It does not have international streaming rights for its content outside the United States and caters to the American audience only.

Vimeo shows a very holistic and welcoming approach to video sharing. Vimeo attracts more professional filmmakers than other sharing sites, and their videos are of higher quality. The community projects and groups also make it easy to find videos of a particular topic or subject matter. There are almost three million members and over 17,000 videos uploaded daily, so the community has a wide choice of videos.

Ustream also allows people to create their own broadcasting channels and their own live shows. It carries live broadcasting from many mainstream media sites. It doesn't allow people to join in with their video chats, but it does have live text chat.

Ooyala, in contrast, has a unique value proposition that is focused on harnessing the power of big data to deliver a broadcast TV quality online video experience globally across many devices. As an SaaS video management and analytics company, Ooyala solutions span enterprises for marketing, publishers for advertising, media and entertainment companies, as well as broadcasters for over-the-top

TV services like Netflix. Ooyala uses big data and real-time video analytics to provide insights to the intended audience, and to connect them with meaningful experiences that are both personalized for the viewers and profitable for the digital publishers. Ooyala maximizes engagement by delivering content based on viewer behaviors for both live and on-demand media. It also helps in streamlining work flows with powerful tools featuring fast transcoding, efficient content management, and robust player customization. Ooyala has all the products and services needed to implement the video capabilities in a system of engagement for a digital business.

The host of Internet-based TV sites based on a cloud computing platform, along with the convergence of social, mobile, and big data, creates the disruptive innovation that brings changes to society. We are familiar with crowdsourcing of breaking news that comes first in the form of video that people have captured at the point of occurrence and uploaded from their smart devices.

Big data and advanced analytics based on metadata information from video footage and predictive analytics based on voice-transcribed text processing provide greater insights into behavioral patterns and predictability. Surveillance cameras across public buildings, airports, security gates, and traffic lights stream video footage that provides great data mining capabilities for predictable behavioral patterns to mitigate or minimize security threats.

Netflix's Evolving Business Model

When Netflix was founded in 1997, the company was built on single-rental DVDs by mail—in effect, the standard Blockbuster model applied to the Internet. It was intended to be a more convenient way to rent movies—and to take advantage of lightweight DVDs that would be much cheaper to mail than bulky videocassettes. But the new firm's first idea flopped. Netflix originally charged a set fee for each movie rented, just like Blockbuster, which didn't catch on. Then CEO Reed Hastings decided to change the business to a subscription model that allowed customers to pay a flat monthly fee and rent as many movies as they wanted—with no late fees. This new business model proved successful and started challenging Blockbuster in a big way.

As Netflix became successful, competitors emerged because its business model seemed simple: Just keep DVDs in a warehouse and mail them out when orders come in. But Netflix's business is anything but simple, and that's why the competition has faltered. Quick delivery, for example, depends on having regional distribution centers in just the right places, and in its early days Netflix suffered from many complaints about slow delivery. It took several years for the company to get its distribution layout right. Managing a huge inventory of movies is another challenge. Ensuring quick delivery means stocking thousands of titles and having plenty of copies of the most popular films. That can get expensive. But a slim inventory that leaves customers waiting for movies would drive business away.

When Blockbuster, the huge video rental chain, set up a mail-delivery service in the summer of 2004, rival Netflix watched its stock price tumble. After inventing the business in the late 1990s, Netflix had already survived one competitive scare when Walmart began dabbling in DVD rentals. But by 2004, Walmart was backing out, having decided that video rentals weren't part of its core business. But Blockbuster, the nation's largest video rental chain, was a much bigger threat. Video rentals were its entire business.

Six years later, Blockbuster was in tatters, leaving Netflix as the undisputed winner in the DVD-by-mail business. Blockbuster's long-anticipated bankruptcy filing was clear proof that the company had clung far too long to an outdated strategy and had failed to understand changes that others eagerly exploited. Blockbuster planned to reorganize and continue to operate its online rental service and its 3,000 retail stores while it came up with a new strategy. But even writing off $1 billion in debt wouldn't make Blockbuster competitive, and the chain's downfall reflects the huge risk any firm faces today by just standing still.

Netflix's secret sauce lies in its business model: algorithms that allow users to rate movies and then receive recommendations for other films they might like, including some they may never have heard of before. This kind of technology is common today, as sites like Pandora and Amazon make it a routine part of their users' experience. But Netflix was an early innovator, and CEO Hastings seems to have understood that enhancing customers' experience would build brand loyalty that is crucial in such a cutthroat industry.

In 2004, Redbox began offering video rentals for $1 a night through vending machines at fast-food restaurants, grocery stores, and other retail outlets, stealing Blockbuster customers with practically none of the overhead that comes from running actual stores. Redbox now has 24,000 kiosks nationwide. Apple is now in the movie-rental business, offering movie downloads for many popular devices. Cable and phone companies have also started offering video on demand straight to their customers' TVs, a service that suffers from a limited supply of movies but obviously offers the ultimate convenience. Netflix, for one, saw this coming, and has been aggressively developing its own on-demand offerings for subscribers, including converters that allow streaming straight to the TV.

Blockbuster copied moves like these, but was also consistently late to the game with no real innovations of its own. The recession sealed the deal, as business declined and Blockbuster was finally unable to make its debt payments, resulting in bankruptcy and eventual closure of stores.

Now with video streaming as its dominant business, Netflix is working to transform what, exactly, that streaming entails. At $8 per month, the company has been rolling out original programming, and it's clear that Netflix will look more like an alternative cable network—except on the Internet.

The Netflix story is also noteworthy due to the disruption of the cable TV industry pay-per-view business proven by the recent Emmy Award nominations for its *House of Cards* series as original programming.

In order to sustain business ecosystem leadership, digital businesses need to develop and execute a customer experience management strategy enabled by the relevant social business technology that will drive a customer-centric value chain as a virtual enterprise. The Ecosystem Hub architecture will continue to be described throughout chapters in the book as well as in the Epilogue with use case scenarios from the travel, tourism, and hospitality industry. Such familiar keystone scenarios utilize a virtual enterprise integration methodology that builds on a virtual Visitor Information Center (vVIC) platform as an example of Ecosystem Hubs developed using an iterative incremental implementation roadmap.

The key for building next-generation digital businesses is integrating the business ecosystem with customer engagement solutions. Remember this approach utilizes two fundamental elements of enterprise information systems engineering:

- Ecosystem Hub architecture that employs the Force 5 Tornado technologies using collaborative commerce principles.
- Ecosystem Hub implementation roadmap that is an extensible, robust, scalable model for digital business transformation in accordance with business agility readiness gap analysis concepts.

These elements provide the foundation of our strategic framework to build systems of engagement for creating business agility.

Travel Industry Disruption by Force 5 Tornado

The travel industry has a history of IT innovation disruption and now digital video is disrupting the marketing of destinations in the tourism industry:

✓ First, the global distribution system changes airlines reservations . . .
✓ Then, disruption via Internet disintermediation of travel agent in 1990s . . .
✓ Now, DMAI *Futures Study* cites destination marketing organization disruption via "Googling" . . .

The travel, tourism and hospitality use case describes a destination marketing industry scenario that illustrates how the Ecosystem Hub Implementation Roadmap can be employed for evaluating

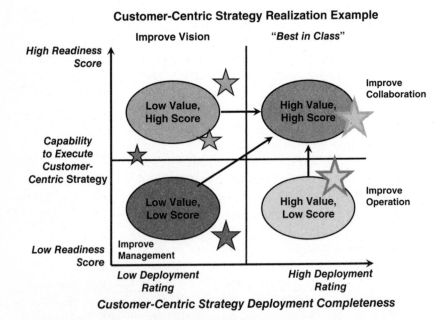

Figure 2.5   Business Agility Readiness Assessment

business agility readiness. The example used is for the Sonoma County Tourism (SCT) Ecosystem as depicted in the example shown in Figure 2.5 for the "to-be" SOE deployed for the next Sneakaway campaign.

The Epilogue contains the keystone scenario assessment of business agility readiness for the SCT Sneakaway campaign. Recall that this use case features an overview of the development of the Ecosystem Hub via the cloud-based Simpleview Social CRM Partner Extranet to further describe the SCT Ecosystem. As such, key issues surrounding cloud, social, mobile, video, and big data analytic applications are discussed.

Remember that this case study will continue to evolve in order to provide an illustrative real-time story of how the Force 5 Tornado technologies can create the business agility needed to gain and sustain your competitive advantage. It may be accessed via the Creating Business Agility blog. Stay tuned for more . . . !!!

References

Castiglioni, F., & M. Crudele 2013, October 22. "Design an SoE Ecosystem to Support Rich user experiences." IBM Corporation.

Levitas, D., I. Berlinsky, S. Ellison et al. March 2012. "Mobile Video Collaboration: The New Business Reality." International Data Corporation.

Supply-Chain Operations Reference-Model: SCOR Users Seminar. 2002, November 13. "From Modeling and Simulation to Real Time Decision Support." Pittsburgh: Supply-Chain Council.

Seave, A. 2014, March 31. "Mobile and Tablet Video Continues Exponential Growth, Reports Ooyala in Quarterly Index." *Forbes.*

Seave, A. 2014, April 1. "Mobile Video Viewers Spend Majority of Time Watching Long-Form Content." *Forbes.*

Webster, M., and R. Perry (October 2013). "The Business Value of Ooyala's Digital Video Solution." International Data Corporation.

CHAPTER 3

Hyperconnectivity Drives Innovation

As you are reading this chapter, you may have already noted the significance of business agility and the roadmap presented using the balanced scorecard in our previous chapters. We have attempted to lay a sound foundation to define various business stakeholders and how these technology forces have helped align chief information officers (CIOs), chief marketing officers (CMOs), and others in the current turbulent business environment. We have also put our best efforts into defining the Business Agility Readiness Roadmap with clear guideposts to help you make rapid progress in your business process optimization. We have made an effort to highlight cases of success and failure that would help you to identify clearly the stage you are at in your business and to transform your business with the impact of these technology forces. You have noticed that it is imperative to transform your current business model and processes to create business agility to survive and thrive in business irrespective of what business sector you are in today. It was okay to run a business independently just a few years ago, but no longer. We introduced and talked about business ecosystems, a concept that brings all stakeholders such as employees, customers, and partners (distributors, value-added resellers, systems integrators, independent consultants, investors, shareholders) to participate in your business to create business agility and to help your business succeed. Considering carefully, you would realize that all play a major role in your business, and none should be ignored or taken lightly.

We have entered the age of hyperconnectivity—the state in which we are always connected to the Internet through a number of devices (computers, PDAs, smart devices, smartphones), accessing applications and content for various purposes. Rapid innovation in the technology sector has continued to drive consumers and businesses to adopt devices that enable increasingly mobile and connected access to their content and services. This new era is about much more than just sheer numbers of new network-connected devices, computers, and applications. It is about providing pervasive access to, and continuous presence on, the network, where anyone or anything can interact with anyone or anything else no matter where they are located. We also referred to a paradigm shift from a system of record (SOR) to a system of engagement (SOE) that is maturing rapidly in adoption both at the consumer level and at the business level.

As Fabio Castiglioni and Michele Crudele at IBM write, online consumers of current age require a rich experience that leverages information from disparate structured and unstructured sources, social channels, and their friends' recommendations. This offers quick information and better resources for effective decision making in general. This has become a norm in the consumer space, and we need to replicate the same in our businesses, too. A SOE enables this rich experience by extracting value from the information that comes from multiple channels and enabling new digitized business models. A cloud operating environment (CloudOE) is the platform that supports SOE workloads. The CloudOE enables the agility and velocity that an SOE needs by providing an ecosystem for developing, deploying, and operating SOE applications.

Hyperconnectivity has led major innovations in the area of emerging technologies such as the cloud, social, mobility, big data, and predictive analytics. In this chapter we stay focused on cloud technology and architecture that would enable business agility. In recent times, cloud computing has emerged as a much hyped and talked-about concept in information technology (IT). It has drawn the attention of not only IT professionals but all industry and management people seeking to understand and reap benefits from it. The IT media have written about it and major conferences are still drawing a large attendance of knowledge workers. It has gone to the extent that software mogul Marc Benioff of Salesforce.com made a sharp statement that "Software is dead," while in response, Larry Ellison of Oracle commented, "If we're *dead*—if there's no hardware or software in the cloud—we are so *screwed*. . . . But it's not water vapor! All of it is a computer attached to a network. What do you think Google runs on? Do they run on water vapor? I mean, *cloud*—it's all databases, operating systems, memory, microprocessors, and the Internet. Then there's a definition: What's cloud computing? It's using a computer that's out there. 'Open source is going to destroy our business, and there'll be nothing but open source and we'll be out of business.' And minicomputers are going to destroy mainframes and PCs are going to destroy minicomputers and open source is going to destroy all standards and all software is going to be delivered as a service. I've been at this a long time, and there are still mainframes— but it was the first industry that was going to be destroyed, and watching mainframes be destroyed is like watching a glacier melt. . . ." Ellison concluded in anger and frustration, "What the hell is cloud computing??"

Bob Evans, senior vice president at Oracle, further wrote some revealing facts in his blog post at *Forbes*, clearing away all doubts people may have had in their minds. You may like to consider some interesting facts in this regard. Almost eight years ago, when cloud terms were not yet established, Oracle started developing a new generation of application suites (called Fusion Applications) designed for all modes of cloud deployment. Oracle Database 12c, which was released just recently, supports the cloud deployment framework of major data centers today and is the outcome of development efforts of the past few years. Oracle's software as a service (SaaS) revenue has already exceeded the $1 billion mark, and it is the only company today to offer all levels of cloud services, such as SaaS, platform as a service (PaaS), and infrastructure as a service (IaaS). Oracle has helped over 10,000 customers to reap the benefits of the cloud infrastructure and now supports over 25,000 users globally. One may argue that this could not have been possible if Larry Ellison hadn't appreciated cloud computing. Sure, we may understand the dilemma he must have faced as an innovator when these emerging technologies were creating disruption in the business (www.forbes.com/sites/oracle/2013/01/18/oracle-cloud-10000-customers-and-25-million-users/).

You will agree with us that cloud computing is undoubtedly the hottest and most commonly used buzzword in IT, and it is undergoing numerous interpretations by various IT service providers for their advantage and benefit. In our endeavor, we will make an attempt to simplify the term, concept, and paradigm of cloud computing and its related technologies for all business executives, technical developers, and knowledge workers. Cloud computing has become a prominent battleground among major IT vendors, offering hardware, software, network infrastructure, and consulting services providers. Enterprises have been slow to adopt it for various reasons, namely immature standards, concern for data security, and the fact that the whole model is not yet fit for running mission-critical applications (P. Hunter 2009).

Cloud computing is becoming a new platform for enterprise and personal computing. It competes with traditional desktop or hand-held computers (including smartphones) that run applications directly on the devices. But SaaS and cloud computing will rise to the level of an industry platform only when firms open their technology to other industry players. For example, Salesforce.com created a customer relationship management (CRM) product and configured it not as packaged software but as software delivered over servers and accessed through a browser. Salesforce.com developed its own in-house platform for delivering the software as a service to its customers. It then developed AppExchange as an open integration platform for other application companies that built products utilizing some features in the Salesforce.com CRM product. Salesforce.com created a new industry platform named Force.com, a development and deployment environment using Salesforce's SaaS infrastructure.

Paradigm Shifts: Mainframes to Client-Server to Cloud Computing

Information technology has undergone several paradigm shifts: from mainframes to client-server to Internet computing and then to cloud computing. We witnessed the advent of mainframes in the 1960s, which were initially meant for single users but gradually evolved in the 1970s as multi-users where several users were connected with terminals sharing computing resources in real time. In this model, the large computing resource was virtualized, and a virtual machine was allocated to individual users who were sharing the system. In reality, these terminals were accessing virtual instances of computing resources of a mainframe. The similar concept of virtual instances has been practiced in cloud computing by many thousands of machines.

We then witnessed the next wave of client-server computing, the concept where the mainframe as the computing center was diluted and computing resources were distributed. As computing power increased, work gradually shifted away from centralized computing resources toward increasingly powerful distributed systems. In this age of client-server, PC and PC-based applications dominated; many routine tasks were moved to the desktop and more resources were deployed on the desktop to run PC- or client-based applications. The mainframe was used only for corporate enterprise resource planning (ERP) and data processing–based applications. The standardization of networking technology simplified the ability to connect systems as Transmission Control Protocol/Internet Protocol (TCP/IP) became the protocol of the growing Internet in the 1980s. The emergence of the web and HTTP in the late 1990s brought computing back to the data center environment.

Next Evolution: Large Data Center—Grid Computing—Cluster Computing

In recent times, there has been an enormous evolution in computing capabilities, including hardware, software, and storage. Hardware and storage devices are mass-produced and commoditized. A few commodity servers can handle extensive data processing that was tackled on large mainframes or minicomputers earlier.

Grid computing enables groups of networked commodity computers to be pooled and provisioned on demand to meet the changing needs of business. Instead of dedicated servers and storage for each application, grid computing enables multiple applications to share computing infrastructure, resulting in much greater flexibility, cost, power efficiency, performance, scalability, and availability, all at the same time.

Cluster computing, consisting of a set of loosely or tightly connected low-cost commodity computers that work together so that in many respects they can be viewed as a single system, provides scalable on-demand flexibility.

Defining Cloud Computing

There have been many interpretations of cloud computing concepts and technology by many vendors and service providers. Some of the leading firms that have defined cloud computing are:

- *Gartner*. Cloud computing is a style of computing where massively scalable IT-related capabilities are provided as a service across the Internet to multiple external customers.

- *Forrester Research.* The cloud provides a pool of abstracted, highly scalable, and managed infrastructure capable of hosting end-customer applications and billed by consumption.
- *The 451 Group.* The cloud is IT as a service, delivered by IT resources that are independent of location.
- *Wikipedia.* Cloud computing is a style of computing in which dynamically scalable and often virtualized resources are provided as a service over the Internet.
- *IBM.* A cloud computing platform dynamically provisions, configures, reconfigures, and deprovisions servers as needed. Cloud applications use large data centers and powerful servers that host web applications and web services.
- *University of California at Berkeley.* The cloud offers the illusion of infinite computing resources available on demand, the elimination of up-front commitments by cloud users, and the ability to pay for use of computing resources on a short-term basis as needed.

Prior to the popularity of cloud computing, there were a number of related service offerings that attracted only minor attention—grid computing, utility computing, elastic computing, and software as a service. The basic technologies from each of these have been incorporated into cloud computing and appear to be attracting more interest than these predecessors. This attraction may be a function of the maturity of the technology and the services offered, or it may be driven by a marketing blitz that has occurred as Amazon, Google, Apple, and other big names have gotten behind it. (Smith, R. 2009).

What Is Cloud Computing?

The National Institute of Standards and Technology (NIST) is an agency of the U.S. Department of Commerce that defines and sets standards for any emerging technology. NIST defines cloud computing as a model for enabling convenient, on-demand network access to a shared pool of configurable computing resources (e.g., networks, servers, storage, applications, and services) that can be rapidly provisioned and released with minimal management effort or service provider interaction. Cloud computing refers to both the applications delivered as services over the Internet and the hardware and systems software in the data centers that provide those services.

According to NIST, this cloud model promotes availability and is comprised of five essential characteristics, three service models, and four deployment models.

Essential Characteristics

1. *On-demand self-service.* A consumer can unilaterally provision computing capabilities, such as server time and network storage, as needed, automatically and without requiring any human intervention with each service provider.
2. *Broad network access.* Capabilities are available over the network and accessed through standard mechanisms that promote use by heterogeneous thin or thick platforms (e.g., laptops, PDAs, and smartphones).
3. *Resource pooling.* The provider's computing resources are pooled to serve multiple consumers using a multitenant model, with different physical and virtual resources dynamically assigned and reassigned according to consumer demand. There is a sense of location independence in that the customer generally has no control over or knowledge of the exact location of the provided resources but may be able to specify location at a higher level of abstraction (e.g., country, state, or data center). Examples of resources include storage, processing, memory, network bandwidth, and virtual machines.
4. *Rapid elasticity.* Capabilities can be rapidly and elastically provisioned, in some cases automatically, to quickly scale out and can be rapidly released to quickly scale in. To the consumer, the capabilities available for provisioning often appear to be unlimited and can be purchased in any quantity at any time.
5. *Measured service.* Cloud systems automatically control and optimize resource use by leveraging metering capability at some level of abstraction appropriate to the type of service (e.g., storage, processing, bandwidth, and active user accounts). Resources usage can be monitored, controlled, and reported, providing transparency for both the provider and the consumer of the utilized service.

Service Models

We can classify cloud computing several ways, such as hardware, infrastructure, platform, framework, application, and even data center.

1. *Software as a Service (SaaS).* The capability provided to the consumer is to use the provider's applications running on a cloud infrastructure. The applications are accessible from various client devices through a thin client interface such as a web browser. The consumer does not manage or control the underlying cloud infrastructure, including network, servers, operating systems, storage, or even individual application capabilities, with the possible exception of limited user-specific application configuration settings. Salesforce.com CRM is an example of this service model.

2. *Platform as a Service (PaaS).* The capability provided to the consumer is to deploy onto the cloud infrastructure consumer-created or acquired applications created using programming languages and tools supported by the provider. The consumer does not manage or control the underlying cloud infrastructure, including network, servers, operating systems, or storage, but has control over the deployed applications and possibly application hosting environment configurations.

3. *Infrastructure as a Service (IaaS).* The capability provided to the consumer is to provision processing, storage, networks, and the other fundamental computing resources where the consumer is able to deploy and run arbitrary software, which can include operating systems and applications. The consumer does not manage or control the underlying cloud infrastructure but has control over operating systems, storage, deployed applications, and possibly limited control on selecting network components. Amazon EC2 and S3 are examples of this service model.

In the IaaS model, users subscribe to uses of certain components of a provider's IT infrastructure. Although the subscribers don't have control of the entire cloud infrastructure, they do have control over selected portions of it, such as firewalls, operating system, deployed applications, and storage. In the PaaS model, a combination of applications forming a platform is subscribed to as a service by users. For example, a combination of software tools may be used as a programming and software platform. The SaaS model can be seen as a special case of PaaS, where a single application can be subscribed to as a service. Such services are often accessed through a web browser.

A private cloud is usually owned and used by the same organization, such as a corporation. It often refers to a proprietary computing infrastructure owned by the organization, and provides computing and information services to its employees behind the organization's firewall.

A public cloud often refers to computing and IT infrastructure that is owned by an organization but provides computing and information services to external users or subscribers. By subscribing to services provided by other well-established companies, new start-ups, for example, can quickly realize their computing and information technology (CIT) needs without investing so much money and time to implement their own computing and IT infrastructure.

Cloud Deployment Models

1. *Private cloud.* Here the cloud infrastructure is operated solely for an organization. It may be managed by the organization or a third party and may exist on or off the premises.
2. *Public cloud.* The cloud infrastructure is made available to the general public or a large industry group and is owned by an organization selling cloud services.
3. *Community cloud.* The cloud infrastructure is shared by several organizations and supports a specific community that has shared concerns (e.g., mission, security requirements, and policy and compliance considerations). It may be managed by organizations or a third party and may exist on or off the premises.
4. *Hybrid cloud.* The cloud infrastructure is a combination of two or more clouds (private, public, or community) that remain unique entities but are bound together by standardized or proprietary technology that enables data and application portability (e.g., cloud bursting for load balancing between clouds).

Executive Insights
Harbinder Khera, Founder and CEO, Mindmatrix

At the very early stages of when cloud computing was talked about in the IT forums and conferences, we seized the opportunity to build and develop software solutions, all leveraging the cloud platform and its deployment models to cater to the needs of marketing and sales automation and offer tools for sales and channel productivity. The cloud technology platform has offered us greater business agility to bring new solutions and services to a large market, breaking all barriers, and has helped our customers reap its benefits by helping provide actionable intelligence to their sales teams with follow-up actions. Cloud deployment models not only offered a choice to our customers, but helped us immensely to manage and maintain our development process as agile and extremely productive.

Savvis Deploys PaaS

Savvis is one of the early cloud service providers engaged in offering platform as a service (PaaS). It partnered with Oracle to deliver a complete suite of tools in a cloud environment. Using the advanced provisioning tools built by Oracle running inside Savvis, administrators now have the ability to create application blueprints—configurable building blocks that greatly simplify the Oracle software stack, reducing costs and improving productivity and speed to market.

SavvisStation: User Interaction Portal

Savvis offers instantaneous visibility into critical IT infrastructure through a simple, user-friendly interface portal that works seamlessly with Oracle Virtual Assembly Builder to provide administrators with simplified access to the Oracle environment.

SavvisStation allows subscribers to track system health, monitor application performance, plan for capacity with trending analysis, view real-time and historical statistics on server resource utilization, receive bandwidth utilization statistics, and monitor status of support tickets in real time.

Executive Insights
Avanish Sahai, Vice President, Salesforce.com

The essence of business computing is being disrupted—and users/customers are driving this disruption or even revolution—at both a demand and a supply level. Let's review some of the big changes that cloud computing is enabling from a customer's perspective:

- *Ongoing innovation.* Users expect innovation in their experience, in their ability to learn how to use apps, and in the ability to connect different apps quickly together. Traditional enterprise computing paradigms of command and centralized control stifle innovation and don't support customer requirements. A cloud-based model that provides constant updates (multiple times a year), much like what customers experience from consumer sites like Facebook or LinkedIn, is the only way to meet customer demand.
- *Consistent and constant access.* Users are carrying and leveraging multiple devices—mobile phones, laptops, tablets. They expect—in fact, require—that whenever and wherever they access apps they should see updated, consistent, and real-time information. By leveraging key tenets of cloud computing such as multitenancy, automatic updates, and minimal downtime for upgrades, they are assured that data are accurate and up-to-date—whether they check in from an iPhone on the subway or over Wi-Fi on an airplane.
- *Social.* Users are experiencing fundamental changes in their personal app experience—feeds, automatic updates, ease of attaching documents, photos, and the like, and rapid inclusion of friends and family. That same expectation has rapidly emerged in their use of enterprise apps. The user experience paradigm is undergoing its most radical change since the days of green monitors—it needs to be engaging, intuitive, and aligned with the device of choice. Once again, cloud-based solutions enable this social experience in ways that traditional computing simply can't even imagine. Beyond the critical elements that provide an end-user, or demand-based, point of view, the cloud is also

creating a fundamental supply-side disruption: software, hardware, and services providers all have to revise their models. On the software front, clearly the subscription pricing models that are inherently tied to cloud computing create a much more transparent and value-aligned model between vendors and customers. Customers buy what they need, add capabilities as and when required, and maximize value capture.

From a hardware perspective, the cloud maximizes utilization of otherwise severely underused hardware—no more gigantic data centers designed for peak use that remain dark or idle most of the time. Hardware costs, already severely commoditized, will continue to decline dramatically and vendors need to review their models and perhaps go up the stack. Finally, services providers need to revisit their business models—no more multiyear deployment cycles with hoards of consultants and analysts. Customers demand rapid value and minimal disruption; this requires new service delivery models—short engagement time lines, value-driven milestones, and agile practices. Thus the cloud revolution is really that: a fundamental disruption of business computing unlike anything we have seen before. And customers are the biggest drivers and beneficiaries, for a change.

Executive Bio: Avanish Sahai is an accomplished entrepreneur, investor, and adviser at numerous technology and services firms. After many years in management consulting, he has been a senior executive at leading technology companies. Avanish is currently Global Vice President of ISV Alliances at Salesforce.com, where he and his team have built the AppExchange into the leading marketplace for business apps.

Key Business Drivers for Cloud Services

We all have witnessed and experienced information and communication technology (ICT) with changing times that have offered greater benefits and challenges to business. In a challenging business and economic environment, businesses have constantly looked for technology and services to optimize cost and increase efficiency. Start-ups and small and medium-sized businesses (SMBs) always look for low investment for infrastructure that requires capital expenditure (capex) and optimized operational cost to run their business. In a tough economy, even large enterprises are pressured to cut costs and rightsize their needs, depending on market conditions and customer demand. Cloud computing, in the recent past, has emerged as a promising technology and services paradigm to address these business challenges.

Business Value Propositions for Cloud Computing

There are a number of business benefits offered by cloud computing, and we enumerate several and support them with some real-life case references to help your business achieve greater agility for sustainable competitive advantage.

- Cloud computing is dynamically scalable. Businesses can draw as much computing power as is necessary on an hourly basis. As demand from internal users or external customers grows or shrinks, the necessary computer, storage, and network capacity can be added or subtracted on an hourly basis.
- The resources can be purchased with operational funds, rather than as a capital expenditure. Many IT departments face a long approval process for capital funding, in addition to the wait for equipment delivery and installation. Cloud computing allows them to bring capacity online within a day and to do so using their operational budgets.
- The equipment does not reside in the company facility. It does not require upgrades to the electrical system, the allocation of floor space, modifications to the air-conditioning, or expand-ing the IT staff. Computers at Amazon.com consume space, power, and staffing support at Amazon instead of within the customer's company.
- There are competing providers for this service. If the first cloud provider does not deliver acceptable performance, a company can always shift its business to another company offering better service or lower prices.

Large Telco Company Embraces Cloud to Optimize Infrastructure Cost

As per the published report by Crimson Consulting Group (February 2012), "BT Operate Boosts Service Levels and Lowers Management Costs by Standardizing on Oracle Database 11*g* for Consolidation onto a Private Cloud."

British Telecom (BT) is one of the world's leading providers of communications solutions and services, with operations in 170 countries. It provides fixed-line, broadband, mobile, and networked IT services as well as TV products and services.

BT has been a communications service provider for more than 100 years. In recent decades, BT's IT infrastructure grew significantly to include 17,000 databases and 30,000 servers. Managing an environment of this size and complexity is a significant challenge, and BT needed to streamline, consolidate, and simplify operations to transform its business.

Like any modern corporation, BT relied heavily on its database infrastructure to support critical business applications. But the complexity of managing thousands of databases representing a mix of products, versions, operating systems, and hardware was highly cost intensive. Application deployment was too slow, operations were too expensive, resource utilization was too low, and the workload on the IT team was too high.

BT deployed Oracle technology stack for the cloud on Enterprise Linux running on Hewlett-Packard (HP) blade servers. BT Operate also expects further gains in operational efficiency and utilization with Oracle Enterprise Manager 12*c*.

Source: www.oracle.com/us/products/database/bt-case-study-1533554.pdf.

President Obama Election Campaign Leverages Cloud to Win

We all know how President Barack Obama's election campaign was successfully executed, run, and managed using all these technologies led by its chief technology officer (CTO), Harper Reed. Similar to any other business operation, data was critical to the campaign and came in various sizes, types, and frequency that needed to be consolidated, integrated, and analyzed in real time to provide insights to Obama to tailor his message to the right audience. Moreover, the team also needed to manage the media, volunteers, and donors to support the campaign. One can imagine that the campaign team must have experienced challenges and limitations of computing infrastructure resources that were required for specific time frames during the campaign.

Cloud infrastructure and especially platform as a service (PaaS) came in handy to the campaign team, rendering scalable computing and storage capacity on demand on a pay-as-you-go basis when they needed it at a crucial time. The team used autoscaling to quickly add cloud resources in order to enable as many as 7,000 volunteers to make more than two million calls to voters in four days at the campaign's end.

Concerns and Risk Assessment of Cloud Computing

Cloud computing offers numerous benefits, but each of these also offers corresponding disadvantages or raises concerns; therefore, it is imperative to assess all risks before implementation and deployment of major business-critical applications on the cloud.

- Security, data privacy, and regulatory compliance are the foremost among many concerns. Many companies are hesitant to host their internal data on a computer that is external to their own premises and that is potentially cohosted with another company's applications. Companies may be concerned about the physical location of the data that are being stored in the cloud. The laws of the host country of the equipment apply to the data on the machines. European and Asian companies have expressed concerns about having their data stored on computers in the United States that fall under the jurisdiction of the U.S. Patriot Act, allowing the U.S. government to access that data very easily.
- Experienced users of cloud computing services have noticed a big variation in the performance of their applications running in the cloud. Because many companies are all sharing the resources, it is possible to arrive in a neighborhood that is extremely busy and very noisy, leaving little room for one's applications to run and communicate.
- Interesting bugs in this large system have yet to be worked out. There have been instances in which entire cloud services have

crashed and been unavailable for hours or days. When this happens, applications will be offline until the larger problem is fixed.

- Each cloud vendor offers unique services and unique ways to communicate with the computer resources. It is possible for subscribers to get so deeply embedded into these unique and proprietary services that they cannot move applications without some major changes to both software and data.

- It appears that a cloud provider has an infinite number of computers and storage disks to meet subscribers' needs. But there is a finite number of these resources available, and the provider is multiplexing these between the thousands of applications that are starting and stopping every hour. If all customers called for services at the same time, the provider could run out of available resources. This is the cloud computing equivalent of a busy signal on Mother's Day or an insurance claim following a major hurricane. These concerns, and others that are much more technical in nature, are well known to the major cloud computing providers and the intermediary support companies.

- Cloud computing refers to both the applications delivered as services over the Internet and the hardware and systems software in the data centers that provide those services. From a hardware provisioning and pricing point of view, three aspects are new in cloud computing.

  1. The appearance of infinite computing resources available on demand, quickly enough to follow load surges, thereby eliminating the need for cloud computing users to plan far ahead for provisioning.

  2. The elimination of an up-front commitment by cloud users, thereby allowing companies to start small and increase hardware resources only when there is an increase in their needs.

  3. The ability to pay for use of computing resources on a short-term basis as needed (for example, processors by the hour and storage by the day) and release them as needed, thereby rewarding conservation by letting machines and storage go when they are no longer useful (Armbrust et al. 2010).

Understanding Cloud Architecture

Having covered cloud terminologies, nomenclature, benefits, and inherent challenges, let us understand its underling architecture that would help in adoption and deployment with ease and confidence. Cloud infrastructure and deployment of various services such as platform, application, infrastructure, and database became possible with the proliferation of virtualization as a robust technology.

Virtualization provides the high server utilization needed in the cloud computing paradigm. It smooths out the variations between applications that need barely any CPU time (they can share a CPU with other applications) and those that are compute-intensive and need every CPU cycle they can get. Virtualization is the single most revolutionary cloud technology whose broad acceptance and deployment truly enabled the cloud computing trend to begin. Without virtualization, the economics of the cloud would not have been viable.

Virtualization Strengthens Cloud Deployment

We can view virtualization technology as part of an overall optimization strategy that includes client and overall server platform (hardware, operating systems, database, and storage). Platform virtualization is a technique to abstract computer resources such that it separates the operating system from the underlying physical server resources. Instead of the operating system (OS) running on hardware resources, the OS interacts with a new software layer called a virtual machine monitor that accesses the hardware and presents the OS with a virtual set of hardware resources. This means multiple virtual machine images or instances can run on a single physical server, and new instances can be generated and run on demand, creating the basis for elastic computing resources. Basically, server virtualization removes physical barriers and isolates one technology from the other, thereby eliminating dependencies. It allows multiple independent virtual operating systems, databases, storage, and applications on the same physical hardware. This reminds us of the IBM mainframes used for time-sharing virtualization in the 1960s to enable many people to share a large computer without interacting or interfering with each other. (See Figure 3.1.)

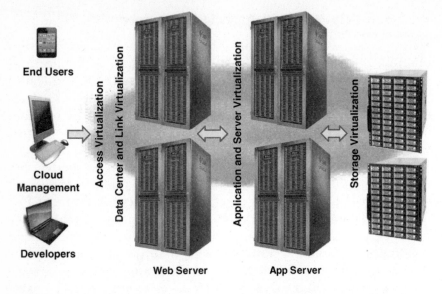

Figure 3.1 **Cloud Computing and Virtualization Deployment Architecture**

Virtualization Enables Server Consolidation

Virtualization helps in server consolidation, which is the cornerstone of the cloud computing deployment architecture and enables economies of scale and elasticity. Server consolidation helps in reducing hardware requirements by a 10-to-1 ratio or better. It accelerates server provisioning time by 50 to 70 percent. It reduces the energy cost by 80 percent and powers down servers without affecting applications. Examining server utilization, we observe that the average server in a corporate data center has typical utilization of only 6 percent. Even at peak load, utilization is no better than 20 percent. In the best-run data centers, servers run on average at only 15 percent or less of their maximum capacity. But when these same data centers fully adopt server virtualization, their CPU utilization increases to 65 percent or higher, and that helps in making cloud services appealing and cost effective. Virtualization reduces capex, operational expenditure (opex), and total cost of ownership (TCO).

In the continued endeavor to increase efficiency and agility in business, virtualization in cloud infrastructure offers server consolidation that reduces overall cost, including capital expenditure (capex), operational expenditure (opex), and total cost of ownership (TCO). Capex cost is minimized as multiple machines are consolidated onto a single host. By consolidation, opex is reduced significantly and in turn this lowers the overall total cost of ownership of all these computing services.

There are two main server virtualization platforms in deployment in many data centers today.

Virtualization Platforms

1. *Hosted virtualization.* This needs general-purpose operating systems such as a Windows server or Linux below the virtualization layer. VMware server and Microsoft Virtual Server are good examples of this deployment.
2. *Hypervisor-based virtualization.* The most popular virtualization platform doesn't need to run on any general-purpose operating systems such as a Windows server or Linux and is also referred to as bare-metal virtualization. VMware ESX server and Oracle VM (based on Xen server) are good examples of this implementation in various data centers.

Cloud Service Models and Security

As cloud computing matures and gains acceptance as the mainstream of business technology strategies and deployments, those engaged in enterprise business computing tend to become concerned regarding security, time to value, public versus private, lock-in, cost, and more. For businesses, these questions are reasonable as cloud adoptions grow rapidly around the world and increasingly essential workloads move from their traditional on-premises location to the cloud.

Cloud computing will not be accepted by common users unless the trust and dependability issues are addressed satisfactorily. (See Figure 3.2.)

Cloud-Based Solutions to Meet the IT Needs of Multiregional Branch Offices

Cloud computing has offered various deployment models to meet the IT needs of companies with multiregional branch offices globally. These cloud-based solutions can be deployed on one or a combination of these deployment models.

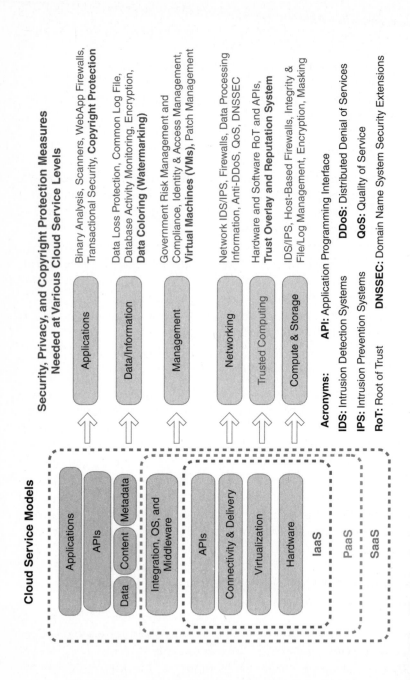

Figure 3.2 Cloud Service Model

88

Australian Government: Maximizing the Value of Cloud Computing

Many agencies within the Australian government have identified the importance of the government's own adoption of cloud services to provide operational efficiency in order to offer the best services to citizens. The recent fire was a learning exercise for other government departments as they watched the Department of Human Services with the cloud service. Any catastrophe of this kind stalls and disrupts business operations and functioning. Australia is not alone. Around the world, public agencies are taking advantage of cloud services to reduce overhead, scale appropriately, and customize solutions.

Individual agencies are already using private, public, and community cloud services. In many cases these are significant information and communication technology (ICT) projects, delivering tangible benefits for the community. These services have provided better value for the money and more innovative services than was possible though traditional ICT sourcing. The U.S. Department of Human Services has deployed a community cloud that provides significant flexibility and scalability, at a low unit cost for client departments.

Source: www.communications.gov.au/digital_economy/
cloud_computing/national_cloud_computing_strategy_html/
maximising_the_value_of_cloud_computing_in_government.

Private Cloud

For organizations that have a well-established computing and information technology infrastructure, such as some high-tech companies in the IT business, a completely private cloud-based solution may be a better choice for providing computing and IT services to new branch offices in other cities or other countries. In such a case, the data center, servers, and all major computing and IT devices reside behind the firewall on the organization's enterprise network, located on-site at the head office, while users in branch offices access the computing and information services through a virtual private network (VPN) or a web browser if a web interface has been made available for accessing the service (Harris 2011).

Figure 3.3 depicts the architecture of a private cloud-based solution.

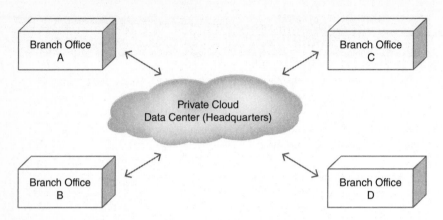

Figure 3.3   Architecture of Private Cloud-Based Solution

In a private cloud-based solution, since everything is under the control of the very same organization, this solution gives the organization total freedom and autonomy in managing all the components of the computing and information technology infrastructure.

National Australia Bank: UBank Offers a Personal Touch with Cloud-Based Services

With a large number of different business units, adopting a private cloud was the most optimal means for standardizing the way application servers are used at the National Australia Bank (NAB) and its UBank. On top of all the software infrastructure is what the bank calls "Web portal-as-service," which is another example of a PaaS with a web portal focus.

UBank as a business, or as a brand, started with no customers initially. According to NAB, "It's a complete end-to-end banking solution from an application level and from an underlying service level."

NAB's journey toward PaaS has given it the confidence to expand the infrastructure beyond new ventures like UBank. The bank plans to transform and renew its core platforms to enable future business models. NAB IT strategists view PaaS as "significantly less complex" and easier to integrate. The architecture also poses less of an IT focus and is less costly to support and adapt as its business evolves.

Source: http://delimiter.com.au/2012/08/27/
nab-shifts-ubank-onto-new-core-it-platform/

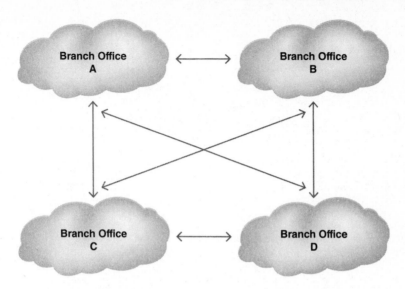

Figure 3.4   Architecture of Federated Cloud-Based Solution

Federated Cloud

Federated cloud computing can be seen as a variant of private cloud computing. As in private cloud computing, in federated cloud computing the information technology infrastructure is still privately owned solely by the organization, but the equipment, servers, and services are distributed among the head office and branch offices. This may be necessary when different branch offices have different missions and each needs more dedicated computing and information services. For example, one branch may be working on data mining, while another branch may be concentrating more on server development. (See Figure 3.4.)

Public Cloud

A public cloud-based solution is for the organization to subscribe all needed computing and information technology services from providers in the public cloud. This solution is suitable for organizations that have no resources or interest in implementing their own CIT infrastructure, or small start-ups. By subscribing to the needed computing and IT services readily available in the public cloud, a start-up can quickly get its business going and have its creative ideas tested.

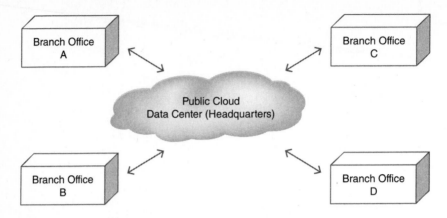

Figure 3.5   Architecture of Public Cloud-Based Solution

If the business doesn't fly, it can easily get off the boat with less to lose. (See Figure 3.5.)

Hybrid Cloud

Consistent with the definition of *hybrid*, a hybrid cloud involves both a private and a public cloud. A hybrid cloud-based solution may be applicable for an organization that has an established computing and information technology (CIT) infrastructure sufficient for its current needs, but doesn't want to invest big money and time to expand its current CIT infrastructure for a new business. In this case, it would rather obtain the needed CIT services from a reliable source in the public cloud. By doing this, it may be more easily turned around if the new venture doesn't go well. (See Figure 3.6.)

Advantages of Cloud Computing-Based Solution

A cloud computing–based IT solution for organizations with multi-regional offices brings both advantages and challenges. The advantages are as follows:

- Cloud computing provides organizations with more agile solutions to meet their IT needs. With cloud computing, subscribers can quickly get the IT services needed to run their businesses. This is especially suitable for new businesses undertaking

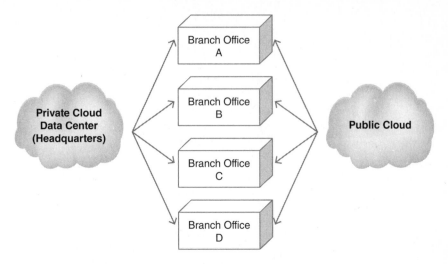

Figure 3.6   Architecture of Hybrid Cloud-Based Solution

Executive Insights
Pankaj Jha, Architect, Brocade

We observe that cloud computing has changed the business competitive framework in ways not seen as possible earlier, by providing a winning formula for both providers and customers—making Michael Porter's classic managerial model of competitive forces analysis less applicable, if not completely irrelevant.

Before we analyze individual elements of the Porter model, an example or two would help to highlight the forces of change. Whereas traditional supply-driven markets required buyers to purchase software from major companies such as Microsoft, Oracle, or IBM, in the new paradigm a customer leases a software functionality over the web on usually a white-labeled platform. Most small and medium-sized companies look to see if the features meet their requirements, and often they ask for and receive an integration of features across multiple product offerings—all customized for look and feel by their cloud services provider.

Elements of the Porter model have lost their relevance in this new scheme of things. The large pool of suppliers that provide cloud services on an original equipment manufacturer (OEM) basis with their white-labeled software includes both large and very small companies. Software development, marketing, and distribution are no longer strictly a big company play. Anyone with the skills for developing software can provide his or her services over the cloud (Amazon, Oracle, GoGrid, Azure, etc.) and sell them on a monthly subscription basis. The cloud computing customer base is so large that it can absorb all companies providing services anywhere in the world. Substitute products (competing SaaS or IaaS offerings) don't affect competitiveness of a company, because services can be had from the large pool without affecting business operations. Similarly, bargaining power of customers is less of a concern. While traditionally customers bargained on product price and shopped across brand names, nowadays customers only care about good and reliable service and don't bargain much, as they already realize significant savings. Infrastructure providers such as those who make servers and network equipment are benefiting immensely because they can supply a large quantity of hardware to cloud infrastructure companies. They no longer need to pursue individual companies to sell and service their wares.

Not only is cloud computing here to stay, but we and the industry in general are looking at cloud computing as a new catalyst for growth of a newly redefined marketplace. While it is true that very large organizations would slowly evolve from private cloud to hybrid cloud and eventually to a pure cloud, a much larger section of the industry, the small and medium-sized business (SMB) market, is quickly adopting cloud computing as a new core framework that brings benefits to all players.

Executive Bio: Pankaj Jha is an architect at Brocade engaged in systems design, switching/routing networking, and embedded software development.

brilliant but risky ventures. By subscribing to services from a third party, an organization can save money on capital investment. It can also save on maintenance because the computing and information technology (CIT) infrastructure is owned and maintained by the third party.

- Cloud computing-based solutions are reliable and offered by trusted cloud services providers such as Amazon, Rackspace, Salesforce, Oracle, and others. Cloud computing solutions provide scalability based on business needs. It can also be easily scaled down if required.

- Cloud computing solutions offer high-end security with high-end data centers equipped and installed with all security tools and technologies.

Design and Deployment Strategy for Cloud Services

In an endeavor to create business agility, as you (or your company) begin to formulate your cloud strategy, you need to understand the inherent capabilities that are offered by cloud computing. These capabilities can help to gain competitive advantage by creating opportunities for cost advantage and organizational agility. We see the following seven capabilities (if not more):

1. Managed interface
2. Geolocation independence
3. Source independence
4. Access from anywhere
5. Digital business setups
6. Audit control
7. On-demand elasticity

In deriving these capabilities, enterprises should consider their information as an asset and should want to find ways of generating and accessing it. When formulating its cloud strategy, a company should consider the extent to which it needs each of the seven capabilities. Subscribing to these services should be based on the company's needs and cost considerations. Cost considerations occur because each capability implies investments in technology, processes, people, and governance. It is recommended that companies evaluate these capabilities before implementing them in order to derive value from cloud computing (Iyer and Henderson 2010).

Managed Interface

This capability creates an infrastructure that is organic and responsive to changing user requirements. As companies develop and deploy application services, each service can be used by other services using an interface called an application program interface (API). In determining the APIs to provide, involvement can vary from highly involved as a gatekeeper and moderator in the provisioning of applications to low involvement by allowing developers to freely write applications.

This results in four strategies for managing APIs. Under the open co-innovation model, companies such as Amazon and Google have a very open and community-driven approach to services. A developer wanting access makes a request through Amazon Web Services' discussion forum, to which both Amazon employees and community members contribute and decide how open and participative they want to make their API processes. Companies that adopt the Apple or Salesforce.com model need to make huge investments in internal resources for staffing and implementation.

The Amazon and Google model requires the creation of forums and ground rules for participation. Internal experts are also needed to track discussions, identify emerging trends, and respond appropriately. The open model followed by Google and Amazon allows unfettered innovation but no quality control of the user experience. The qualified model, on the other hand, guarantees a level of user experience but may cause developer consternation with the certification process. Overall, creating an API-based interface to existing applications unlocks their potential by making them more accessible to internal and external requests, creating immense opportunities for collaboration and innovation.

Geolocation Independence

This capability controls access to services and information assets from anywhere within an enterprise without needing to know their location. Today, organizations with large data sets typically employ experts whose sole role is to know where data elements exist within their databases. Usually, these experts work for the IT architecture group to ensure that each application follows the internal architecture policies and that proper approval is given to access data. The downside is that business unit personnel often feel that these experts slow down responses to competitive pressures by increasing application development times.

Application development at Google follows a different path. Google has made huge investments in an infrastructure that is "built to build." This infrastructure allows developers to build new applications that can access information assets without knowing the exact location of their physical storage. The infrastructure ensures that applications access the right data sources, keeping data integrity high. When a few software engineers in Bangalore set about building it, they were able to tap into many of the preexisting features, such as discussion forums and news feeds that already existed in Google's infrastructure, and reuse them to create a new product.

Source Independence

This capability of cloud computing enables a company to control access to services and also helps to switch service providers easily and at low cost. The current model of information systems development carries the risk of a company being locked into a vendor or solution. With cloud computing, the functionality that an application delivers is based on a call to a service, which should make it easy and less expensive to move to a different vendor to obtain the same functionality. The key factor enabling a choice to be made is that access to both existing data and the metadata allows the existing data to be imported easily into a new application. The same principle must apply to a service inside the company firewall. Just as a company can move from one vendor to another, so business units must be able to use or disassociate from their internal IT service, leading to the sourcing independence described here.

The data that users create and store within their favorite social networking sites can be accessed by applications that conform to the OpenSocial Foundation API specifications. Prior to this initiative, each application required a proprietary development effort to enable it to run on a social networking site. Using the OpenSocial standards, application developers can now write a program once and have it run on any social networking site conforming to these standards. Social networking sites gain value by having many applications run on top of their data. Users benefit from this sourcing independence because of the many applications that run using their data.

Access from Anywhere

This capability of cloud computing allows users to access any company service from any platform or device via a web browser. The first generation of the web ensured that information was linked via hyperlinks, with access by pointing and clicking. In the current mashup era, every bit of information should be accessible via a program. A second expectation is that information assets should be accessible from any device. However, to prevent performance problems with ubiquitous access, companies may have to implement intelligent caching techniques and provide high bandwidth connectivity.

A digital business environment can be defined as a suite of integrated applications (processes) and tools that support specific major business capabilities or needs. With cloud computing, this capability provides decision makers with integrated and seamless access to all the capabilities needed to analyze and execute business decisions. Application is done by configuring various services (memory, processors, and so on) to suit a business need. With EC2, all the work of configuration is preserved and reusable. If the same environment is required at a later time, it can be mirrored by Amazon's servers and invoked identically at a future date. A digital business environment is analogous to the long-established concept of a virtual machine (VM).

Audit Control

This cloud capability enables users and the usage of every information service within an organization to be tracked. The ability to verify the history, location, or application of an item through recorded documentation is crucial for ensuring that companies comply with internal and external constraints. Internally, it may be important to track the services partner's use. In other instances, safe harbor compliance rules may require companies to audit the use of their data from other parts of the world.

On-Demand Elasticity

On-demand elasticity provides a self-service capability for rapidly scaling service usage up or down, transparently and automatically. Most organizations plan their processing capacity to cope with peak loads. As a result, much of the capacity remains unused most of the time. In addition, the pricing scheme for using cloud computing should match the needs of the organization; however, this has proven difficult to enforce.

Five Steps in Cloud Apps Deployment

It is highly recommended to follow the best practices of cloud applications deployment in various steps and based on proven guidelines.

1. Populate the cloud application with initial data.
2. Provide user access.
3. Manage user access.
4. Integrate applications and their data.
5. Optimize business processes.

Challenges

- Extracting, transforming, and loading large volumes of data across the various cloud deployments
- Connectivity with diverse systems
- High performance requirements

Provisioning with Identity Manager

- Autodetection of new employees from the human resources (HR) system
- Approval work flows for auditing and traceability
- Role-based profiles to provision users based on job function
- Password policies to set initial passwords and force password reset

Manage User Access Challenges

- Reconciling who has access to what applications and entitlements
- Detecting excessive access and dormant accounts
- Password aging and detection of orphaned accounts
- Self-service account management and password reset
- Automated account disabled upon termination
- Certification review reporting and role management

Integrate Applications and Their Data

- Extracting, transforming, and loading bulk data in real time
- Capturing, transforming, and updating transactions in real time
- High performance requirements with a nonintrusive solution
- Connectivity with diverse systems

Obstacles and Opportunities for Cloud Computing

Now let us examine various obstacles and opportunities pertaining to cloud-based services deployment. The first three affect adoption, the next five affect growth, and the last two are policy and business obstacles. Each obstacle is paired with an opportunity to overcome that obstacle, ranging from product development to research projects (Armbrust et al. 2010).

1. *Business continuity and service availability.* Organizations worry about whether utility computing services will have adequate availability, and this makes some wary of cloud computing. Ironically, existing SaaS products have set a high standard in this regard. Google Search has a reputation for being highly available, to the point that even a small disruption is picked up by major news sources. Users expect similar availability from new services, which is difficult to do.

2. *Data lock-in.* Application programming interfaces (APIs) for cloud computing are still essentially proprietary, or at least have not been the subject of active standardization. Thus, customers cannot easily extract their data and programs from one site to run on another. The difficulty of extracting data from the cloud is preventing some organizations from adopting cloud computing. Customer lock-in may be attractive to cloud computing providers, but their users are vulnerable to price increases, to reliability problems, or even to providers going out of business.

   One solution would be to standardize the APIs in such a way that an SaaS developer could deploy services and data across multiple cloud computing providers so that the failure of a single company would not take all copies of customer data with it. One might worry that this would lead to a race to the bottom of cloud pricing and flatten the profits of cloud computing providers. There may be two arguments to minimize this fear. First, the quality of a service matters as well as the price, so customers may not jump to the lowest-cost service. Some Internet service providers today cost a factor of 10 more than others because they are more dependable and offer extra services to improve usability. Second, in addition to mitigating data lock-in concerns, standardization of APIs enables a new usage model in which the same software infrastructure can be used in an internal data center and in a public cloud. Such an option could enable hybrid cloud computing or surge computing in which the public cloud is used to capture the extra tasks that cannot be easily run in the data center (or private cloud) due to temporarily heavy workloads.

3. *Data confidentiality/auditability.* Despite most companies outsourcing payroll and many companies using external e-mail services to hold sensitive information, security is one of the most often cited objections to cloud computing. There are also requirements for auditability, in the sense of Sarbanes-Oxley Act and Health Insurance Portability and Accountability Act (HIPAA) regulations that must be provided for corporate data to be moved to the cloud. Cloud users face security threats from both outside and inside the cloud. Many of the security issues involved in protecting clouds from outside threats are similar to those already facing large data centers.

   In the cloud, however, this responsibility is divided among potentially many parties, including the cloud user, the cloud vendor, and any third-party vendors that users rely on for security-sensitive software or configurations. The cloud user is responsible for application-level security. The cloud provider is responsible for physical security, and likely for enforcing external firewall policies. Security for intermediate layers of the software stack is shared between the user and the operator; the lower the level of abstraction exposed to the user, the more responsibility goes with it. Amazon EC2 users have more technical responsibility (that is, they must implement or procure more of the necessary functionality themselves) for their security than do Azure users, who in turn have more responsibilities than AppEngine customers.

4. *Data transfer bottlenecks.* Applications continue to become more data-intensive. At $100 to $150 per terabyte transferred, these costs can quickly add up, making data transfer costs an important issue. Cloud users and cloud providers have to think about the implications of placement and traffic at every level of the system if they want to minimize costs. This kind of reasoning can be seen in Amazon's development of its new cloud front service. One opportunity to overcome the high cost of Internet transfers is to ship disks. While this does not address every use case, it effectively handles the case of large delay-tolerant point-to-point transfers, such as importing large data sets.

5. *Performance unpredictability.* Multiple virtual machines (VMs) can share CPUs and main memory surprisingly well in cloud computing, but that network and disk input/putput (I/O) sharing is more problematic. As a result, different EC2 instances vary more in their I/O performance than in main memory performance. One opportunity is to improve architectures and operating systems to efficiently virtualize interrupts and I/O channels.

6. *Scalable storage.* Three properties whose combination gives cloud computing its appeal are: short-term usage (which implies scaling down as well as up when demand drops), no up-front cost, and infinite capacity on demand. Storage is offered on demand according to business needs.

7. *Bugs in large-scale distributed systems.* One of the difficult challenges in cloud computing is removing errors in these very large-scale distributed systems. A common occurrence is that these bugs cannot be reproduced in smaller configurations, so the debugging must occur at scale in the production data centers. One opportunity may be the reliance on virtual machines in cloud computing. Many traditional SaaS providers developed their infrastructure without using VMs, either because they preceded the recent popularity of VMs or because they felt they could not afford the performance hit of VMs.

8. *Scaling quickly.* The pay-as-you-go model certainly applies to storage and to network bandwidth, both of which count bytes used. Computation is slightly different, depending on the virtualization level. Google AppEngine automatically scales in response to load increases and decreases, and users are charged by the cycles used. Amazon Web Services (AWS) charges by the hour for the number of instances you occupy, even if your machine is idle. The opportunity is then to scale quickly up and down automatically in response to load in order to save money, but without violating service-level agreements.

9. *Reputation fate sharing.* One customer's bad behavior can affect the reputations of others using the same cloud. For instance, blacklisting of EC2 IP addresses by spam prevention services may limit which applications can be effectively hosted. An opportunity would be to create reputation-guarding services similar to the "trusted e-mail" services currently offered (for a fee) to services hosted on smaller Internet service providers (ISPs), which experience a microcosm of this problem. Another legal

issue is the question of transfer of legal liability—cloud computing providers would want customers to be liable and not the providers (e.g., the company sending the spam should be held liable, not Amazon).

10. *Software licensing.* Current software licenses commonly restrict the computers on which the software can run. Users pay for the software and then pay an annual maintenance fee. Many cloud computing providers originally relied on open source software in part because the licensing model for commercial software is not a good match to utility computing. The primary opportunity is either for open source to remain popular or simply for commercial software companies to change their licensing structure to better fit cloud computing. For example, Microsoft and Amazon now offer pay-as-you-go software licensing for Windows Server and Windows SQL Server on EC2.

There are a few challenges and concerns surrounding cloud computing–based IT solutions as described below: The operational costs may be high. The capital cost can be much lower when a cloud computing–based solution is chosen. However, the company's operational cost may be higher than when running its own CIT infrastructure because it may be required to pay higher subscription fees for the subscribed services. A cloud computing–based IT solution should provide reliable computing and information technology (CIT) services if care is taken in selecting the providers. However, there are two factors that may cause the CIT services obtained from cloud computing to be unreliable:

1. Unpredictable failure of network external to the organization. Since those portions of the network are not under the organization's control, it cannot really do anything to avoid such failure, or to ensure a quick recovery once such a failure has occurred.
2. Services discontinuity. It is very important to choose a reliable and trustworthy service provider. Financial stability and their proven services should be the major criteria in selection. As organizations become increasingly global in their business, supply chains and transaction management become more complex. For most businesses, growth is tied to the ability to operate both domestic and overseas, with the addition of each location increasing complexity.

Driving Growth More Efficiently

Global transactions and sourcing are becoming increasingly important, and in this area, cloud solutions have a significant impact on efficiency and cost savings. The major benefit of cloud technology versus typical on-premises software is the elimination of IT staff and support. Transacting with new global partners is significantly easier and less expensive using the cloud, thereby allowing businesses more flexibility to transact with multiple business partners in different regions. In today's environment, it's evident that businesses require an adoption methodology for flexibility and responsiveness to changing dynamics.

In this scenario, however, chief financial officers (CFOs) struggle to manage risk as business becomes increasingly dependent on layers of global partners and suppliers. A massive amount of risk exists in the following areas:

- *Trading partner risk.* Who are partners? Are there hidden suppliers that could put brand and business at risk?
- *Compliance risk.* Is there visibility into documents and data to file and comply with Sarbanes-Oxley and other regulations in a timely manner?
- *Finance-related risk.* Is credit or liquidity an issue that will hinder suppliers, and hence business? Is the business making money and benefiting in the supply chain? Are rising costs in China going to impact margins?

Cloud technology provides a standard platform that generates visibility into transaction parties, payments, and documents. Visibility, agility, and a collaborative environment can mitigate the risks associated with trading partners, compliance, and credit. The average consumer product transaction can involve anywhere from five to 20 different parties in the steps leading from product manufacture to the store shelf. Each of the parties involved in a supply chain poses several elements of risk.

Database Services on a Private Cloud

For database environments, the PaaS cloud model provides better IT services than the IaaS model. The PaaS model provides enough resources in the cloud that databases can quickly get up and running and still have enough latitude for users to create the applications they need. Additionally, central IT management, security, and efficiency are greatly enhanced through consistency and economies of scale. Conversely, with the IaaS model, each tenant must build most of the stack on its own, lengthening the time to deployment and resulting in inconsistent stacks that are harder to manage. A private cloud is an efficient way to deliver database services because it enables IT departments to consolidate servers, storage, and database workloads onto a shared hardware and software infrastructure. Databases deployed on a private cloud offer compelling advantages in cost, quality of service, and agility by providing on-demand access to database services in a self-service, elastically scalable, and metered manner. Private clouds are a better option than public clouds for many reasons.

Shared Services

Information technology departments can leverage shared services to reduce costs and meet the demands of their business users, but there are many operational, securities, organizational, and financial aspects of shared services that must be managed to ensure effective adoption. Consolidation is vital to shared services, as it allows IT to restructure resources by combining multiple applications into a cohesive environment. Consolidation goes beyond hard cost savings; it simplifies management, improves resource utilization, and streamlines conformity to security and compliance standards.

- *Server consolidation.* Reduce the number of physical servers and consolidate databases onto a smaller server footprint.
- *Storage consolidation.* Unify the storage pool through improved use of free space in a virtual storage pool.
- *Operating system consolidation.* Reduce the number of operating system installations. Reducing server footprint does not always provide the best return on investment (ROI), but reducing the number of operating systems will improve overall manageability.
- *Database consolidation.* Reduce the number of database instances through schema consolidation. Consolidate separate databases as schemas in a single database, reducing the number of databases to manage and maintain.

- *Workload consolidation.* Merge the redundant databases that support business intelligence or operational data store systems. When consolidated into a single data store, these workloads benefit from the additional resources and scalability provided by the private cloud infrastructure.

Security Considerations in Private and Public Clouds

Cloud computing offers promising convenience, elasticity, transparency, and economy. But with the many benefits come some challenging issues of security and privacy. The history of computing since the 1960s can be viewed as a continuous move toward ever-greater specialization and distribution of computing resources. First we had mainframes and security was fairly simple. Then we added minicomputers and desktop and laptop computers and client-server models, and it got more complicated. Tim Mather, Subra Kumaraswamy, and Shahed Latif outlined information security and privacy issues in depth pertaining to various cloud deployment models in their publication *Cloud Security and Privacy* (Mather et al. 2009).

Components of Information Security

We need to consider broadly three components of infrastructure-level security and their various implications in cloud deployment.

1. *Network level.* Shared infrastructure such as a virtual local area network (VLAN) (private and public) and Dynamic Host Configuration Protocol (DHCP) server, firewall, and load balancer have limitations of point-to-point encryption, extranet security, and monitoring. This may cause a threat of domain hijacking due to domain naming systems (DNS), denial of service (DoS), or distributed denial of service (DDoS). However, this may be mitigated by deploying a virtual private cloud and virtual private network (VPN)–based solution with strong authentication.
2. *Host level.* Shared infrastructure such as hardware (CPU, memory, disks, network) or software (virtualization layer [e.g., Xen], Web Console) provisioning also offers limitations of patch, configuration management of a large number of dynamic nodes, host-based intrusion detection system (IDS), and access management. This offers a threat of image configuration drift and vulnerabilities, targeted DoS attack, and

attack on standard OS services. However, we can mitigate these threats by such strategies as: secure-by-default, harden image, turn off OS services, use software firewall, enable logging, access provisioning, patch, or configuration management.

3. *Application level.* Shared infrastructure such as virtualized host, network, firewall (if hosted on IaaS or PaaS), virtualized stack (e.g., LAMP), and database versus dataspace (e.g., SimpleDB, BigTable) also offers limitations in SaaS and SaaS/PaaS deployment. In cloud deployment, application-level security is highly critical, especially with denial of service (DoS) or economic denial of service (EDoS)—an attack against the billing model that underlies the cost of providing a service with the goal of bankrupting the service itself.

Data Security and Storage

Data security and storage are other major issues that need attention during cloud deployment.

Data Lineage

- Knowing when and where the data was located within the cloud is important for audit/compliance purposes.
- Example: Amazon Web Services (AWS)
  - Store <d1, t1, ex1.s3.amazonaws.com>
  - Process <d2, t2, ec2.compute2.amazonaws.com>
  - Restore <d3, t3, ex2.s3.amazonaws.com>

Data Provenance

- Computational accuracy (as well as data integrity)
- Example: Financial calculation: sum $((((2*3)*4)/6)-2) = \$2.00$
  - Correct, assuming U.S. dollars
  - How about dollars of different countries?

Lack of Control in the Cloud

Most security problems stem from consumer's loss of control and lack of trust (mechanisms).

- Data, applications, and resources are located with provider.
- User identity management is handled by the cloud.

- User access control rules, security policies, and enforcement are managed by the cloud provider.
- Consumer relies on provider to ensure:
  - Data security and privacy
  - Resource availability
  - Monitoring and repairing of services/resources

Identity and Access Management

Managing access for diverse user populations (employees, contractors, partners, etc.) is a critical administration task of a cloud administrator. More and more personal, financial, and medical data hosted in the cloud will need increased authentication. Software applications hosted in the cloud require access control, and there will be greater need for higher assurance authentication, including authentication from mobile devices.

What Are the Key Privacy Concerns?

Privacy rights or obligations are related to the collection, use, disclosure, storage, and destruction of personal data or personally identifiable information (PII). They are about the accountability of organizations to data subjects, as well as the transparency to an organization's practice around personal information.

Some considerations to mitigate privacy concerns are storage, retention, and destruction; auditing, monitoring, and risk management; and privacy breaches.

Storage.   The aggregation of data raises new privacy issues. Some governments may decide to search through data without necessarily notifying the data owner, depending on where the data resides and whether the cloud provider itself has any right to see and access customer data. Some services today track user behavior for a range of purposes, from sending targeted advertising to improving services.

Retention.   It is important to determine who enforces the retention policy in the cloud, and how exceptions to this policy are managed. Also, policy needs to clearly define how long personal information (that is transferred to the cloud) is retained. And does the organization own the data, or does the cloud service provider (CSP) own it?

Destruction. Cloud service providers usually replicate the data across multiple systems and sites, and increased availability is one of the benefits they provide.

- How do we know that the CSP didn't retain additional copies?
- Did the CSP really destroy the data, or just make it inaccessible to the organization?
- Is the CSP keeping the information longer than necessary so that it can mine the data for its own use?

Auditing, Monitoring, and Risk Management. If business-critical processes are migrated to a cloud computing model, internal security processes need to evolve to allow multiple cloud providers to participate in those processes as needed.

These include processes such as security monitoring, auditing, forensics, incident response, and business continuity.

Privacy Breaches. It is critical to define a clear policy regarding privacy breaches with cloud service providers, such as:

- How do we know that a breach has occurred?
- How do we ensure that the Cloud Service Provider (CSP) notifies us when a breach occurs?
- Who is responsible for managing the breach notification process (and costs associated with the process)?
- If contracts include liability for breaches resulting from negligence of the Cloud Service Providers(CSP):
  - How is the contract enforced?
  - How is it determined who is at fault?

Virtual Machine Introspection

IBM Research is pursuing a similar approach called "virtual machine introspection." It puts security inside a protected VM running on the same physical machine as the guest VMs running in the cloud. The security VM employs a number of protective methods, including the whitelisting and blacklisting of guest kernel functions.

It can determine the operating system and version of the guest VM and can start monitoring a VM without any beginning assumption of its running state or integrity.

Instead of running 50 virus scanners on a machine with 50 guest VMs, virtual machine introspection uses just one, which is much more efficient, says Matthias Schunter, a researcher at IBM Research's Zurich lab. "Another big advantage is the VM can't do anything against the virus scan since it's not aware it's being scanned," he says. In another application, a virtual intrusion detection system runs inside the physical machine to monitor traffic among the guest VMs. The virtual networks hidden inside a physical machine are not visible to conventional detectors because the detectors usually reside in a separate machine, Schunter says.

Service-Level Agreement

The following are some of the key areas that need to be addressed by the cloud computing contract, generally referred to as a service-level agreement (SLA):

- A clear articulation of fees for base services and modifications over time.
- Well-defined performance metrics and remedies for service failures and an understanding of how the metrics may change over time.
- Security, privacy, and audit commitments that will satisfy regulatory concerns, including an understanding of where data and information (including intellectual property) reside.
- Clear delineation of the affiliated entities that may receive services under the contract as well as provision for the continued receipt of services by divested entities during a transition period.
- Understanding the process for changes to the solution over time and the impact on connections between the cloud solution and other systems and processes used by a customer.
- Adequate provision for termination of the contract and moving to a substitute provider, including termination assistance and recovery of all data.
- Addressing business continuity, disaster recovery, and force majeure events.

- Clear restrictions on use and ownership of customer data and any intellectual property of the customer resident in the cloud.
- Access to and recovery of customer data as needed, and an understanding of the customer's rights with regard to litigation holds and e-discovery requirements.
- A reasonable allocation of risk for breaches of contract and for third-party claims related to the solution.
- Understanding subcontractors that may be used by the service provider and the conditions for the service provider using subcontractors.
- Addressing the resolution and impact of disputes and bankruptcy (e.g., software escrow arrangements for SaaS offering).

Intellectual Property Rights

In an IaaS environment, the customer maintains all intellectual property ownership rights related to any applications that it runs using the IaaS platform. Of course, reasonable confidentiality provisions will need to be included to protect any trade secrets that the customer places on the IaaS platform. The obligations to acquire third-party consents should also be straightforward in the cloud computing environment, with the provider being responsible for any consent required for it to operate its solution and the customer acquiring necessary third-party consents required in connection with any application or data that the customer brings to the public cloud platform. The intellectual property and licensing structure for an SaaS or a PaaS solution could be more complex, depending on the intellectual property at issue. The provider will retain ownership of its solution, but the customer will need to consider the ownership of any intellectual property for any interfaces or add-ons that the customer develops in connection with using the services as well as the ownership of applications developed on a PaaS platform.

References

Armbrust, M., A. Fox, R. Griffith, A. D. Joseph, R. Katz, A Konwinski, and M. Zaharia. 2010. "A View of Cloud Computing." *Communications of the ACM*, 53(4): 50–58.
Harris, W. 2011. "Cloud Computing-Based IT Solutions for Organizations with Multiregional Branch Offices." Proceedings of the European Conference on Information Management & Evaluation, 435–440.

Hunter, P. 2009. "Cloud Aloud [Cloud Computing in Enterprises]." *Engineering & Technology (17509637), 4* (16): 54–56. doi: 10.1049/et.2009.1612.

Iyer, B., and J. C. Henderson. 2010. "Preparing for the Future: Understanding the Seven Capabilities of Cloud Computing." *MIS Quarterly Executive, 9*(2): 117–131.

Mather, Tim, Subra Kumaraswamy, and Shahed Latif. 2009. Cloud Security and Privacy: An Enterprise Perspective on Risks and Compliance. O'Reilly Media.

Smith, R. 2009. "Computing in the Cloud." *Research Technology Management, 52*(5): 65–68.

4

Breaking the Barrier of Physical Infrastructure

If you are reading this chapter, you already know how the innovative technologies of cloud, social, mobile, video, and big data with predictive analytics have impacted our businesses and fueled business agility in all dimensions. These technologies have enabled us to carry out most of our business functions remotely without being physically present on site. They have not only removed the barriers of physical infrastructure but have also helped greatly in reducing the cost of operations and in carrying out business globally with minimum cost.

Effective Use of Technologies

The recent innovations in technologies and in business models have broken the barrier of physical boundaries. They have allowed us to go beyond the physical infrastructure to carry out all sorts of work and study, to purchase, sell, exchange information, trade, and carry on commerce across the globe. A simple task like holding a meeting previously required us to travel to offices within a city or across cities, countries, and at times, continents. Now with technologies like Cisco's WebEx, Microsoft's NetMeeting, Join.me, and Oracle's Beehive, we do not need to commute to offices or travel across countries or continents to hold meetings unless face-to-face meetings are absolutely necessary. In a global environment, workplaces have practically no boundaries, with employees located all over the world.

Technology like Join.me has helped us in collaborating on content while writing this book. We both usually used Join.me in our real-time collaboration for sharing and discussing the manuscript in progress irrespective of our geolocation, breaking the physical boundaries and increasing our efficiency. We made sure that our manuscript for the book that you are reading was reviewed jointly without our being in the same room. Our writing activity did not suffer despite our work-related travel to other countries in different time zones. The technology offered greater efficiency in our goal to write the book on schedule for the publisher. It is fair to say that we had minimal or no in-person meetings with all the project's stakeholders such as the creative, editorial, and printing teams located in different places. This all became possible with the effective use of technologies that we are using today.

Reduce Cost to Your Advantage

With the ever-increasing prices of real estate, the virtual office has become an attractive phenomenon to many businesspeople. Companies can be located at a particular place but the employees conduct their day-to-day office work from different locations such as a hotel, café, or home. New technologies such as Web 2.0, wiki, chat, forums, tags, and RSS (Rich Site Summary/Really Simple Syndication) have enabled teams to maintain effective communication and content collaboration. These technologies have not only broken the barrier of physical infrastructure but have also provided business agility to launch any business with low cost and expand existing businesses globally with minimal cost of operation. We are living and working in the twenty-first century era in which Thomas L. Friedman, the author of *The World Is Flat: A Brief History of the Twenty-First Century*, says that the playing field is being leveled. Globalization has removed all barriers, supported by technological innovation in the areas of information and communication technology (ICT) and transportation. This helped first with outsourced manufacturing and assembly in remote locations with low-cost labor supplies, primarily in India and China, to bring down the cost of assembly, manufacturing, or services in the areas of call centers, medical transcription, accounting, legal, publication media, and films. And, subsequently, business process outsourcing (BPO) or better-defined as knowledge process outsourcing (KPO) evolved in all areas of jobs and at various locations, providing the business agility and efficiency needed to run business operations smoothly.

The cloud computing infrastructure and the fast-emerging cloud operating environment (CloudOE) (Castiglioni and Crudele 2013) with its major ecosystem have enabled access to elastic computing and system application resources deployed across pervasive mobile devices, breaking the physical boundaries. The cloud computing infrastructure has not only enabled access to a system of record (SOR) such as customer relationship management (CRM), enterprise resource planning (ERP), and supply chain management (SCM), but has also offered a system of engagement (SOE) via social interaction on social media, access to geolocations via maps, voice over Internet protocol (VoIP) telephony, chat, and wiki for real-time collaboration in the context of business applications to make the right decisions without being limited by physical location.

Customer Interaction Center in Offshore Locations

We are accustomed to receiving a direct marketing call from vendors promoting their products and services from remote offshore locations. But when we call a local merchant regarding a query or a desired service, we are surprised when that call is routed to a call center agent responding from an offshore location in one of the BRIC countries (Brazil, Russia, India, and China) to reduce the cost of customer-facing interactions, breaking all geographical boundaries. It is an accepted norm to implement customer relationship management (CRM) functions to offshore locations with the help of these technologies that provide business agility. Today, new sets of CRM suites of applications such as Salesforce.com, Oracle Sales Cloud, and many others can be easily implemented on cloud software as a service (SaaS) with a pay-as-you-go model integrated with voice over Internet protocol (VoIP) telephony. These applications and technology solutions enable call center agents to know the details about customers on incoming calls and answer effectively despite their geolocations and time zone differences. In fact, time zone differences help businesses in their continuity of customer services, ensuring that someone is responding to customer requests 24/7 all through the year.

Some of key back-office operations such as payroll, human resources (HR), and accounting are also distributed to various locations, breaking the physical boundaries and sometimes performed by third-party companies as outsourced services leveraging these technologies. It would be insane in the current business context not to consider and implement these technologies and deploy these business models to stay competitive in fiercely competitive business scenarios. These business processes and models are applicable across industries and are rapidly deployed to provide agility and sustainability. Whether we are making hotel reservations, purchasing airline tickets, checking our appointment schedule with health care services providers, obtaining auto repair and maintenance services, or renewing insurance policies, we are witnessing this rapid change in business scenarios, and it would not have been possible without these emerging technologies. It is interesting to note that major innovations in all these major technologies are contributed by software design and deployment, and these vendors are actively embracing the changing paradigm. Major software vendors are setting up their development and back-office support infrastructures in offshore locations, cutting down their operational costs and allocating best resources to design innovation. They are not only deploying their applications across industries but using the applications themselves and implementing them to their advantage. Amazon established a large data center to support customer demand for its e-commerce transactions, and now the same infrastructure is available for computing and storage in the form of Amazon Elastic Compute Cloud (EC2), discussed in Chapter 3.

Let us examine some of the leading sectors that are early adopters of these emerging technologies and are leading innovation and providing business agility within a collaborative ecosystem.

Amazon and eBay Business Models: Breaking the Barrier of Physical Infrastructure

Amazon and eBay in the retail sector have led the e-commerce phenomenon and changed the bricks-and-mortar model of doing business by breaking the barrier of physical infrastructure. Online shopping is the best-known activity in e-commerce. It allows shoppers to buy via the Internet, and, in turn, it lets business owners sell products online at any time. The access to an e-commerce portal 24/7 from across the globe deployed on the cloud environment via all devices powered by social collaboration has not only broken the physical barrier but enriched the decision making process, making it highly effective and predictable.

Amazon Business Model

Amazon.com is designed to perform electronic trade, and consumers are satisfied through comfortable processes. Amazon started by selling books and then expanded its niche market by selling other products. The Amazon website allows businesses and individuals to create listings of the items that they have for sale, and those items then go live on the Amazon website. The items will stay up for as long as it takes for them to sell, or until the seller decides to delete them manually from the listing. The Amazon business model and strategy is to earn a small percentage of the sale price of each item that is sold through its website (like a commission).

The simplicity of the strategy has allowed Amazon to take its business to the next level with an innovative business model.

The eBay Business Model

With a similar business model, eBay has built an online person-to-person trading community on the Internet, leveraging the emerging Internet-based technologies and platforms. Buyers and sellers are brought together in a manner where sellers are permitted to list items for sale, buyers bid on items of interest, and all eBay users are allowed to browse through listed items in a fully automated way. The items are arranged by topics, and each type of auction has its own category. With its web interface, eBay has both streamlined and globalized traditional person-to-person trading, which has traditionally been conducted through such forms as garage sales, collectibles shows, flea markets, and more. The web interface enables sellers to list items for sale within minutes of registering, and facilitates easy exploration by buyers.

Browsing and bidding on auctions is free of charge, but sellers are charged three kinds of fees:

1. When an item is listed on eBay, a nonrefundable insertion fee is charged, which ranges between $0.30 and $3.30, depending on the seller's opening bid on the item.
2. A fee is charged for additional listing options to promote the item, such as a highlighted or bold listing.
3. A final value (final sale price) fee is charged at the end of the seller's auction. This fee generally ranges from 1.25 percent to 5 percent of the final sale price.

At the end of the auction, eBay notifies the buyer and seller via e-mail if a bid exceeds the seller's minimum price, and the seller and buyer finish the transaction independently of eBay.

eBay has successfully leveraged these technologies to their advantage in establishing leadership in the field of e commerce.

* * *

The success of Amazon and eBay in leveraging these converging technologies established the legendary milestones in the field of e-commerce and led the way for businesses across industry sectors to transform in order to survive, thrive, and grow for sustainable competitive advantage. In the current tornado of technology storms, business will not have the success they desire if they do not possess a web storefront to inform, educate, and carry out business transactions with their customers. Moreover, in order to survive in today's tough economic climate, many businesses, whether established, new, or global, will be looking to drive efficiency and reduce costs by leveraging these emerging technologies.

Virtual Support Removing Physical Boundaries

Customer services and support are other major business areas that strongly leveraged these emerging technologies and optimized costs by breaking the boundaries of physical infrastructure and geolocation. With virtual, anytime, anywhere, Internet-based applications, businesses can sell more effectively in geographic markets that were previously unreachable and unprofitable. Even small companies can now deliver services to customers and partners in distant places using these technologies. Communications (VoIP, Skype) and web-based support capabilities can reduce or eliminate on-site travel, minimize downtime, and optimize productivity for customers and overworked information technology (IT) staff.

More important, customer services and support have undergone dramatic changes in the recent past based on these technologies breaking the physical infrastructure and geographic boundaries completely. When we call the customer support desk, we really do not know where the person is located. The call gets routed to remote locations in India, Ireland, and sometimes the Philippines, depending on the time zones.

Today, the help desk needs a better way to manage the realities of today's enterprise dynamics, such as:

- Mobile and remote workers using a multitude of computing devices and operating systems, including smart devices

- Leaner budgets than ever for help desk operations, yet business demands for greater help desk productivity and service quality
- Varying, yet ever more strict, security and compliance mandates for data management by region or by country

With the emergence of solutions, companies have a significantly better way to troubleshoot, fix, administer, and maintain their systems. Banks support their customers using a variety of web-based tools, including chat, remote control, VoIP, and video; these solutions enable managers to track customer services virtually via the Internet. This capability helps eliminate costly visits to customer locations and long distance calls. Exceptional customer service must be the backbone of businesses in today's tough climate. Now the challenge of providing high-touch customer service has never been easier while also dramatically reducing operational costs and enhancing customer satisfaction. These next-generation support solutions add the vital human element to communication with customers and create a new level of attention that ultimately improves client retention and loyalty.

Oracle Advanced Support Ensures Uptime of Mission-Critical IT Environments

Oracle Advanced Monitoring and Resolution delivers monitoring and resolution services across the entire information technology (IT) stack (from servers to applications) that help maximize uptime of mission-critical environments. Experts from Oracle Advanced Customer Support Services provide 24/7 monitoring and mission-critical support that helps drive continuous system optimization and deliver better service levels while controlling both costs and risk through proactive monitoring and resolution services.

Today's complex IT infrastructures require specialized expertise in networks, servers, applications, and storage. But, with tightened IT budgets, it can be difficult to retain IT specialists to manage complex IT environments across a broad range of products.

Oracle Advanced Monitoring and Resolution leverages intellectual property, tools, and best practices to continually optimize the IT environment. The service consists of two principal services for mission-critical systems:

1. *Advanced monitoring.* Predictive monitoring provides 24/7 proactive system monitoring. These services leverage proprietary Oracle technologies and provide coverage for complex Oracle, Sun, and supporting third-party systems from the network layer to the applications layer. Monitoring services helps to ensure uptime and to deliver increased service levels via proactive notification of potential issues, enabling staff to focus on core business activities.

2. *Advanced resolution.* Resolution services include proactive monitoring and provide the Information Technology Infrastructure Library (ITIL)-based processes and technological expertise for system administration and incident resolution. A dedicated team of technical experts delivers proactive and preventive maintenance.

Proactive monitoring and resolution services are delivered via a global network of local experts and fully disaster-recovery-compliant control centers in the Americas, Europe, and Asia. Resolution services are uniquely designed for businesses with options ranging from fully remote solutions breaking all physical and geographical boundaries to fully on-site solutions, or the appropriate combination.

Education: Going beyond Physical Boundaries

Education is yet another sector that can leverage these emerging technologies such as cloud and collaborative technologies and reach remote locations, breaking physical boundaries. In many ways, education is timeless. Its purpose has been to help learners expand their understanding of how things work, improve their capabilities and skills, and grow as successful individuals. However, education today is far different from what it was just a decade ago. Technology has been a major driver, but other resources are converging to reshape the way we think about, and deliver, learning:

- A heightened focus on educational outcomes and institutional accountability
- Learner-centric learning that recognizes that different people have different learning styles and different pathways to acquiring an education

- The need for lifelong continuous learning and the emerging importance of reaching nontraditional students and people with disabilities
- Globalization and the fact that our students graduate into a world that is more competitive, faster paced, and more information driven
- Economic pressures to cut costs and, for higher education and private schools, to increase revenues as well

These forces are re-architecting education, which today may blend traditional elements with online learning, both self-paced and in real time. Instruction may be delivered entirely in a live, virtual classroom. It may be based on "learning by doing" projects that prepare learners to navigate their personal and professional lives in an interconnected, always-on world. It may fall anywhere on the continuum from formal, structured classes and professional development to in-the-moment, informal problem-solving sessions and ad hoc meetings.

Many technology solutions such as Blackboard, Edmodo, Huddle, and Moodle deployed on cloud platforms enable collaborative education and are easily accessible and available even in remote locations where Internet access is available. OpenStudy (http://openstudy.com) is a unique learning platform and a sound effort in the right direction to break the boundaries of physical and geographical infrastructure, where students collaborate, ask questions, give help, and connect with other students studying the same things regardless of their locations, time zones, and institutions. This endeavors to make the world one large study group, regardless of school, location, or background.

Now major universities in the United States have joined the initiative to provide free, open online courses, breaking all physical boundaries and enabling students/learners across the globe to learn with mere Internet access.

Massive Open Online Courses: Breaking Physical Boundaries in Education

Although there has been access to free online courses on the Internet for years, the quality and quantity of courses have changed. Access to free courses has allowed students to obtain a level of education that many could only dream of in the past. This has changed the face of education. In the *New York Times* article "Instruction for Masses

Knocked Down Campus Walls" (March 4, 2012), author Tamar Lewin stated, "In the past few months, hundreds of thousands of motivated students around the world who lack access to elite universities have been embracing them as a path toward sophisticated skills and high-paying jobs, without paying tuition or collecting a college degree."

Although massive open online courses (MOOCs) are the latest trend, not everyone agrees that schools should offer them. Joshua Kim's *Inside Higher Ed* article "Why Every University Does Not Need a MOOC" (March 6, 2012) noted that offering free material may not make sense for the individual university.

Since a MOOC is voluntary and there is no penalty for dropping the program or lagging behind, there may be issues with course completion. Although a student may have received an excellent education, there will not be a corresponding diploma.

For those who desire a free education and have the motivation, the top 10 sites for information about MOOCs are:

1. *Udemy free courses.* Udemy is an example of a site that allows anyone to build or take online courses. Udemy's site exclaims, "Our goal is to disrupt and democratize education by enabling anyone to learn from the world's experts." The *New York Times* reported that Udemy "recently announced a new Faculty Project, in which award-winning professors from universities like Dartmouth, the University of Virginia and Northwestern offer free online courses. Its co-founder, Gagen Biyani, said the site has more than 100,000 students enrolled in its courses, including several, outside the Faculty Project, that charge fees." [https://www.udemy.com/]
2. *ITunes U free courses.* Apple's free app "gives students access to all the materials for courses in a single place. Right in the app, they can play video or audio lectures. Read books and view presentations." [www.apple.com/education/ipad/itunes-u/]
3. *Stanford University free courses.* From quantum mechanics to the future of the Internet, Stanford offers a variety of free courses. Stanford's Introduction to Artificial Intelligence was highly successful. According to Pontydysgu (www.pontydysgu.org), "160,000 students from 190 countries signed up to Stanford's 'Introduction to AI' course, with 23,000 reportedly completing." [http://see .stanford.edu/]
4. *University of California at Berkeley free courses.* From general biology to human emotion, Berkeley offers a variety of courses. Check out

Berkeley webcasts and Berkeley RSS feeds. [http://webcast .berkeley.edu/]

5. *MIT free courses.* Check out MIT's RSS MOOC feed. [http://ocw .mit.edu/help/rss/]

6. *Duke University free courses.* Duke offers a variety of courses on ITunes U. [http://itunes.duke.edu/]

7. *Harvard University free courses.* From computer science to Shakespeare, students may now get a free Harvard education. "Take a class for professional development, enrichment, and degree credit. Courses run in the fall, spring, or intensive January session. No application is required." [www.harvard.edu/faqs/free-courses]

8. *UCLA free courses.* Check out free courses such as the writing program that offers more than 220 online writing courses each year. [https://www.uclaextension.edu/pages/search.aspx?c=free+courses]

9. *Yale University free courses.* At Open Yale, the school offers "free and open access to a selection of introductory courses taught by distinguished teachers and scholars at Yale University. The aim of the project is to expand access to educational materials for all who wish to learn." [http://oyc.yale.edu/]

10. *Carnegie Mellon University free courses.* Carnegie Mellon boasts "No instructors, no credits, no charge." [http://oli.cmu.edu/]

Khan Academy: Making a Great Impact in Education

With emerging technologies, the face of education is changing rapidly and the world should benefit immensely, breaking all physical boundaries. Anyone in the world with Internet access can learn from the best and brightest for free.

In 2004, Sal Khan, a former hedge fund analyst living in Boston, Massachusetts, began tutoring his cousins in need of a deeper understanding of mathematics. Khan began with short and focused instructional videos teaching unit conversion using a virtual blackboard and talking through the logic of solving these problems, and expanded to a library of over 5,000 instructional videos, including 100 self-paced practice exercises and metrics to analyze the learner's progress, available for anyone in the world to consume and learn. He formed the Khan Academy to share his video lessons on YouTube via the Internet and to help students better understand various math and science topics explained in ways that were different from how he was taught in the classroom and through textbooks.

Khan refers to himself as a teacher of the Khan Academy since he creates all of the instructional videos. The Khan Academy has become extremely popular; students and parents have found Khan's resources exceedingly beneficial and a supplement for their foundational understanding of math and science.

Health Care Services Leveraging Outsourced Services

These technologies have enabled the health care sector as well, and many in this industry are turning to outsourced health care management solutions as a strategic alternative to manage their office functions, as well as selected administrative, financial, and IT services. Health care providers will need to find new business models to support operational and clinical quality, reimbursement, and stakeholder management. Services such as case and policy administration, member enrollment, profile management, claims management, benefits administration, billings and collections, and provider relations can be rendered remotely from distant locations, breaking barriers of physical boundaries and time zones, lowering the costs, and enhancing agility and efficiency. Emerging new process models can help organizations control costs and focus on growth while improving operational efficiencies and optimizing existing resources.

Health care delivery organizations can meet the objectives of reducing operational costs, minimizing administrative overheads, and maximizing profitability by strategically outsourcing their business processes to specialized service providers at offshore locations. There are various front desk services such as patient registration, scheduling and appointment management, eligibility verification, referral management, appointment confirmation, follow-up appointment reminders, and scheduling that are efficiently carried out by professionally trained staff at offshore locations, breaking physical boundaries by business process outsourcing (BPO) service providers. Back-office services such as medical billing, accounts receivable (A/R) management, denial management, patient statements, trending, and reporting have become a proven business model for optimizing operational efficiency.

Assembly: Outsourced by Apple in China

Manufacturing broke geographical barriers a long time ago with outsourcing to offshore locations, causing a lot of uproar that U.S.

jobs were being taken by India and China. As the previously cited *New York Times* article pointed out, when President Obama asked Steve Jobs, Jobs answered bluntly: "Those jobs are not coming back." Foxconn is contracted by Apple to assemble iPhones in a southern Chinese city, Shenzhen, and employs 230,000 workers. The Foxconn campus has banks, supermarkets, bookstores, fire brigades, a police station, a hospital, and many other facilities. It is sometimes referred to as "iPod City." By locating the same iPhone factory in the United States, Apple would add more than $25 billion in labor costs a year, which would completely wipe out its 2010 profit of $14 billion.

As these emerging technologies are creating a revolution, businesses need to focus on research and innovation and create more companies such as Apple, Facebook, Google, and Tesla.

Manufacturing Outsourcing: Levi Strauss & Co.

We all know that today Levi Strauss & Co. products are sold under the Levi's, Dockers, Denizen, and Signature brands. The products are sold in approximately 55,000 retail locations in more than 110 countries, including approximately 1,900 dedicated retail stores. Levi Strauss & Co. was founded in San Francisco by Bavarian immigrant Levi Strauss in 1853.

In an endeavor to survive and remain in the business, the company changed its business model to embrace manufacturing outsourcing. It shut down many of its sewing factories in the United States and outsourced to offshore countries, breaking physical boundaries, and brought back a focus on innovation to meet customer demand and responsiveness with agility.

Travel and Hospitality Sectors: Breaking Physical Boundaries

With the convergence of these technologies (cloud, social, mobile, video, and big data) continuing to diversify, the travel and hospitality industry is no exception and has offered greater customer engagement for airline ticket booking packaged with hotels, car rentals, and package tours all at the click of a button on any device from any geolocation. In addition, today's customers demand a personalized experience with real-time information and assistance via voice, online, e-mail, text, and chat media.

Expedia, Travelocity, Orbitz, Kayak, CheapoAir, Bestfares, MakeMyTrip.com, Cleartrip, and Carlson Wagonlit Travel are a few of the many travel and hospitality portals that offer elegant services via an interactive portal with a rich web experience for all travel and hospitality needs, breaking physical boundaries. We no longer need to visit any physical offices to accomplish these jobs—we can do so with the use of smart devices from anywhere at any time.

MakeMyTrip.com is an example in the travel and hospitality industry to establish rapid growth over a decade, crossing the limit of geographical boundaries and leveraging these major technologies. The company was founded in the year 2000 with the aim of empowering Indian travelers with instant booking and comprehensive travel and hospitality packages in one web environment. It aimed to offer a range of best-value products and services based on leading technologies for interactive customer engagement supported by round-the-clock support staff. With greater customer engagement based on cloud deployment, the company expanded its reach to global customers, breaking all geographical boundaries, and today it is extremely successful among Asian diasporas globally, including those in the United States, Australia, Europe, the Middle East, and Africa.

Software Development Leverages Global Resources

It is not an exaggeration to say that we do not need a software development team in one room at one office location at any given point in time. In fact, all major software development work is carried out with distributed resources all across the globe, breaking physical geographical boundaries and optimizing cost. Maximizing IT development resources is a common problem facing many large companies, especially those with information-intensive business models such as financial services, telecommunications, high technology, and manufacturing. Priorities and workloads fluctuate continually—from team to team, department to department, and project to project.

Convergence of these technologies has also helped software development across the board in several ways. Cloud infrastructure has helped global IT teams to provision the right development resources to the team on a virtual consolidated infrastructure and has eliminated diverse setups at numerous places that entailed lots of duplicate effort to make sure each lab had the proper versions and updates for each server and storage array.

AEC Industry Removes Barriers

The architecture, engineering, and construction (AEC) industry can maximize project collaboration, make business more agile, and reduce operational costs by leveraging these emerging technologies and deploying services based on cloud infrastructure. As we all know, construction professionals are constantly challenged to deliver successful projects due to tight budgets, short time lines, geographically dispersed teams, and difficulty in accessing information.

Architects and construction engineers would be able to access their blueprints, computer aided design (CAD) files, and contracts hosted and managed by content storage offered by cloud service providers. Box, a leading online storage services provider, recently announced its services named Box OneCloud apps to better serve customers in architecture, engineering, and construction. These services can be accessed remotely from anywhere, at any time, and on any devices, removing any geographical barriers and providing greater business agility and efficiency. Site engineers and architects conduct site inspection and many other jobs such as quantity surveying, validation, and correction with the help of smart devices on-site, accessing all contents accessible from their cloud services.

With these technologies (cloud, social, and mobile), architects would be able to create the architectural drawings remotely located at any location, supported by structural engineers providing structural drawings, again from remote locations, and executed by site engineers to carry out the construction work with real-time active collaboration with the architects and structural engineers.

Many large construction projects are executed with the use of sophisticated software services offered by Intergraph, Autodesk, and Bentley in cloud deployment models to create business agility in the AEC sector.

As we further examine all these technology forces in the next chapter, we dig deep on the power of collaborative management providing greater capabilities to manage tasks more efficiently with powerful collaborative tools. We have endeavored to provide some guidance on leading tools that may help in transforming your business with new modes of collaborative management and execution with various stakeholders in business with the single mission of creating business agility and providing greater efficiency.

Converging Technology: Inside the Force 5 Tornado for the Perfect Storm

The convergence of cloud, social, mobile, video, and big data provides synergy for determining what the vision, mission, and strategy of the next generation of digital business is using collaboratively internally to align functional resources and externally to leverage trading partner capabilities with compatible core competencies. In this manner we can use the digital business value chain to develop a market-leading ecosystem where the power of the whole is greater than the sum of the parts.

Accordingly, *CIO Insights* are provided by Dean Lane, founder of Office of the CIO (www.oocio.com) and author of *The Chief Information Officer's Body of Knowledge* (John Wiley & Sons, 2011). His insights focus on how CIOs may leverage their understanding of these converging technologies for CIO success to deliver the business value of IT for digital businesses.

Transformation, Synergy, and Innovation through the Cloud[1]

Technology has become an extremely important part of many people's lives. It is having an impact and successful effect on their goals in both their professional and personal lives. Gradually, they are having more alternatives and more flexibility in the technology they use every day, and as that technology spills over into their professional lives, the line between personal and professional is blurring. People want to be able to choose what technology they use or operate, and they increasingly want to use that same technology in all aspects of their lives, not just either at home or at work.

Actually, according to an analysis by Unisys conducted by International Data Corporation (IDC), 95 percent of information technology personnel use at least one self-purchased system at work. The analysis also found that information technology personnel "report using a combination of four client devices and several third-party

---

[1] This section is written by Dean Lane, Office of the CIO.

plans, such as online sites, in the course of their day." The Unisys-IDC analysis also revealed a somewhat worrisome difference between what information technology personnel are actually using at work and what their organizations believe they are using. For example, "69% of [information technology] workers say they access non-work-related online (Cloud) sites, while only 44% of their organizations evaluate this to be the scenario" (Unisys 2012).

For IT, it's about understanding usage and creating a balance of goals and enterprise requirements. Cloud technology, without a concern, creates risks to the business such as to security and compliance. However, there are also many benefits to the cloud that organizations can implement with the right design and technique. People and employees like their cloud technology because it makes it much easier for them to be connected with others, it is convenient for exchanging information, and it all functions together. Significantly, for organizations, the amount of data that can be accessed, analyzed, reviewed, and used to benefit the company represents tremendous benefits. Those benefits that are there for the taking by organizations require a partnership between the information technology department and other functional business units. To get the right balance— to decrease the risks and increase the benefits—in some circumstances could mean using certain consumer technology in the workplace and in others it could mean providing enterprise alternatives that will keep both clients and professionals excited.

Information Technology Revolution.   The landscape of the technology architecture is being changed by employees who are carrying out their own alternatives to buy, learn, and use a variety of well-known cloud consumer technical improvements and program alternatives to get things done in the workplace.

These improvements and alternatives are challenging and reducing old restrictions in the work environment. At work, at home, and everywhere in between, tech-savvy employees and clients are using the same successful, accessible alternatives and plans. From smartphones available in the open market to iPads to websites and instant messaging, people are staying knowledgeable, linked via the cloud and successful in their professional as well as their personal lives. Accelerating the situation are changing usage needs of an always-on atmosphere and anytime/anywhere accessibility that is primarily changing support and service requirements.

This cloud-based consumer-powered IT architecture is already turning conventional IT styles on their collective heads. It's a successful new way to operate that will boost companies for years to come and usher in a new design of business productivity. And yet, unfortunately, most companies are not ready to take advantage of this cloud-based productivity increase.

Some of the latest Unisys research, conducted by IDC, shows a distressing gap between the actions and goals of new "iWorkers" and their employers' capability to deal with, secure, and support this movement and then implement it. The iWorkers are not so much demanding change as they are generating it through contract usage motivated by flexibility and interconnectedness. While iWorkers are very familiar with available capabilities and are adept at recognizing the value of technological innovation, they have little comprehension of the security risks, administrative concerns, and additional administration resulting from a huge launch of client gadgets and plans into the work environment. When the enterprise embraces this new paradigm, it means improved productivity from new ways of connecting. Additionally, the cloud will provide a sharp competitive edge over the competition. Those IT organizations that choose to implement the opportunities and facilitate these changes will earn a reputation as a contemporary organization offering a flexible, agile work environment that is just as secure as those that do not embrace this change (Unisys 2012).

Organizations, meanwhile, are still mostly dealing within the constant, command-and-control IT styles of the past. Those styles are very good at addressing risks and expenditures, but they sometimes prevent the organization from generating the immediate benefits obtained from the cutting edge. They also lack the consideration of improvements found by designing for productivity.

To administer the full power of this new productivity architecture, companies need to update their IT activities in order to:

- Manage and support these well-known client technologies.
- Protect significant information and alternatives against online hackers, malware, and other widespread client threats.
- Offer the engaged app actions that clients are looking for when transacting with their suppliers.
- Manage the estimated fourfold improvements that these off-the-shelf apps can bring while incorporating the necessary changes into the IT infrastructure.

- Attract and sustain the new technological innovation of employees coming into the firm.

Companies that take the initiative and implement the new cloud architecture being spawned by this consumer-powered IT will find that the user acceptance is incredible, employees are more engaged and successful, the capability to leapfrog is enhanced, and, yes, they even obtain cost avoidance (Preston 2011).

Root of IT Consumerization. Anyone who views the consumerization occurrence as being encouraged by just technology is missing an important point. The real change—and why it's gradually not an IT selection—is in the enterprise itself. The 1950s were a military-style "company man" enterprise, which was an outcome of the incredible influx of militarily trained World War II soldiers returning to the staff. In the 1960s and 1970s companies found benefits not only from individuals but also from teams and other types of associations. This beginning saw a decomposition of the enterprise into a thinner style with less middle-level experts and more staff energy (Gruman 2012).

This became amazingly codified using methods from administration experts such as W. Edwards Deming. His use of Six Sigma as well as workers' co-ownership and Toyota's "anyone can quit the setup line" perspective were a new way of operating. The 1990s and early 2000s saw a continuous hollowing out of centralized administration as a result of part-time work, contracted work, and the alternative of strategy work through programs (in organizations that mostly had no individual-empowerment culture).

That gradual progression eventually left many organizations with a smaller set of knowledge workers being maintained because they could think for themselves, as well as use their feelings and knowledge to generate revenue, client support, items style, or other various functions (Gruman 2012).

Information Technology Personnel Living in a Fool's Paradise. The unpleasant reality for IT and enterprise leaders is that most are managing in a fool's paradise when it comes to the cloud paradigm. Recent IDC research reveals that although 40 percent of IT choice creators say they let workers access enterprise information through the cloud from employee-owned gadgets, 70 percent of workers say they access enterprise information that way. That means in many organizations IT has no real control over what is actually developing in the environment it is managing. IDC's analysis also reveals that the use of individually run devices is and will continually increase (O'Neill 2011).

Other IDC studies have shown some IT detachment from the consumerized technological innovation that is already within their own organization. Let's look at an example of the mismatch between IT's and users' opinions of guidelines with regard to who will pay for cellular services. IT believes that the enterprise decides and immediately will pay for business-related accessibility that it implements by distributing only BlackBerry devices to customers. Users of other cellular technologies say they will accept the expenditures themselves or allocate them back to the company as a cost. In other words, these IT organizations see the BlackBerrys as standing for the preconsumerization state of their organizations whereas their users see other personally provided technologies as the path to increased productivity (O'Neill 2011).

Information Technology in the New World.   The consumerization of IT, enabled by the cloud, requires a different way for many in IT to think, as it begins with soft principles and needs IT to share possession of administration and technological innovation selection with enterprise workers and their business divisions. So as the consumerization pattern is motivated by soft people concerns, an excellent idea to explore is that the administration reaction to it be based in people techniques (Kemp 2011).

On the technological innovation side, the approach would be to use guidelines as opposed to firm limitations to guide workers to the right results while enabling appropriate independence and imagination. It says the IT monoculture at the end point stage is a dead end. Instead IT should think of technological innovation as an "onion cloud" with several layers. The external, employee-oriented layers should be versatile and easily tailored to the individual, while core IT processes should be consistent and secured as much as possible. For example, allow any cloud application that conforms to your program guidelines but add levels of validation and safety measures such as protection for those online functions that are truly susceptible within the system. Even if you allow personnel to move their work group to the cloud and access it from an iPad, it doesn't mean that the same personnel can access your HR information resources.

The bad part is that not all the technological innovation is available to deal with this layered onion approach. The view of detailed privileges administration is hardly ever integrated into common business information items or techniques, and even more rarely into cloud applications and gadgets. Another thing to remember is that the cloud is not new. Payroll provided by a third-party service provider began this voyage. The Internet took it to a whole new level, as data became unbounded, not just processing functionality. Yet not only have companies lived through this, but they've benefited greatly from that new power. Think back to the view that prevailed then and remember how stringently controlled it was. End users with their own computing resources once seemed terrifying, but it ended up not being so bad. Then you designed (as it became clear you had to) ways to take advantage of the enhanced capabilities in a secure way. Now utilize that same thinking when considering this latest wave of technological change (Kemp 2011).

Security Challenges Raised by the Cloud. Generally, IT organizations offer to run personal computers and laptops interacting within the business's trusted network or via a successful, effective, and properly secured virtual private network (VPN). Now, with the bring your own device (BYOD) model, you have customers making IT choices from outside the trusted environment using their own personal computers or mobile devices. The substitution of IT choices outside the trusted zone for IT choices in the trusted environment is developing, and later on IT segments will contain several on-premises and off-premises choices.

This change in IT choices from within to outside the trusted zone is increasing the overall cost to businesses, but this cloud capability is also broadening the use of IT within those companies. Generally, IT has been about automating the centralized system worker's environment circa 1970. Think of the vintage inbox and outbox and how they are being replaced by outsourced providers, and in many cases texting or instant messaging. The consumerization/bring your own (BYO) phenomenon has IT providing services that require broadening capabilities to all customers within an organization. Many customers who typically may have not used the cloud (e.g., scientists, top income earners, etc.) are now being given use of devices and programs to produce new productivities (O'Neill 2011).

Some may characterize movement to the cloud as ascending but still a far way off. Vendors and others portray that an organization is behind the times if it is not fully embracing the cloud. That being said, and given that most enormous companies don't like to change something that functions (e.g., many around the world are still interacting with mainframes), it's difficult to see companies looking to instantly rip out something that is currently part of their IT structure. This indicates that business and IT will be providing several on-premises and off-premises IT choices with the off-premises-based IT choices incrementally and gradually improving in flexibility, capabilities, and functionality. But no matter what this pattern of clouds and hybridization represents within IT, organizations right now are suffering from a significant task of managing and complying with security concerns. To cope with increasing demand and still protect the company's data, IT must have end-to-end knowledge and administration over clients, plans, servers, and devices. This will allow IT to ensure that the business is properly secured while still being nimble enough to easily provide solutions to changing business conditions. Typically, this involved getting and obtaining on-premises devices, servers, and plans. Now the same type of security capabilities must be utilized for IT technologies that are outside the trusted environment and are not directly managed by the IT department.

So just as there is a multibillion-dollar market for PC administration (e.g., antivirus, etc.), certainly a comparative market for cloud and cell phone administration will eventually evolve. In much the same way that there is a big market for provisioning clients and offering them personal sign-on to on-premises systems, such as those of SAP and PeopleSoft, there is little doubt that a large market will appear for SaaS solutions where clients can have a single sign-on to many systems.

It remains to be seen if the classic on-premises pushed security model organizations such as Symantec, McAfee, or Computer Associates can properly switch to a consumerized and cloud-based method for providing information security. Also yet to be answered is whether the new cloud-based organizations such as Google or Salesforce.com will provide these capabilities or if one or more pure-play small businesses can develop the requisite capabilities and offerings. At the same time, IT organizations are now looking at available options for getting on-premises IT security alternatives and also investigating a personal set of best-of-breed solutions for off-premises IT security alternatives, as well as exploring whether they can use one solution to, for example, secure both PCs and mobile phone devices ("Consumerization of IT Gone Wild" 2011).

The prospective drawback of inadequate knowledge and functionality to successfully administer security over off-premises IT alternatives may prevent realization of some of the benefits even as productivity is enhanced by new BYO devices, plans, and services. Established organizations, the new cloud-based organizations, and lots of venture-backed small businesses are attempting to cope with those concerns that in the end will further increase the effectiveness of a BYO cloud-based IT group.

The Use of Business Intelligence in the Cloud Is a Game Changer. The use of business intelligence (BI) in the cloud is what is creating an alliance between chief marketing officers (CMOs) and chief information officers (CIOs). This will be the first of several alliances between the CIO and business unit leaders. The data most readily available enables companies to gain insight into consumer behavior, identify sales opportunities, and make data-driven decisions without hefty investments in IT infrastructure.

The CMO-CIO alliance is a prime opportunity for CIOs to better collaborate with an organization's other business leaders. In fact, IT leaders with the right cloud know-how can help drive revenue and reduce costs—achievements that are likely to impress other business leaders and create opportunities for additional alliances.

But as more and more companies migrate from on-premises to cloud BI, challenges arise. Here are the five most important issues that IT leaders need to carefully consider when evaluating cloud BI:

1. Deliver trusted data.

    Blending disparate sources of data within a cloud BI solution is key to deriving actionable insights about your business. Unfortunately, inaccurate and untrustworthy data can significantly skew results. Whether it's customer contact details in a CRM system or inventory reports generated by an ERP tool, IT leaders must both properly test and validate algorithms and always ask the right questions of the data to get the right answers.

2. Consider a hybrid model.

    There's no such thing as a cookie-cutter approach to BI. While a growing number of companies prefer cloud-based BI solutions to on-premises ones, in-house hardware is still important. For instance, companies extracting valuable consumer intelligence or conducting traditional financial trending analyses using large volumes of highly sensitive data are likely to prefer the control and security provided by an on-premises BI system. The secret is having the next-generation infrastructure in place to support multiple approaches to BI.

3. Keep your data secure.

   Security concerns continue to arise around cloud-based and BI solutions. The good news is companies can take matters into their own hands. First organizations must figure out what data can be put in the cloud safely and securely. Next, it's necessary to ensure that a cloud BI provider offers network segmentation through firewalls, up-to-date security patches, password protection, and security management services so that the same levels of data protection can be achieved as with an on-premises setup.

4. Build the right infrastructure.

   Managing a cloud strategy is no easy task. That's why it's critical that IT leaders have the necessary infrastructure capabilities to support cloud BI. This requires IT leaders to design and communicate with the CMO an integration plan so that corporate data as well as big data from various sources can be seamlessly migrated to the new cloud system. This effort must be conducted working hand in hand with the CMO and other business line leaders to ensure that a next-generation infrastructure supports not only cloud BI but also business goals.

5. Facilitate change management.

   It's common for many cloud BI tools to be largely underused. That's a shame given the time and money invested in cloud BI. Fortunately, greater adoption is possible by offering the CMOs and other employees extensive training in BI tools. Proper change management as well as educating employees on how they stand to benefit from a BI system's capabilities also requires plenty of up-front planning. After all, making the most of technologies like cloud BI can help companies save money that can be reinvested in growing the business or in strategic projects.

Effects on the CIO. While the use of the cloud and personal devices such as smartphones, notebooks, and other products on the market is creating more effective and efficient personnel, it is handcuffing many IT departments. For every sales rep using his or her personal iPad to access enterprise e-mail or CRM, there are IT professionals behind the scenes having difficulties dealing with the intersection of personal devices and enterprise detailed information, and making sure that everything is complying with policy (O'Neill 2011).

Many cloud and consumerization of IT methods are hit-or-miss, rattled and shaken by protection issues and unclear detailed recommendations about how to administer them or provide the proper security, according to a frontline study of 750 IT professionals conducted by Point of View Analysis (Gibbs 2011).

But despite the benefits to personnel, the cloud and consumerization of IT are a thorn in the side of most IT departments, according to the research. Most (82 percent) surveyed say they are concerned about the use of individual devices for work requirements, with the biggest situation being potential program security breaches (62 percent), followed by possible loss of customer enterprise data (50 percent), potential theft of intellectual property from home (48 percent), and issues with compliance requirements (43 percent).

As with any change in a business, the cloud and consumerization of IT will become a priority, and big changes will occur within IT to aid in the use of personal devices at work. It's a certainty that this will not be going away soon.

Conclusion

All in all, one will find that use of the cloud will grow and it is something that is going to make your life interesting, for want of a better word. It is not certain what the end user side of the IT catalog of your upcoming services will look like. However, it is fairly certain that the baseline services will have to support nothing but wireless connectivity to diverse mobile devices utilizing a cost-effective strategy characterized by details all over the place driven by comprehensive security methods. And may the gods help you if you're in a regulatory industry.

With that as the impact on the CIO, there's only one answer on what to do: Change; take the alteration. Be sensible. You know that you are already attached to the reins of the enterprise. The items exercising the future are on their way and coming directly at you. Not only will these items defy conventional procedures, but someone has jammed the velocity controls to "comprehensive on."

References

Castiglioni, F., & Crudele, M. (2013, October 22). *Design an SoE ecosystem to support rich user experiences. IBM Corporation.* "Consumerization of IT Gone Wild." 2011. *Network World, 28*(13): 7.

Friedman, Thomas L. 2005. *The World Is Flat: A Brief History of the Twenty-First Century.* New York: Farrar, Straus & Giroux.

Gibbs, M. 2011.Gibbs, M. 2011. "IT Consumerization: It's Biblical!" *Network World, 28*(20): 34.

Gruman, G. 2012. "The Real Force Behind the Consumerization of IT." *InfoWorld.*

Kemp, T. 2011. "Consumerization of IT Raises New Security Challenges." *Forbes.*

O'Neill, S. 2011. "Consumerization of IT Taking Its Toll on IT Managers." *CIO.*

Preston, R. 2011. "Consumerization of IT Is No Fad." *Information Week.*

Unisys. 2012. "Consumerization of IT." Retrieved January 18, 2012, from www.unisys .com/unisys/ri/topic/researchtopicdetail.jsp?id=700004.

CHAPTER 5

Power of Collaborative Management

If you are reading this chapter, you have realized the fact that we are working in both a real and a digital business environment where there are no geolocation boundaries. Internet and cloud technology solutions have enabled us to work from anywhere, at any time, on any devices. It is only the mind-set that has to change rapidly and start thinking globally from any business execution point of view. In this chapter, we enumerate and outline some of the leading tools that may provide effective collaboration in the context of business to optimize cost and help in growth.

As a business owner or as a line of business leader or even as a manager of a department, one has to ask a simple question: How do you perform your day-to-day tasks or make business decisions on a critical business matter? Do you decide all on your own or based on collaborative insights from team members? In today's dynamic environments, we have to examine whether traditional management provides enough value where business agility, adaptability, and survivability are required. In the context of ecosystemism, we discussed the significance of customers and partners all playing greater roles of influence. It would not be prudent for managers or business leaders to work in isolation when executing business functions, despite their capability, knowledge, and experience. Making decisions completely on gut instinct and experience of a business leader was a normal practice in the past but not anymore. In a multiple-location, multicultural, widely distributed business environment, collaboration is the name of the game, and the power of effective collaboration simply cannot be ignored.

Collaborate for Better Execution and Effective Decision Making

The power of collaborative management and use of collaborative tools cannot be underestimated in driving business agility. In a rapidly changing business environment, at the higher levels in an organization, leadership may show the path, present the options for direction, and define the boundaries for the decisions that teams will make in the various spheres of influence. Effective leaders push decision making to the edges of the organization where information is more relevant, available, and real time. Management facilitates the creation of the agreed processes and then acts as guardian to ensure that they are not broken, either by a change of context or by those operating the processes. In this role, management does not make process decisions but facilitates the creation of the process and then identifies when the process needs to be upgraded.

As anyone who has worked in a sizable organization knows, there is no guarantee that the organization as a whole will perform efficiently and achieve its goals, even if each employee is individually efficient and every team has a high level of productivity. To achieve enterprise productivity, it is necessary not only for individuals and groups to "do things right" by working productively but also for the enterprise as a whole to "do the right things"—form the right teams, make the right decisions, allocate resources correctly, and effectively coordinate activities across the entire organization.

Most organizations fall short of the optimal level of enterprise productivity because of one or more of the following reasons, all at a great cost to the business:

- They are disconnected from themselves, with various parts of the organization unintentionally working at cross-purposes with each other.
- Information that exists is not getting shared or reused.
- Human talent is not being applied where it is most needed.
- The same problems are being solved repeatedly by multiple groups.

Intelligent collaboration through automated business processes has the ability to alter the course of any important business activity, with a potentially dramatic impact on the financial performance of the business. Whether it is a simple e-mail exchange, a physical or virtual meeting, a task force, or a large-scale project, the activity is inherently collaborative. In fact, collaboration can be defined as the work that takes place among people when a business process is not predetermining how the work should take place. Collaboration is many things: information sharing, brainstorming, problem solving, best practices negotiation, innovation, coordination of activity, alignment of purpose, and so forth. Collaboration is the white space between the business processes; it is the glue that holds an organization together, as well as the lubricant that allows the machinery to keep running.

Let's visualize a dynamic business environment with collaborative tools and systems that enable people to work and collaborate efficiently to perform and execute their tasks. In a sales scenario, Steve, based in the United Kingdom, receives a request for proposal (RFP) from a prospect that he needs to respond to and submit before the due date within four weeks. After initial study of the document, Steve knows that he will have to seek information and content from various team members located in different cities in different countries in multiple time zones. Does it sound familiar to you? Steve identifies his key team members who would provide the content and contribute with their inputs for the proposal. In order to collaborate with his team for this RFP, Steve first creates a wiki page and uploads the RFP document; he then invites his team members to review the RFP. The wiki allows Steve and his team members to review, upload, and edit content remotely, breaking the barrier of geographical locations and time zone differences and enabling him to submit the response to the RFP in time.

In this chapter we evaluate and examine the power of various collaborative tools that help provide business agility in this dynamic business environment. Collaborative tools, popularly known as Web 2.0 technologies, are rapidly transforming user expectations of enterprise systems. Today's knowledge worker is typically overwhelmed by e-mail and conference calls and frustrated by an inability to intuitively derive answers from the applications at hand. But through highly customizable applications and collaborative services such as blogs, wikis, and social communities, businesses can empower their employees with access to information and content in context and optimize the connections among people, information, and applications.

Enterprise 2.0 is the new paradigm that has emerged rapidly and gained adoption at a fast rate. The term was coined by Andrew MacAfee, a professor at MIT. It is all about easy communication and collaboration with other workers, team members, customers, vendors, and clients. The acronym SLATES, which stands for search, links, authorship, tags, extensions, and signaling, refers to the key elements in Enterprise 2.0, which is primarily driven by Web 2.0 technologies, increased socialization, and business cultures that enable companies to collaborate among employees, partners, and customers. Internet computing technology has experienced at least two revolutions. The first wave, referred to as Web 1.0, provided the platform to publish information about products and services to external and internal consumers. Currently, technology is advancing through a second revolution, referred to as Web 2.0. We have already started witnessing the evolution of Web 3.0, which focuses on semantic web and personalization. Web 3.0 is where the computer is generating new information, rather than humans doing so.

Rich Web 2.0 technologies such as wikis, blogs, tagging, linking, discussions, and RSS (Rich Site Summary/Really Simple Syndication) provide dramatic efficiencies to people working together with global virtual teams, partners, and customers. Social media tools like blogs and microblogs (Twitter) offer new dimensions to publish the content on the Internet via smartphones and smart devices. Enterprise-wide networking, content, and voice collaboration have been the second driver of Enterprise 2.0, moving from data-centric models to people-driven applications. Web 2.0 allows for the collection and dissemination of increasing amounts of intelligence, and social applications are bringing data to the right people, allowing them to collaborate in real time and in a virtual environment. The third key to Enterprise 2.0 is emerging new business cultures, which are the most important part in the adoption of Enterprise 2.0. Social applications rely on the people, process, and technology, and therefore it becomes important to obtain senior management participation and support. This also enables senior management to get real-time feedback from employees, partners, and customers via chat, forums, and blogs. It eliminates all barriers and bureaucracy within the organization and brings transparency.

In order to deploy and have successful implementation of Enterprise 2.0, all these tools and artifacts need to be integrated and implemented on a highly secured and robust platform.

Use of Wiki in Enterprise-Wide Team Collaboration

Wikis are an example of collaboration software that solves all these problems with ease of use; they are simple enough for nontechnical employees to adopt quickly. Wikis (wiki meaning "fast" in Hawaiian) are a promising new technology that supports conversational knowledge creation and sharing. A wiki is a collaboratively created and iteratively improved set of web pages, together with the software that manages the web pages. Inspired by Apple's HyperCard programming environment, the first wiki software was created in 1995 by Ward Cunningham as a way to manage the Portland Pattern Repository's site content. The best-known example of a wiki is Wikipedia, an online encyclopedia that is written and maintained by anybody who feels like it. A wiki is a website where every page can be shared and edited in a web browser with secured access and validation.

Conversational knowledge creation emerged as the most popular way for organizations to create knowledge, largely in the context of online or virtual communities. In conversational knowledge creation, individuals create and share knowledge through dialogue with questions and answers. The conversational model of knowledge creation is different from other models, where knowledge is created through abstraction or aggregation of information, as in data or text mining.

Discussion forums are a key online conversational knowledge exchange and the core technology for many online communities. The leading online community platform, such as ezboard/Yuku, manages the discussions of millions of communities. Instant messaging is promoted through a number of free services, including ICQ and AOL Instant Messenger, each of which serves tens of millions of users. Instant messages enable multiple conversational modes from one-to-many to many-to-many.

The wiki's uniqueness lies both in its software and in the use of the software by collaborating members. It enables web documents to be authored collectively. It uses a simple markup scheme, usually a simplified version of HTML. Wiki content is not reviewed by any editor or coordinating body prior to its publication. Creating and editing wiki pages are necessarily a simple activity. The wiki author uses a web-enabled form field to enter the comment he or she wishes to publish. Authors can use plaintext or often a simplified markup language, although more sophisticated implementations (e.g., TikiWiki) may also allow the use of HTML. Wikis use a common repository (i.e., a database server), an application server that runs the wiki software, and a web server that serves the pages and facilitates the web-based interaction. Wikis are thus available at any time and in any place where there is web connectivity, and have a single common knowledge repository. As a result, they enable and empower multiple users to collaborate whenever and wherever on the same centrally stored knowledge product, and are able to see and use the entire work product. The basic unit of information in a wiki is a web page. In a wiki, if there is a mismatch between knowledge concepts and wiki pages, it can be adjusted either by breaking the content into multiple pages or by combining multiple pages into one.

Wikis as groupware stress the collaborative capabilities of wikis in areas where knowledge may be changing dynamically or where viewpoints differ about the knowledge.

We can very easily implement and use wikis across enterprises in the following 15 ways:

1. *To-do list.* A wiki helps in creating the most productive list, the to-do list.
2. *Project management.* A wiki can be a great way to plan and manage a project, from conception to completion. Assign tasks, make a time line, add notes, paste images, and incorporate other media— whatever you need for a project; there's no simpler way to organize it all.
3. *Operations manuals.* Documentation such as user and operational manuals can be created online and updated when things change, so that anyone can view the updated version at any time. Things change so quickly these days that a printed version of a manual is outdated as soon as it's printed and distributed.
4. *Checklists.* Wikis can be used for creating the checklist.
5. *Plan an event.* Conferences, weddings, off-site meetings, parties— events of all kinds have been planned with wikis, because they're perfect for that purpose. Multiple people can access the plans, create checklists, and add notes, ideas, images, contact info, and much more.
6. *Log client work.* Track client work either by hours spent on a project or by number of projects completed along with dates, rates, and other notes.

7. *Track invoices.* Wikis help in tracking invoices to each client, the work done, dates, rates, and so on, along with when the invoices were submitted, when they're due, and when they are paid.

8. *Notes and snippets.* Web workers take notes, pull snippets from pages, and save images all the time, and yet it can be hard to keep track of all of them. A wiki will help in keeping them at one location.

9. *Goals.* A wiki helps in setting and measuring goals.

10. *Contacts.* A wiki can be an easy and quick way to add contacts and find them at any time and any place you need them.

11. *Workspace.* Besides being a place to keep notes and snippets and images together, a wiki helps in keeping articles, reports, and the like together.

12. *FAQs.* A wiki helps in publishing FAQs to eliminate frequent calls by customers.

13. *Collaboration.* Changes are made and tracked, and collaborators can revert to previous versions if necessary.

14. *Reference.* A wiki helps in quick reference to lists, documents, codes, instructions, and the like that may be referred to regularly.

15. *One place for everything.* One of the best reasons to have a wiki is because it can do all of the preceding tasks, and more. It's versatile—more so than most other tools on the web.

New technologies such as Web 2.0, wiki, chat, forum, tags, and RSS have enabled teams to have effective communication and content collaboration. Many software applications based on these technologies have attempted to address these challenges, targeting different consumers across industry sectors.

Central Desktop: Powerful Tool for Effective Team Collaboration

Central Desktop is one of the many software solutions in this segment. It has drawn attention due to the fact that the Obama campaign used it to manage precinct captains—volunteers who get out the vote and spread the campaign message in specific precincts across the state. Although it might seem that choosing the right software depends on several factors and the team's preference within the enterprise, there are some general guidelines that apply to all, such as:

- Ease of installation
- User accounts (so name is automatically attached to all changes you make)
- Page change subscription by e-mail and RSS
- Page history and stored revisions
- Document attachments
- Page edit locking
- An easy-to-remember syntax

As per its website (www.centraldesktop.com), Central Desktop claims the following:

> Central Desktop delivers a pure web-based social technology platform for next-generation business teams to interact, share, and manage their daily work activities from anywhere at any time. Built collaboratively over four years with direct feedback from its users, Central Desktop's collaboration software platform provides enterprise-grade functionality without enterprise solution resource requirements. Founded in 2005 by Isaac Garcia and Arnulf Hsu, Central Desktop is a privately-held company located in Pasadena, California and offer[s its] software services SaaS (Software as a Service) based Social Technology Platform.

It is extremely easy to create a workspace and upload the document one wishes to collaborate on with the team members in real time. With the platform's web meetings and audioconferencing features, one can also collaborate with customers or partners by voice, sharing the desktop, or remote presentation. It offers integration with Skype (with voice supported), Yahoo!, MSN Messenger, AIM, ICQ, and Jabber, centralizing all communication, and also provides an option to integrate with Microsoft Outlook. In order to collaborate with a virtual team, one can create, edit, and store online docs and spreadsheets in a secure workspace environment in real time.

Central Desktop also offers the ability to track document history and revisions. Its extensive search feature allows for full text and document search for fast retrieval, even if it's in a document, a conversation thread, or a different workspace. As this application is based on software as a service (SaaS), which does not require any local installation or setup, it becomes ready to use up front and provides the ability to access workspaces from anywhere. Although mobile browser-based access is possible with a smartphone, it's a bit cramped and not technically supported currently. Considering the fast adoption and use rate of smartphones such as iPhone and BlackBerry devices, they need to address and provide the integration.

Central Desktop is ideally suited for project collaboration and management. One can create a variety of workspaces, each with a slightly different feature set. These workspaces are all very useful, and include a wiki workspace, a project management workspace, a public workspace (no login required), a user forum workspace, a corporate blog workspace, and a database workspace that allows the capture of data with a web-based front end, which is very useful for surveys, client questions, or just general data capture. I think the most powerful part of Central Desktop is the reporting module, which allows the creation of custom, ad hoc reports on all data in one or any workspace managed in Central Desktop. This is useful for all kinds of tasks, from executive status reporting to day-to-day management of a project.

For project management in particular, Central Desktop is one of the best lightweight solutions. One can easily create tasks or task lists and assign each task to a milestone. Unlike some other products, one can assign due dates and priorities at a task level, which is incredibly important when managing even the simplest milestones. The file management interface is interesting, and allows setting it up in a familiar file folder hierarchy, which helps in managing lots of files. The ability to check in and check out files for version control and to capture all comments about the files as they are being discussed is really helpful. The project dashboard is easy to use and informative. Overall, I think the only things that Central Desktop is missing are the more complex project management features such as task dependencies and resource-leveling features that the more expensive solutions offer.

Mindjet (Spigit): Great Tool for Collaborative Ideation

Spigit, acquired by Mindjet, is one of the innovative collaborative solutions giving organizations the platform they need to make sustainable, ongoing innovation a part of everyday work. Employees and customers have a community and a rich set of features for sharing and collaborating around ideas. Managers have visibility into the ideas that will become the next innovations. As per their website (http://www.spigit.com/), Spigit integrates the collaboration tools of social software with traditional enterprise work flow and quantifiable metrics to bridge the innovation gap, such as:

- Source ideas through focused innovation campaigns and on an open-ended basis.
- Drive the front end of innovation with contributions, assessments, and interactions by community members.
- Collaborate with a full suite of social software tools: forums, wikis, blogs, reviews, voting, and tagging.
- Leverage social network's diversity of viewpoints to refine and build out ideas rapidly.
- Surface the best ideas, track the idea portfolio, and identify key contributors through analytics and administrative controls.
- Build for the enterprise with role- and event-based work flow, integration with internal systems, application programming interfaces (APIs), and high configurability.

Connecting ideas with colleagues and with management's objectives is both a revolutionary opportunity and a significant challenge for organizations. Every day, employees generate ideas for new businesses, products, and process improvements. Enabling others to collaborate on these ideas, and surfacing those with the most merit, is a powerful new approach to accelerating internal innovation.

InnovationSpigit is the enterprise platform built for internal innovation communities. InnovationSpigit integrates emergent social collaboration with traditional work flow and analytics.

InnovationSpigit features include:

- An intuitive and engaging user experience
- Configurable idea templates that support graphics, videos, file attachments, and links
- Work flow through idea stages, role-based requirements, and criteria for idea advancement
- Full suite of social software tools: forums, blogs, wikis, social profiles, activity streams, and tags
- Advanced analytics engine for finding the best ideas among all contributions

- Dashboard providing real-time updates on activity, hotspots, and employee contributions
- Idea trading market that allows employees to buy and sell ideas
- Participation-based currency with redemption for rewards through internal or external stores
- Enterprise authentication through LDAP/Active Directory and single sign-on
- InnovationSpigit widgets that can be embedded in SharePoint, portals, intranets, and other applications
- Full set of APIs for deeper enterprise application integration

IdeaSpigit features include:

- Customizable site skins to reflect company branding
- Easy access via customer self-registration
- Configurable idea templates for simple text ideas or more advanced media support
- Lightweight voting and ratings that capture crowd sentiment
- Discussion forums for each idea as well as site wide
- Advanced analytics engine that surfaces the best ideas among all contributions
- Optional sharing of ideas via popular social media sites
- Multiple communities that can be established for different businesses
- Engagement events to drive participation and ideas for specific areas
- Dashboard providing real-time updates on activity, hotspots, and customer contributions
- Full set of APIs for integration with other applications and sites

In order to meet these challenges, large enterprises are considering enterprise-class solutions that meet key criteria such as open standards, technology platform and architecture, ease of use, security, total cost of ownership, flexibility to customize and adapt to changing business needs, minimal learning curve and training, shorter implementation, and all under a portal framework. Enterprise-wide deployment must consider consolidation of content repository and virtualization of hardware, database, and application to eliminate any downtime and redundancy.

Oracle WebCenter: Enterprise-Wide User Experience Tool

WebCenter makes it easy for users to get the information they need and to collaborate with others to make the necessary changes to business applications and processes. It provides a single, modern framework for the development of all styles of websites, portals, and composite applications. It provides a composer or workspace for users and site administrators to highly personalize the behavior, look, and feel of the portal to meet user needs. It offers direct integration with Oracle's Enterprise Business Dictionary and provides prepackaged integration with applications, content and rich media, business processes, and business intelligence applications in an integrated architecture. With an integrated set of WebCenter tools and services, it empowers end users and IT to build and deploy next-generation collaborative applications and portals that take advantage of the creativity and intellect of every user to improve internal and external business processes for effective collaboration and integration in a real-time environment.

Enterprise-class collaboration software is making an effort to encapsulate all these tools and features within suites under a flexible framework and architecture. Oracle WebCenter Suite is one of the enterprise-class solutions providing all these technologies such as wiki, tags, RSS, chat, forum, bulletin, whiteboard, presence, workspace integrating with all other widgets such as Outlook, smartphones, and the like. All departmental and virtual team-level applications for collaboration will need enterprise application-level integration and consolidation for better manageability and security, and therefore large organizations need enterprise-class solutions.

Rapid growth of wikis, blogs, and intranet portals experienced internally at Oracle has challenged the internal IT team for their manageability, security, and centralized content repository. It has also had a severe impact on the cost to provide separate servers, database, and backup recovery. Therefore, tools like WebCenter offer comprehensive solutions for enterprise-wide deployment on a secured platform.

Enterprise knowledge workers are invariably engaged in starting, moving forward, or completing a process, assignment, or enterprise work flow, including actions that need to be performed on a regular and ongoing basis. This could be preparing to present to a new client, opportunity updating in sales forecasting, customer support case resolution in customer relationship management, general ledger reconciliation in finance, or bringing a new team member up to speed on a project. Many actions driven from enterprise applications or systems of record are inherently collaborative, and for any deviation from the ideal process (typically conceptualized when a specific enterprise application was installed and configured), collaboration is required. This collaboration takes place outside of the application, and is typically not recorded completely or in one location. This means that it is not available for later reference to provide understanding as to how the decisions were made, when an exception reoccurs, or to identify when a process or policy change may be needed. If it is in an activity stream, entries will have swept by, or as e-mail, pieces of the collaboration are caught in individual inboxes (depending on the whims of the individuals involved). Social network posts, voice, and instant messaging (IM) discussions are typically lost forever.

Without a record of the previous and ongoing discussions, it is difficult for participants to garner sufficient context for their deliberations and decisions, especially if they are brought into the process late. At best, a great deal of time is lost educating new stakeholders. At worst, decisions are made without critical information that was available elsewhere in the organization. Current software-based collaboration solutions also require that the user choose the communication in advance—picking up a phone, sending an e-mail, microblogging—before determining if that is the appropriate mechanism or group for the discussion. This is exactly counter to an ideal face-to-face interaction where additional people, voice, text, documents, presentations, and whiteboards can be brought to bear as needed or desired. This results in a need to replay or reschedule discussions again and again until the right combination of context, history, tools, and people is found.

Enterprises have begun to turn to systems of engagement (SOEs), modeled after consumer social tools, which provide an environment in which their staff willingly spends time and which allow the staff to communicate, participate, find, and offer expertise and broaden their networks to enrich and improve both their work deliverables as well as their personal engagement with the business. Traditional systems of record reflect the reverse of systems of engagement: The individual sees little or no value to themselves through participation, and they are of restricted personal interest and are generally treated as a burden to maintain. The ideal is the easy maintenance of system-of-record data, providing managerial and corporate insight, with the communication of valuable changes or updates being efficiently disseminated to appropriate but potentially unknowing individuals throughout the organization. A cohesive, designed interaction between the systems of record and engagement offers that potential.

What is needed, then, is a solution for handling enterprise collaboration that reflects the best of consumer-style social models, preserves both context and history, allows the widening of the participant set as needed, and provides the appropriate media required for a given communication. It also must preserve the ease and fluidity of e-mail, IM, and short message service (SMS), and stream posts while tightly integrating with enterprise applications and software infrastructure. It must extend into as well as out of systems of record, placing the collaboration in context and equally bringing the key record data of the context into the collaborative application. Otherwise, it risks becoming yet another enterprise work flow application with its own set of exceptions (project management applications are notorious for this failing) or just another inbox, a further silo of collaboration data to deal with.

Canadian Partnership Against Cancer

Canadian Partnership Against Cancer is an independent organization funded by the federal government to accelerate action on cancer control for all Canadians. The organization is a partnership of cancer experts, charitable organizations, governments, patients, and survivors and their families.

Canadian Partnership Against Cancer was looking for a unified knowledge management platform to manage a vast amount of cancer-related information and to enable it to easily collaborate with various entities to support the overall mission of reducing the incidence of cancer and bringing change to the cancer control domain.

The new technology platform, WebCenter Spaces, enabled a broad user base, including various local entities to create and customize collaborative communities to support local work and connect with other groups. This provided various Enterprise 2.0 capabilities, including blogs, wikis, and discussion forums to meet user needs.

> Our sole purpose as an organization is to reduce the impact of cancer on Canadians by helping to coordinate improvements to the cancer system. Oracle WebCenter enabled us to quickly implement an integrated set of tools for connecting people, so that we can all fight cancer more effectively.
> —Wayne Roberts, Director of IT,
> Canadian Partnership Against Cancer
> http://apps-systems.com/userfile/files/Apps%20Systems%
> 20Success%20Story%20-%20CPAC%20Migration%20to%
> 20Cloud.pdf

Oracle Social Network: Cloud-Based Enterprise-Class Collaborative System

Oracle Social Network addresses the collaboration gap through stream-based conversations that are designed to capture information from people, enterprise applications, and business processes to facilitate collaboration between individual users and teams of people both within and across enterprises. As a system of engagement, individuals can collaborate, network, drive decisions, and update data, both in the focused pursuit of business objectives as well as in the serendipitous discovery of information and expertise.

With a unique integration of communication, coordination, and social functions into a single tool, Oracle Social Network enhances productivity through contextual collaboration, as a stand-alone tool, or embedded into enterprise applications. Extending beyond the organizational boundaries to connect the enterprise with its suppliers, partners, and customers, Oracle Social Network enables social networking without the noise.

By socializing enterprise applications, business processes, and content, Oracle Social Network enables the social business. By providing a collaboration and networking platform that connects applications, processes, and content to people as well as to each other, Oracle Social Network provides a system that engages the individual rather than being yet another system that demands action. This system allows for cross-enterprise knowledge rather than adding to the silos of lost information.

In Oracle Social Network, collaboration is based on a context that evolves in form, structure, and content, as dictated by the particular needs of a given collaboration. Within that context, Oracle Social Network provides a rich set of tools to choose from. These tools provide for communication, coordination, content management, organization, decision making, and analysis—all essential aspects of collaboration. Every collaborative interaction will evolve differently; therefore, the Oracle Social Network tools utilized will change with each interaction. Some interactions will evolve to represent work spreading over the course of years and involving a large, distributed team, whereas others may involve a few people and some may not evolve at all. Regardless, all collaborative contexts are built from the same parts, utilize the same concepts, and start the same way. The principle of graceful escalation is that you use only the tools and structure you need, so you incur only the complexity you need.

Most communication has an extremely short shelf life; that is, it may not be very useful a few hours or even a few minutes from now. But as we do not know when communication will need to turn into collaboration, it is best to provide the capabilities, latent and available, and let the conversation evolve as needed.

Real-time interactions and presence information as a core capability throughout Oracle Social Network give the participants a sense of social engagement and the application a sense of life that goes beyond even consumer applications today. While real-time communications are being added to networking applications in the form of chat, every interaction within Oracle Social Network happens and is reflected without refreshes in real time. Individuals can see the flow of updates, the volume of participation, their friends' and colleagues' focus, and the trending groups and themes, but remain able to drive decisions (albeit with reduced latency) with all the required and up-to-date information available.

Oracle Social Network enables business users to find and collaborate with the right people within their enterprise and across enterprises—for example, with suppliers, partners, and customers—using information from the human resources system and their own private social network. Oracle Social Network enables business users to collaborate with each other using a broad range of collaboration tools, including personal profiles, groups, activity feeds, status updates, discussion forums, document sharing, cobrowsing and editing, instant messaging, e-mail, and web conferencing. Oracle Social Network is seamlessly integrated with Oracle Fusion Applications, business intelligence, and business processes, allowing users to receive real-time information feeds from these systems and to collaborate and resolve business issues quickly and effectively, including updating applications and business processes from Oracle Social Network.

Oracle Social Network is designed to allow mobile users to stay connected always and to participate in business conversations by providing native applications on a variety of devices, including iPhones, iPads, and Android devices, as well as a modern, easy-to-use browser interface. Oracle Social Network is designed to meet corporate demands for security, privacy, and information protection by providing each enterprise and its users with a virtualized and private instance for collaboration with configurable retention and audit policies for traceability.

Oracle Social Network helps salespeople to identify potential prospects, build effective teams, prepare convincing sales presentations, resolve issues with customer service and contracts, collaborate with partners on joint opportunities, and build lasting relationships with customers.

Oracle Social Network helps marketing teams to design more creative marketing campaigns, target the right customers and partners, and collaborate with sales teams to generate the highest-quality leads.

Oracle Social Network helps human resources professionals and managers to collaborate on workforce planning and staffing, build effective compensation and benefits programs, set goals and objectives, and drive more effective talent management processes. Oracle Social Network can be used by project managers and project teams to build effective project plans, collaborate on project tasks, resolve issues and change requests, and track and update project milestones. Oracle Social Network provides personalized and configurable alerts that enable users to stay informed of actions but to filter out superfluous chatter, enabling them to pay attention to important information.

Businesses are offered a plethora of choices in the collaborative platforms and technology solutions. These solutions on the cloud with a scale-out model will be more appropriate for enabling digital businesses.

CIO-CMO Collaborative Alignment

Digital business success stories share the common feature of relationship management being a core competency that enables business agility. Here we focus on the relationships between the chief marketing officer (CMO) and the chief information officer (CIO) in delivering the business value of IT. The best practices for a CIO-CMO partnership in terms of digital business management are viewed through the lens of business agility readiness.

Use cases presented are in conjunction with the "CMO-CIO Partnership for Collaborative Marketing Agility" scenario. This business value theme is developed using a strategy of innovation for CMO-CIO alignment around big data analytics based on collaborative marketing best practices. A Business Agility Readiness Roadmap, using a balanced scorecard as a framework to describe and measure the alignment gap, provides the context of evolution from a system of record to a system of engagement. Such a tool may be used to assess how to best vet the internal/external collaboration activities associated with management of big data for driving prescriptive analytics. This is a critical success factor in managing the digital business for competitive advantage of the business ecosystem as a whole. CMO insights focus on how CMOs may leverage their understanding of these converging technologies to communicate better with their customers through the media they prefer, engage prospective customers through common interests, and utilize information to build stronger, more personal and more lasting relationships.

The following CMO insights are offered by Blake Yeaman, who is a seasoned marketing and information management veteran. Blake has decades of experience as a leading marketing executive and consultant. Here he shares his lessons learned as marketing chief at Hornblower, Inc.

Marketing Technology Applications at Hornblower, Inc.

An interesting case study about marketing automation and data involves a medium-sized company in the hospitality sector, San Francisco–based Hornblower, Inc. From 2004 to 2012 the company grew its annual revenue in the excursion dining cruise business from $27 million to over $40 million.

In 2012, the company operated about 20 vessels in seven California ports and New York City.

The Problem

Hornblower faced four main strategic challenges:

1. Getting happy customers to return more often
2. Increasing marketing effectiveness on a limited budget
3. Obtaining real-time data with which to make decisions
4. Reducing the long sales cycle and cost of sales

So the problem was really how to replicate great experiences with existing customers and to find new prospects similar to those customers.

The on-the-water dining experience can be an elegant occasion, which is what Hornblower focuses on. Enjoying spectacular vistas and upscale food from a luxury yacht is very appealing. Although often thought of as a tourist experience, about 75 percent of Hornblower customers were local residents. Customer satisfaction was very strong, hovering in the 90 percent range.

Perhaps the biggest challenge facing Hornblower was shortening the time frame for its satisfied customers to return for another experience. The average time for customers to repeat was about two to three years. Management believed that if that cycle time could be cut to one year, it would have a significant impact on revenue.

The mission of Hornblower was and still is to satisfy all of its guests all of the time. While that is a tough ideal to achieve, it required the company to listen to its customers, understand their needs, resolve each issue where possible, and improve the business process to reduce operational challenges.

Hornblower's business is very segmented. Its customers experience the Hornblower nautical charm from different perspectives. Some are out on the town celebrating an anniversary or a birthday. Others might be showing out-of-town guests a little local experience. Still others may be invited guests attending a wedding, a company event, or a high school prom night. However, even though most guests had a fabulous experience, they didn't realize—if they had been attending a company event or a wedding—that they could also come out on a dining cruise as a couple.

So the main challenge Hornblower had was to communicate the variety of options to its customers in an effort to encourage more frequent ridership.

The Current State

Hornblower had the foresight in its formative years in the early 1980s to automate. What it created was a very advanced, state-of-the-art computer system that could support the sales, customer relationship management, operational needs, accounting, employee data, and management reports.

In the late 1990s, Hornblower joined the rest of the business world on the web. The first version was mostly informational, had a very limited method of e-commerce, and was Web 1.0 in layout and design. The data captured from it was distinct from the primary system, though there was a method of sharing some of the information, mostly from daily data synchronizing of the prior day's data.

The current system, the original core computing system, and the addition of the website provided the competitive edge into the early 2000s, at a very low cost of deployment, support, and licensing to the company. However, with the rise in web technology, the cloud, SaaS applications, social media, and big data, the current system showed its limitations and was holding back the growth potential of the company.

The Plan of Action

To achieve a breakthrough in (1) shortening the time for a customer to come back and (2) finding new customers, Hornblower determined that it would need to migrate its current state of technology to a new visionary state. This would reinvent the way customers did business with the company and the way that sales and management could capture business and deliver the experience.

1. Determine business readiness by creating a gap analysis of the current state to the visionary state.
   a. Audit the company data captured in the current state.
   b. Align with critical key performance indicators and data critical to the process.
   c. Create a data warehouse to capture this critical data.
   d. Create prototype reports based on this data.
   e. Identify the functionality required in the visionary state.
2. Modernize the website to elevate the brand and create the capability for:
   a. Customers to:
      i. Easily find what they are looking for.
      ii. Purchase directly online, when possible.

       iii. Expand their awareness of the variety of options and locations available to them.

       iv. Use their mobile devices to access.

   b. Corporate and field marketing to:

       i. Maintain the site without technical help.

       ii. Create and publish new promotions locally and instantly.

3. Build internal competency to manage and affect web analytics.

   a. Hire experts initially to establish a program.

   b. Have experts train internal talent to take over the program.

4. Track in detail all advertising and marketing activities for revenue generation over a year. Realign the budget around high-revenue-generation activities.

5. Implement a new customer relationship management (CRM) system and data warehouse to capture all customer data generated from more than 20 internal and external unique sources of customer information.

6. Use this CRM to:

   a. Launch and track marketing campaigns.

   b. Generate real-time management information.

   c. Allow the sales department to know much more about customers and prospects.

7. Go social.

   a. Launch on Twitter, Facebook, Foursquare, Groupon, and almost any other high-volume social tool.

   b. Create internal responsibilities to read customer posts and respond properly and promptly.

   c. Use a reputation management tool and respond where needed.

8. Make the experience visual.

   a. Create virtual tours for the website.

   b. Make short videos to populate travel sites like Expedia and Travelocity.

Experimentation: Taking a Risk

As innovation in SaaS products in the cloud was introducing new and compelling ways to go to market almost daily, a great degree of faith in their claimed values was required. It was very much like the spaghetti method of testing. You'd throw a bunch of technology solutions at the wall and see what sticks. Quite a few solutions could not live up to their promises, which required a tolerance for failure to develop a learning curve on these new technical spaces. Some integrated easily into the ecosystem of solutions leading to the visionary state, whereas others required tedious custom API development.

As budgets with most companies are limited, it was critical to focus on those solutions that could be integrated with the rest, and that delivered on the promise of the developer. In many cases, a relatively low-cost, powerful solution required new hardware and new human resources to operate it, which quickly killed the return on investment (ROI) expected from that solution. This required getting clear baseline metrics at the beginning and measuring the impact on the business, allowing for quantitative decision making. This was a balanced scorecard approach to measure where we were and where we wanted to be.

This trial-and-error approach was the only way to discover what would work in the early days of SaaS and cloud computing. It took patience and understanding from senior management. In the end, an effective combination of new technology emerged that was unique to Hornblower requirements. The ROI grew as the successful components were built upon and the less valuable ones eliminated. This required a business culture that encouraged innovation and entrepreneurialism, and didn't stigmatize errors. With focus and quick decision analysis, a powerful ecosystem emerged.

Putting the Technology Together

To create a better customer service, Hornblower needed to incorporate several technologies. The key was going to be to figure out how use the information generated to make timely and meaningful decisions to create a better customer experience.

As mentioned before, cloud computing was just emerging at the time. Hornblower built its prototype website driven by a robust customized content management system (CMS) all on cloud-based services.

The e-commerce online store was also deployed as cloud based, utilizing leading e-commerce back-end transaction systems. All of these transactions were integrated with the legacy operational system.

At the emergence of social media in 2006, Hornblower recognized the need to embrace the new social technologies. The company assigned people to generate social content and others to respond promptly to the social media posts. Hornblower tried several cloud-based reputation management tools, and settled on a leading product. However, new tools entered the market monthly and required evaluation. In some cases, the existing tools were replaced with more powerful and often less expensive tools.

As the mobile industry introduced smartphones, especially the iPhone in 2007, Hornblower created mobile views of the web information to make it easy for customers to connect and purchase. The company also deployed new cloud-based, location-driven mobile promotions.

With the demand for visual experiences for the customer, the website was designed to use photography effectively and boldly. However, there was a need for putting video content on the site about the products. Hornblower took two approaches. First, it created video content that could be put on its website and on third-party travel websites. Second, it deployed an engaging cloud-based virtual tour so people could get a better grasp of the experience and the options available to them.

All of these new technologies generated new forms of data. Existing systems weren't capable of capturing the data. Hornblower deployed a new customer relationship management (CRM) system and captured some of the data by customers there. Additionally, it created a data warehouse to collect data from all of the systems. This allowed reporting to be done from across the different systems.

With so many pieces in the technology and data puzzle, and new technology emerging on a constant basis, individual elements could be replaced as needed. The new virtual side to the traditional business created a new way for Hornblower to capture and retain customers.

Aligning Marketing and Information Technology

With marketing requirements dependent on emerging technology, and integration with legacy systems critical to operations, marketing became the number one user of new technology in the company and, correspondingly, the most demanding internal customer of IT. This required a close alignment between the CMO and the CIO. The CIO needed to understand the strategic direction envisioned and what technical development, deployment, and support would be required from the IT team.

The rate of change and complexity of systems presented a challenge for IT, as the IT staff was preoccupied with the management and uptime of the rest of the company's infrastructure. Bimonthly sessions were required to communicate and prioritize the action items. Perhaps the biggest challenge was how to integrate the legacy data with the onslaught of new data in a manner that would allow for the CMO to identify new opportunities for revenue growth and customer satisfaction.

A 2013 CMO Council report, *Big Data's Biggest Role: Aligning the CMO & CIO*, accurately described the challenge Hornblower was facing:

> Marketers agree that there is no shortage of data; in fact, data is
> seemingly everywhere and for many, the lure of collecting everything

has led to a scenario where data repositories are overly bloated. Rather than fueling the enterprise with fact-based decision-making tools, the organization has slipped into a state of "analysis paralysis." In this world where data is everywhere, it is easy to see why both IT and marketing executives feel the strain. (p. 4)

The report goes on to point out that while there was alignment in technology and strategy, at the same time IT was challenged with the customer-focused priority, perhaps because IT primarily focused on internal customers rather than external customers.

In fact, the two are fundamentally in agreement about key direction, strategy, and even roles in the advancement of technology and the criticality of data across the organization. What is lacking is the mandate that customer centricity is the core value, goal, and direction of the organization, eliminating any of the barriers to partnership and aligning both CMO and CIO around the data that powers the customer-centric enterprise.

> "It's a complete partnership between marketing and IT, and they're equal partners in helping define the strategy and understand its implications in terms of technology and information," notes Paul Kadin, Head of North America Marketing Operations and Strategy for Citi. "It takes equal doses of both perspectives to come to a conclusion about what we need to do next." (p. 5)

The report points out the role of the CMO as a primary user of the company data and the CIO as needing to provide access to it.

> Marketers view their role in the journey to customer centricity as being the primary architect of customer engagement strategies. There is also a sense that marketing is ready to take on the load of analyzing the aggregated data—brought from across the organization with the help of IT—into actionable intelligence that powers the customer-focused touchpoints across the entire enterprise.
>
> According to marketing, ownership of insights and competitive intelligence resides with the CMO. But the CIO should be ready and willing to tackle the advancement of marketing operational and measurement platforms, as well as work to optimize the security and availability of technology platforms. (p. 6)

This alignment described in the report between the CMO and CIO is what was experienced at Hornblower. It was a time of rapid development and change, requiring a melding of the minds, joint commitments, and a CMO respect for the existing IT demands for the rest of the business. Compromise, focus, and commitment were paramount.

Lessons Learned

As much of the technology was emerging, unproven technology, and industry standards were still in flux, much of this was try it out, measure the results, and do more of the things that produced results. Technology is always changing and evolving, so what happened here is very relevant to future technology ecosystem restructuring. The takeaways of how to proceed effectively in this kind of process are:

- *Get CXO alignment at the beginning.* While the CMO and CIO worked well on alignment, this key transformation of the business would have been much smoother if all CXO-level staff were aligned. Make it part of the strategic plan. The mandate and support from the top is critical.
- *Establish a realistic budget for internal resources, external resources, and technology.* It will cost more than you think. Double your initial estimate. Measure everything. Eliminate the losers and time wasters.
- *Align all stakeholders at each phase of development.* All stakeholders must feel that they own their part of the solution and that the overall solution is a good plan. IT needs to be involved with solution development and sustainable implementation. Sales leadership needs to be involved with solution development and features, as they are the ones touching the customer. Sales also has to use tools such as the CRM in real time with customer interaction. It must empower the salesperson, not slow the sales process. The operations department needs to be involved with what is being proposed as products, how it will get the orders, and how it will deliver high-quality services in line with the brand and marketing strategy. Marketing needs to drive all parties to engage. Marketing also needs to define its rules of engagement. And perhaps most overlooked, all stakeholders need to define the reporting needs of the system or combination of systems before development occurs.
- *Have a clear picture of where you want to be at the end of the process.* Utilize the services of a professional data architect to do this for you. You wouldn't construct a building without an architect. Your data is one of your most valuable business assets. Invest in a professional.
  - *Start with the data and reporting as the objective.* The goal is to facilitate faster decision making based on accurate data from

multiple systems. If you rely on the canned reports of different systems to be your sources of information, you will find yourself trying to piece together data after the fact.

- *Identify your critical data.* What data is critical to your key performance indicators? Where is the source of each specific data element? At Hornblower, there were over 25 different sets of data from isolated systems in the technology ecosystem. Conduct a data audit to identify the source of critical data, where it's stored, and how to get access to it. Oftentimes critical data has been corrupted from the source to its downstream use, which creates reports that should be reporting the same information, yet they show different results. The audit process will identify superfluous steps and manual labor prone to error. These process steps can be replaced with direct access to the critical data from one system to another.

- *Create a data warehouse.* This is creating big data. The warehouse can be simple and small or more complex, depending on the data you are capturing for the reporting you will need. It's pulling together all of the relevant data elements in a structure where you can find opportunities for business improvement and growth. Deposit the critical data you found in your data audit. Once that data is deposited into the data warehouse with a time stamp, it is an unchanging data point that can reported on with consistency.

- *Develop prototype reports as your first step.* Determine how each stakeholder needs to see information to empower decisions. Is it a lookup, a daily e-mail, a persistent dashboard, or something else? By working out these elements in the beginning, independent of any built-in reporting system, you can engineer powerful information that will be available when you roll out your new integrated ecosystem, while being efficient with your engineering resources.

- *Plan the conversion process from the outset.* Convert at the beginning of a slow sales season, not during a peak season. Build in realistic implementation. Some elements will come online early, while more complex elements require integration and support of existing systems. Data transfers must be planned carefully. What legacy data is included? What data normalization and cleanup are required? When is the data from the existing systems frozen? Before the conversion, a training and migration plan for users must be established. How will employees get their work done in the transition period? And finally, support the transition through the end of life of the existing systems and the successful adoption of the new systems. It takes longer than you think, but it will happen.

In the next chapter, we further expand and discuss mobility and use of mobile and smart devices that have changed and revolutionized the current business environment, thanks to Steve Jobs of Apple, who created iPhones and iPads that revolutionized the whole new concept of technology convergence of voice communication, e-mail communication, video communication, music, navigation, payment, and many more in one device. This technology has surpassed many innovations of the recent past and opened the door for unimaginable creative applications and usage that will further accelerate business agility.

References

"What Is Wiki?" Available at http://wiki.org/wiki.cgi?WhatIsWiki.

Central Desktop. Available at http://www.centraldesktop.com/.

Oracle WebCenter Portal. Available at https://www.oracle.com/us/products/middleware/webcenter/portal/overview/index.html.

Oracle Cloud. Available at https://cloud.oracle.com/social_network.

"The Canadian Partnership Against Cancer Teams with Apps Systems and Oracle on Demand to Improve Customer Experience and Manageability of Their Portal and Knowledge Management Platform by Moving to the Cloud." Available at http://apps-systems.com/userfile/files/Apps%20Systems%20Success%20Story%20-%20CPAC%20Migration%20to%20Cloud.pdf.

CHAPTER 6

Mobility Drives Agility

We are about halfway through our book that so far must have enlightened you with a fascinating paradigm shift in business model, business processes, new delivery and deployment platform, whole new tools and technologies for collaboration, and applications to transform your business and to help you create business agility. In this chapter, we touch upon mobility, mobile devices management (MDM), and mobile applications management (MAM) in greater detail.

Gone are the days when mobile phones were used for telephonic conversation alone. Now we check our smart devices for e-mails, text messages, and various applications such as searching for any web content, music, video, and many business applications. It is not an exaggeration to say that we are carrying a smart computer in our pocket all the time to provide us the agility we need in a dynamic and ever-changing business environment. Our lifestyle has changed dramatically in the past few years, and we are getting accustomed to using these smart devices for everything, including business transactions, communication, entertainment, shopping, and leisure.

In the past decade, we have witnessed a smart revolution in the mobile space. The number of mobile devices has increased fivefold from one billion to five billion, with an astonishing increase in the number of connected people from 400 million to over two billion. This unprecedented growth of connectivity has created an overwhelming range of new possibilities that include communication, collaboration, socializing, and performing e-business transactions. Mobility and mobile smart devices have changed people's lifestyles, work patterns, and ways of doing business. Mobile technologies have revolutionized the way in which we work today. Mobility provides two crucial advantages to organizations: location independence and personalization. The past decade has seen the rapid development of the Internet, the advent of cloud computing, and the lowering of costs of both mobile hardware and services. As a result, mobile technology has become a viable and some would say essential way of conducting business. Hugely successful organizations such as Apple Computer have been able to fundamentally alter the user experience, forcing other organizations to change the way they conduct business, interact with key constituents, and collaborate with one other.

The adoption of smart devices has accelerated at a rapid rate, and businesses have relied on mobile devices for their hyperconnected employees for driving business agility. Calls, messages, teleconferencing and videoconferencing, e-mail, music, camera, and access to a corporate network are common utilities to talk about at least. The list of applications on these smart devices has grown considerably, solving some common problems like flashlights, working as remote devices, card swipe for payment authentication (Square), navigation, and many more. The recent acquisition of WhatsApp by Facebook for a whopping $19 billion has forced many telecom service providers to guess about the next transformation and convergence of many services.

Convergence of Consumer Electronics into Smart Devices

Consumer electronics (CE) devices, once driven by their ability to provide specific functions, like music playback, video, or voice communications, are increasingly providing multiple functions and Internet connectivity for information, communications, and entertainment. This is resulting in the overlap of features and functions between product categories not only in the mobile segment, but also in other CE devices like digital televisions and set-top boxes. As a result, this entire category is morphing into a larger category often referred to as smart devices. There are three leading platforms in the mobile segment: smartphones, tablets, and notebook PCs. In-Stat (www.in-stat.com) research forecasts that this category of mobile "magnet platforms" will grow at a compound annual growth rate (CAGR) of 25.7 percent through 2015, compared to 8.7 percent for the overall mobile market.

"The technology driver of all these smart devices is the mobile technology, because it represents the largest and fastest-growing segment of the entire electronics market," says Jim McGregor, chief technology strategist. "Even in PCs, where increasing performance was once the mantra, CPU vendors are now focused on the performance efficiency of mobile computing and using the resulting products to drive advancements in other forms of computing, including desktop PCs, servers, and embedded applications. The innovation of the mobile market is being driven by four key factors: richer content, network access for communications and content, increased bandwidth to enable this access, and new technologies."

Executive Insights
Jeetu Patel, General Manager, Syncplicity Business Unit, EMC Corporation

Faced with the megatrends of mobile, social, cloud, big data, and video, the patterns inherent in our society are in the midst of a complete refactoring. Culture, behavior, work, technology use, how software is developed, and how consumers use it—none of these are static.

As we ponder this further, it's clear that visionary business leaders have an opportunity to act now. The starting point is recognizing what values are essential in the transformed world, in order to successfully harness this refactoring and swell productivity and agility levels. Values are the guiding compass, pointing in the right direction, even at times of disorientation.

Design is one such enduring value. How it gets surfaced, acted upon, and predicted can catapult the organization from outright failure to successful implementation.

Just like shelf space in a grocery store, where moving from knee level to eye level immediately impacts purchases, so too will device screen room and interface constructs alter the user's behavior. Particularly in an environment of well-designed apps and heightened user expectations for design quality, the design value will matter considerably moving forward.

Similarly, amidst the backdrop of big data, focusing on the right set of visualization can have a far greater effect than if that crucial step is bypassed. Data that is visualized to show rapid deterioration in a product line renewal rate reverberates faster than columns of numbers directly exported from an order-tracking tool.

This rethinking of design is already emerging within the mobile enterprise software space, the likes of which we will look back upon one day with awe.

In the first wave of mobile software development, incremental innovation simply brought old functionality to a new device. In the process, fundamentals were often missed. How frustrating was it to see a document for review on your mobile screen, yet be unable to edit it? Design was simply your desktop basic functionality, brought awkwardly to your smartphone or tablet.

The second wave brought mobile on par with the desktop. Functionality was refactored amid the new memory and added capabilities of our favorite gadgets. Fewer and fewer research and development (R&D) teams argued if a mobile version of their software was next. But such design was still a parallel effort, a passenger alongside the driver of monolithic application development. SharePoint is now in the cloud? Interesting, but it doesn't solve my problems.

The reality is that mobile technology itself is the new design baseline, cleanly isolated and independent of any lingering PC notions. Mobile is the superset form factor, under which all functionality must be derived and considered.

Let it be clear, there will still be coexistence between different form factors, with each finding its own suitable usage. Mobile technology will be used "also," "first," or "only" in relation to PCs or tablets, with a more single-purpose approach for each case. It might be used "only" when it comes to driving navigation, "first" when it involves voice calls, and "also" after writing a document on a PC and then just approving it through e-mail on a mobile device.

But it is this third wave of mobile design that will ignite the imagination and drive brilliant new solutions. Once we unleash imagination, it's only a matter of time before the way we think about values will change our world in thrilling ways.

Productivity is the other value, in addition to design, that will pervade and sometimes overtake other factors that prioritize how an organization should change. Shortening the time to complete a task, eliminating the time held captive by inefficiencies, and increasing abstract thinking time are varied ways this value can manifest itself, if implemented correctly.

Consider one example: remember what "taking pictures" used to mean? It was a time-consuming and disparate routine of carrying camera equipment with you, buying film, configuring the camera settings, and at last waiting to process the film.

By rethinking "taking pictures" as "sharing moments," however, those inefficiencies not only disappeared, but new worlds opened up. Ubiquitous devices brought image capture to the masses. Apps made photos easy and addictive to share. And social media created a place where all the people to share photos with are constantly present.

The same thing will occur as we prioritize productivity as a core value, and leverage it from the mobile implementation perspective. Many technical attributes of mobile are barely tapped today: proximity, location, and personalization, for example. Yet we already see new segments quickly embracing that third wave of mobile design; these are inklings of what's to come:

- Retail workers processing credit card payments without the customer ever waiting in line.
- Flight attendants logging meal orders as they walk the aisle with their devices.
- Citizens never bothering with the red tape to turn on a landline for making phone calls.
- Executives at airports sharing presentations delivered live from their devices.

It's time to plan: How else can we eliminate knowledge workers' wasted time, speed their transactions, and heighten their ability to share value?

Yes, the mobile platform itself offers rich new design inspiration, especially alongside the other megatrends. But for those leaders who embrace and fight for the values of design and productivity, their path through the crowded forest of these trends will be the straightest. While we cannot know how and where exactly the megatrends will impact each part of our lives, we can prioritize these key values that are enduring, and thereby steadily develop business agility.

Executive Bio: Jeetu Patel is currently managing the business at Syncplicity, acquired by EMC in 2012. Prior to this assignment, Jeetu was CTO at EMC and was in charge of the long-term strategic vision that helped formulate the cloud, big data, mobile, and collaboration strategies.

We have focused on mobile technologies as a means of creating and improving existing business, enabling digital business, and driving business agility. The past decade has witnessed the disruptive innovation and business model in the area of cloud, social, mobility, big data, and power of collaboration as discussed in Chapter 5. Mobile technologies with handheld capabilities are unique, as they provide personalization, location, and time independence. Apple Computer has disrupted the mobile market by combining voice and data communication, digital photos and video films, entertainment, and gaming all together with ease of use and a rich user experience. As a result, mobility can drive agility in businesses with unlimited potential. Mobile technologies and smart devices are influencing our social, cultural, and business patterns.

"Mobile is not just about conveniently selling on a mobile device; it's about giving customers all the information they need while they're in the store, and making it a better experience," says Jon Kubo, CIO of Wet Seal. "One of the trends we're seeing is retailers looking to put tools in the hands of customers that basically empower them. Customers want to be empowered in their shopping experience."

Bhuvan Unhelkar, national director at the Australian Institute of Business Analysis, defines mobile business (m-business) as evolution of both internal and external business practices through the adoption of suitable mobile technologies and processes, resulting in a mobile enterprise. He argues that m-businesses primarily want to engage with customers and business partners in location-independent and time-independent manners. This allows them to provide customers with new and valuable services and products. Moreover, m-businesses also want to exploit the location and time independence of mobility to improve internal business processes. Because of the dynamic and instantaneous nature of mobile technologies, m-businesses can be in close and even constant contact with customers, partners, other external partners, and internal stakeholders.

In the fall of 2011, Oracle commissioned a survey to look at consumers' perceptions of their experience when they shop across different retail channels. This online study, conducted by an independent service, polled 2,169 U.S. and Canadian consumers aged 18 years and older. It analyzed their use of channels including computers, mobile devices, brick-and-mortar stores, catalogs, and customer service representatives to gain more information about a product or to complete the purchase of a product or service. The survey also gathered data about consumers' experiences with these channels, as well as how they are incorporating social media into their online commerce activities.

According to the report, mobile commerce is a vital link between channels, especially for consumers 18 to 34 years old. Twenty-seven percent of consumers who own smartphones use them to browse or research products more than once a week, up from 13 percent of consumers in 2009. Because smartphones are capable of doing things such as completing in-store and online purchases, special offers, and notifying retailers when the customer enters a store, they are poised to serve as a common platform for the cross-channel experience.

Consumers age 18 to 35 are moving faster than others to use their smartphones to pay in stores and online. Retailers and mobile service providers first must assure consumers that the mobile phone is safe to use as a payment device.

As security measures improve, however, adoption will soar. Wholesalers and retailers should move aggressively to understand unique opportunities to connect with customers via their mobile phones and create a more seamless and personalized cross-channel experience. The following are the results when consumers were asked whether they use their mobile phones to complete purchases in a store, and how secure they believe the mobile device to be:

- For those who have a smartphone, 44 percent of consumers age 25 to 34 and 30 percent of consumers age 18 to 24 say they are using or soon will use their mobile phone as a payment device, though that number drops to 22 percent of consumers age 35 to 44 and to 9 percent of consumers overall.
- For adopters, 52 percent say they would use a smartphone to pay in stores because it is faster and more convenient than getting out your wallet or using a credit card.
- Security concerns are a barrier, as 25 percent of consumers worry that someone will steal payment information if they use their mobile phone to pay in stores, and 68 percent of consumers globally say information stored or transmitted on their mobile phone is not secure.
- When it comes to making purchases online, 45 percent of consumers age 18 to 34 who own a smartphone will use it to purchase products online as often as a few times each week, a number that drops to less than 6 percent among older consumers.

- Eleven percent of U.S. consumers use their smartphones to make an online purchase at least once a month, compared to just 5 percent of Canadian respondents.

Increasingly, the mobile web is a primary touch point for individuals to interact with an organization and find information on products and services.

Executive Insights
Naeem Zafar, Cofounder, Bitzer Mobile, and Faculty Member, University of California at Berkeley

While some companies are asking, "Why do I need mobile technology?," progressive companies ask, "How can we do things differently with mobile technology so that we improve productivity and reduce costs?" And that is exactly what has happened with the proliferation of mobile technology in the enterprise. There are tremendous cost benefits in being able to disseminate searchable information easily via the web and mobile to customers, partners, and employees rather than having call centers or expensive printed brochures for the same objective.

The adoption of mobile technology at work is as dramatic as the introduction into the enterprise of the Internet in the mid-1990s. When the Internet came into the workplace, it was thought to be a fad. However, that proved to be wrong, as there is a huge cost benefit and competitive advantage associated with delivering information in an efficient and timely manner.

Mobile technology in the workplace may be even more profound than what the Internet first caused. For 200 years we put on the monkey suit, fought traffic, and came to a building to go to work. What was special about that building was that it contained all the data and that was where the people were. Employees no longer need to come to the office to get access to the information and connect with people, as most tasks can be accomplished with e-mail, videoconferencing, phone, collaboration tools, and so on. The definition of work stands to be redefined forever as mobile technologies are adopted within the workplace.

We've seen some large corporations be very effective in using remote workers. In many cases people don't even know where their manager is located, but they have conference calls, video-conferences, and other collaboration tools to get the job done. That is one of the reasons we have not seen the unemployment rate go down much while productivity and profits are at an all-time high for corporations. We have learned to be extremely productive, and that is changing the concept of work.

Mobile Transforming Work Flow

Let's consider a few cases where adoption of mobile technology is changing the way people work. When an insurance agent talks to Mr. and Mrs. Johnson at their home, not only is he able to have a conversation and understand their needs, but he can now pull up the right rate quotations on his iPad, explain nuances, and get them to sign the contract right there on the spot. That's the new paradigm that enables the insurance agents to do several more deals a day. The economics are so powerful that it will be hard for an insurance company or other service-based agency not to adopt this model.

Imagine coming to address the claim for a traffic accident and being able to take the pictures, pull up the right cost structure, settle that account, let people sign on the iPad from the scene of the accident, and have the company transfer the claim settlement money into their bank account. That's possible today.

A doctor is able to consult with patients all over the world on videoconference. Using a mobile device, the doctor does not have to travel to each hospital, and patients don't have to travel for a week from the village to come to the hospital to consult the doctor. These are very profound changes that have an economic impact that is multi-fold; that's what mobile technology enables.

Mobile Infrastructure Needed

What building blocks are needed to make all this possible? Those building blocks include authentication, data security, user experience, ability to access applications, and ability to have different applications access each other to fetch the data between them. Bitzer Mobile has put many of these pieces together. Going forward, we will see all of this become as normal as it is today to use the Internet to access anything that was not available 20 years ago. That's what the promise of mobile technology is. It will profoundly change how you think of work and how people get paid for doing work.

New Ways to Work

Education is another area that is being completely transformed. Today, the role of teacher in any part of the world is to create curriculum, do the instructional teaching, generate conversation in the classroom, and also manage the social aspect. That's a lot to ask from a teacher, and there is lack of uniformity among the teachers.

Now, imagine that you can access some of the best content created at Stanford, Berkeley, MIT, Harvard, Brown, and similar institutions. You can also consume it anywhere from Uganda to Australia to South America. The teacher now only has to do half the things and can focus on social interaction among the students, and just look at analytics to figure out who is stuck where and how to help them. All of that is possible with the mobile tablet. It is possible today, and adoption and wide use are happening right now. Khan Academy is in 60 languages today and has more than 5,000 videos that are available for free while the Khan Academy is providing analytics and teaching tools to help the teachers in the classroom. That's just a start. I just began teaching my first massive open online course (MOOC), on financing new ventures with the University of California at San Francisco on the NovoEd platform, and 6,000 students have signed up from all over the world.

Adopting Mobile Technology in the Enterprise

There is a great disadvantage to a company if its employees are not set up to access information and data easily today. With regard to mobile access, there are ghosts of security that hound the IT teams; but all these issues are being addressed by new technology solutions that are available in the market today, and most of those do a much better job when enabled via the cloud and mobile. So not adopting mobile early and not asking the question of what can we do better as a company with mobile technology puts a company at a severe competitive disadvantage.

There is demonstrated return on investment (ROI) by not investing money in equipment such as company-owned computers and mobile phones. Companies used to supply these devices in order to control the data network and access and to ensure security. Today there is no need for that. With the bring your own device (BYOD) movement, you can implement enterprise-grade security for data access and control. A secure container from mobile devices can achieve a level of security that is equivalent to or higher than that of earlier networks that were strictly controlled by IT teams.

Once we have the security in place, we can now focus on leveraging the data and apps. Those companies that are not focused on utilizing the data will pay a severe penalty in a competitive landscape. Firms need to be focused on how to increase productivity while reducing capital and operational expenses, and mobile technology has to be a big part of that conversation.

Executive Bio: Naeem Zafar is a serial entrepreneur who just sold his sixth start-up to Oracle in 2013 in the enterprise mobility space. He has taught entrepreneurship and innovation at the University of California at Berkeley since 2005 and is the author of five books. He has degrees in electrical engineering from Brown University and the University of Minnesota.

Mobility Strengthens Ecosystemism

We discussed the concept of a business ecosystem in Chapter 1 that provides a model for sustainable competitive advantage via a collaborative commerce synergy to develop and execute a customer experience management strategy enabled by social business technology to drive a customer-centric value chain. Mobility with smart devices renders pervasive access of content, and information strengthens the business ecosystem and offers enhanced agility. Customers, employees, and business partners of any organization can reap significant benefits with the help of mobility and smart devices.

Let us examine some use cases that businesses can leverage by deploying mobility across the enterprise.

Mobility Empowers the Workforce

Mobility and mobile technologies have empowered the workforce on the move such as sales, service, shop floor, retail outlets, hospitality, health care, banking, travel, and many more. It is a common sight to find sales or service persons irrespective of industries walking with smart devices such as tablet PCs or iPads to demo their products or services with their customers or simply to capture some facts and obtain authorization for carrying out some services.

Enabling Sales Team to Get Smarter

Mobility has provided access to powerful systems such as customer relationship management (CRM), enabling salespeople to perform their jobs more effectively than before and helping them to talk to their customers with all resources at hand at all times remotely in front of their customers. With the help of smart devices, the sales team is getting smarter and more efficient, whether they have to deal with the marketing cycle (prospecting, cold calling with customer intelligence, lead generation, e-mail marketing) or handle requests for proposals (RFPs), proposal submission, or customer presentations and demonstrations. They are now able to carry out all of these tasks simply on smart devices with all resources available to them delivered via the cloud infrastructure, discussed in Chapter 3.

Most of the leading enterprise CRM systems, such as Oracle Sales and Marketing Cloud, Salesforce.com CRM, Microsoft Dynamics, Sugar CRM, and SAP CRM, are offered on the cloud infrastructure and are accessible on smart devices, making sales teams smarter and more efficient to help them achieve their sales quotas. Mobility has not only helped sales teams get smarter; it has also helped customers to get the right solutions for their business needs, cutting the sales cycle drastically.

Helping Services Team to Get Proactive

Mobility has also helped service personnel to serve their customers proactively with the help of smart devices and iPads, accessing their systems of records and guiding them with facts and figures at hand. Integrated CRM systems with service deployed on the cloud assists them with scheduling warranty and routine services and helps them with greater intelligence about previous history on breakdown and maintenance service. For example, if we take our car in for scheduled maintenance service, a service adviser of a reputed car manufacturer comes with an iPad to pull the details of the car history and its maintenance record. Based on inputs, the service adviser records tests and diagnostics to be carried out and takes our signature for parts and labor for the maintenance service. Isn't it a neat, smooth, and pleasant experience that we get these days thanks to mobility and smart devices?

Enabling a New Mode of Communication and Customer Interaction

Smart devices have improved accessibility and communication among ecosystems. Customers, employees, and partners can access information in different ways and access different information altogether. Mobility has offered more availability to ecosystem users. For example, an airline passenger can access flight times while being driven to the airport in a taxi without actually calling the airline. It is common to print the boarding pass with a bar code on smart devices and pass through security check-ins at the airport. Similarly, accessibility to sports scores, medical information, and other types of information is increasing every day. Rapid growth and availability of hotspots is enabling connectivity around airports, hotels, restaurants, schools, and universities, providing greater agility in information access, consumption, and execution of significant tasks.

Executive Insights
Harbinder Khera, Founder and CEO, Mindmatrix

"Mobility Playing the Role of a Catalyst"

Mindmatrix empowers sales and marketing teams to engage with customers and prospects through both direct and indirect channels and seamlessly across a combination of online, social, mobile, and offline mediums. Using the Mindmatrix Revenue Growth Platform, sales and marketing teams are able to spend less but sell more. Adding to this revolution is the ever-increasing use of Internet-enabled mobile devices that make information available on the go to the sales and channel personnel, at the touch of a finger. As a result, companies are now dealing with empowered prospects who are more informed than ever before. For companies, keeping up with such prospects requires being able to engage them across multiple channels in real time; mobile devices offer all information such as sales and marketing information at their fingertips, and those assets get personalized and delivered using Mindmatrix services. Mindmatrix has added agility to sales and services personnel by helping them with actionable and follow-up actions for their customers and prospects, and mobility has played the role of a catalyst.

Location-Based Targeted Customer Outreach

Smart devices also offer location presence, enabling marketers to target and communicate about their products and services in real time specific to the location. For example, if we go to any mall and check in to services offered by Foursquare or Google Places, all subscribers to these services will know about our presence in the mall. Merchants in the mall may target us with their products and services promotion by sending brief alert messages while we are in the mall. This has opened up a new targeted communication in the field of marketing and advertising. It helps merchants to target customers walking near their stores and also helps customers to get good bargains of products and services.

Mobility Enables Crowdsourcing

The current smart devices (such as iPhone and Samsung) are powerful with all their built-in gadgets such as cameras, sound recording, and access to all apps, including social media (i.e., Twitter, Facebook, LinkedIn, Skype, Viber, and many others that enable crowdsourcing). Many breaking news stories these days come first via Twitter, Facebook, or LinkedIn updates with the help of smart devices capturing photo or video on the site of occurrence. Active journalists also refer to Twitter pool or crowdsourced news for credibility and authenticity.

Government agencies are seeking public help to curb crime and report incidents with the help of smart devices, uploading photos or videos of a crime at the scene. Neighborhood watch is a great initiative to monitor. Nextdoor is great example of portal services where we can update, report, or upload any findings in the neighborhood that are observed by residents, and counsel authorities. Smart devices are enabling us with smart walk, capturing any issues with roads, pathways, streetlights, or abnormal activities and behavior, and report them live instantly.

Mobility Strengthens Health Care Services

Mobile networks and smart devices combined with social networking, cloud technology platforms, and big data analytics have laid a strong foundation for patients to receive health care not only in hospitals and clinics but also in the communities where they live. Mobility is becoming a core attribute of patients, practitioners, providers, and payers, helping them to work together toward greater access of health care services and better outcomes. One of the most visible patient empowerments is at the intersection of mobile and social networking. Patients are now actively participating in health-related discussions in online community forums and blogs, often using smart devices. Patientslikeme.com, one of many community portals, has more than 150,000 users who share and discuss conditions, symptoms, and treatment information on over 1,000 health issues.

More interestingly, patients have started using smart mobility for their fitness and wellness. The list of social and mobile fitness apps is long and growing every day. Some examples are Nike FuelBand and Abvio RunMeter, Walkmeter, and Cyclemeter, all mobile based and with GPS capabilities. Monitoring of chronic diseases by these devices is another great application that is growing significantly. For example, patients are able to enter blood sugar information by Internet and mobile devices, and their care provider is then able to provide coaching and corrective care.

More advanced capabilities such as blood pressure cuffs are being connected directly to smart devices for measuring blood pressure and transmitting the readings to care providers in case of any anomalies.

Mobile Development Framework

In order to provide a robust enterprise-class development platform for developers, Oracle recently introduced a mobile enterprise application platform comprised of Oracle ADF Mobile, Oracle Berkeley DB, and Oracle Lite Mobile. ADF Mobile and JDeveloper enable application developers to rapidly extend enterprise applications to mobile devices. These mobile applications use Berkeley DB for reliable device/local data management. The Oracle Lite Mobile server runs on the Web Logic server in the middle tier and provides connectivity between the Oracle Database server applications and mobile devices. This allows for automatic and bidirectional synchronization with the data center, as well as robust remote management of devices.

Medtronic Reaps Benefits of Implementing Mobility Across the Enterprise

Medtronic has become a world leader in medical equipment and therapies for cardiovascular, neurological, and musculoskeletal disorders, chronic health conditions, and surgical procedures with its technological innovation in health care services. First it introduced a battery-powered pacemaker, a device that is saving many lives today, and now it has taken yet another major innovative step by introducing an iPad system to deliver its state-of-the-art medical technology to physicians and patients worldwide. With recent advances in information technology, Medtronic had an opportunity to build a system that could share documents and presentations to explain complex and highly technical products through a visually rich, interactive, easy-to-use mobile platform. The solution needed to be a system that is very accessible—requiring little or no training while abiding by the Medtronic security policies already in place.

"Our mission is to alleviate pain, restore health, and extend life," says Linnea Burman, director of marketing and drug delivery systems in Medtronic's Neuromodulation division. "We're working every day to help more patients have access to our therapies. The iPad helps us communicate with clinicians; it helps our stories come to life. The sales representative can pull up information quickly and use graphics to tell a story in a very memorable way."

Putting iPads into the hands of thousands of employees gives Medtronic the ideal platform to present and explain its visionary medical technologies to health care professionals, individual patients, and patient advocacy groups. "IPad lets us get information to our customers much quicker than we could before," says Michael Hedges, Medtronic's chief information officer.

Since 2010, Minneapolis, Minnesota–based Medtronic has purchased nearly 13,000 iPads and created its own app store for internal-use mobile applications. Working with Oracle Partner Fishbowl Solutions, also a Minneapolis-based company, Medtronic IT staff has extended its Oracle WebCenter content-based system for managing and distributing documents. This mobile content management system (mCMS) for the iPad links to Medtronic's Oracle WebCenter-based back-end system and enables field sales staff to provide current and accurate product and therapy information to customers, with content designated by audience or topic.

Source: www.apple.com/ipad/business/profiles/medtronic/; www.fishbowlsolutions.com/fishbowl/groups/public/documents/case_studies/031170.html.

Next Generation of Applications Leverages Mobility Platform

New applications are getting built and developed, which are keeping mobility in mind that can be extended across mobile platforms and devices. Oracle's next-generation Fusion suite of applications is built with that vision with the Application Development Framework (ADF) Mobile and offers cross-platform, rich on-device mobile capabilities with tight device services integration, and a mobile-optimized user interface. ADF-based applications enable enterprises across industries to meet frequently changing mobile requirements by allowing developers to rapidly and visually develop applications once, and then deploy them to multiple devices and channels.

Fusion Tap is a collection of mobility application modules that work across the Oracle Fusion Applications suite to provide mobile workers the ability to be productive anywhere and anytime. By taking an information-driven approach to mobility, Oracle Fusion Tap enables mobile workers to know what they need to do through a common exception-based work list, what they need to know through embedded analytics, and whom they need to connect with for immediate resolution.

Fusion Mobile Sales drives further sales team productivity by enabling direct access of Oracle Fusion CRM within iPhone and BlackBerry, and allowing instant access and team sharing of important customer, contact, and opportunity details within smartphones. Through mobile technologies, employees can spend more efficient time with customers. Employees are now able to access enterprise applications, such as customer relationship management (CRM), self-service, and many other applications on their smart devices remotely from anywhere. Employees can gain a better understanding of their internal inventories and respond immediately to changing customer demands. Mobile customer relationship management (M-CRM) must create close relationships with customers by providing value. Customers want reliable and fast service, and CRM provides those services to enable the business to gain more customers. The CRM is crucial in a mobile business, as it is the system that provides the business with the ability to directly contact the customers and users. Furthermore, personalization of the customer's interaction is extremely valuable in M-CRM. The combination of technology, software, people, and reengineered business processes converges to provide value through CRMs.

Enterprise Mobility Platform

Enterprise mobile platforms are becoming increasingly vital for businesses. With wider use of smart devices, large enterprises are forced to formulate plans and strategies to encourage a bring your own device (BYOD) policy by employees. When employees are encouraged to bring their devices to the enterprise, they need to have access to corporate applications and data. That may pose a challenge for businesses to provide secure access to data and applications with identity and access validation. An enterprise mobility platform must deal with mobile device management (MDM) as well as mobile applications management (MAM).

Major technology vendors such as IBM, Oracle, Hewlett-Packard (HP), and SAP have formulated comprehensive strategies to offer enterprise mobile solutions and introduced their robust mobility platforms. Oracle recently acquired Bitzer Mobile while IBM snapped up Fiberlink to strengthen its BYOD security offerings (http://investorplace.com/2013/11/oracle-buys-bitzer-mobile-bring-device-bid/#.UqnVp_QW0lo).

Oracle's mobile platform is robust and comprehensive to help developers build cross-platform, multichannel, and multidevice applications. It helps in integrating data and services across the enterprise and mobile devices. It leverages their identity and access authentication services to provide secure information uniformly across all layers of enterprise and mobile applications. Most important, the platform enables deployment and management on the cloud as well as on the premises for multidelivery. With the Bitzer acquisition, the platform adds BYOD security capabilities, enabling employees to bring their own devices, and, with single sign-on (SSO), they get access to all enterprise applications segregated from their personal applications on their devices.

Mobile Deployment Framework

Companies are changing how they conduct business due to the growing demands for mobility and access to business applications. As the corporate enterprise network evolves into a wireless-centric, cloud-based, mobility-applications-driven environment, mobile solution providers have developed a comprehensive suite of products and services that address this market known as mobile device management (MDM). Such solutions enable enterprises to:

- Manage and control subscriber inventories.
- Control and optimize the expense side of corporate mobility.
- Secure and protect the enterprise infrastructure.
- Monitor and manage usage.
- Manage applications and security.
- Manage users and access on a real-time basis.

Business Considerations for Mobile Platforms Deployment

It is very important for businesses to consider each of the following factors before deploying mobile platforms across their enterprises:

- Different approaches to the content carrier versus the business partner that is going to provide the content and services
- Pricing model for the relationship with the carrier and the partner
- Ownership, privacy, and security issues in terms of mobile contents
- Licensing to ascertain and use location information on customers in order to promote business
- Quality of service (QoS) based on mobile network technologies and their coverage
- Collaborations and service-level agreements (SLAs) with location-based service providers
- Strategies for the development and management of contents for mobile services
- Managing the changes to the business model and organizational structure resulting from mobile technology adoption
- Managing the changes to the relationships with clients and suppliers resulting from mobile technology adoption
- Development of mobile applications that will create value for customers
- Integrating online and offline contents and services in order to provide a unified view to users
- Using extranets and intranets to enable clients and partners in the dynamic decision-making process required in mobile business
- Handling quality and testing issues related to dynamically changing business processes

- Providing for regulatory compliance by business, especially in a global mobile context

Mobility has increased real-time collaboration (discussed in Chapter 5) and improved accessibility and communication among the employees, customers, and partners ecosystem. Oracle Social Network addresses the collaboration gap through stream-based conversations that are designed to capture information from people, enterprise applications, and business processes to facilitate collaboration between individual users and teams of people both within and across enterprises. As a system of engagement, individuals can collaborate, network, drive decisions, and update data, both in the focused pursuit of business objectives as well as in the serendipitous discovery of information and expertise.

Mobility can enhance knowledge management (KM) within an organization by making it more robust, accurate, reliable, and accessible. Mobile technology is a rapidly expanding part of everything we do, from how we reach customers to how we access information to how we collaborate with colleagues. End users can update key documents or add new ones anywhere and at any time.

Smart Devices Protection Is Important

Use of smart devices offers great benefits, but it may also pose severe threats to businesses if not protected with security measures and strict policies. In businesses today, smart devices are commonly used for corporate e-mails, documents, and many times for accessing corporate applications via VPN access. These devices also provide access to corporate contacts databases and repositories of information, and sometimes valuable financial information systems. In these cases, the confidentiality of sensitive business data must be secured and protected. These devices when logged to corporate systems may become vulnerable to unauthorized access by other users. For example, corporate e-mails, contacts databases, and financial information should not be available to unauthorized users, and these devices should be protected from such vulnerability.

It has been common practice for companies to protect their servers, workstations, and other IT systems and services, and protecting and securing smart devices should also be taken to the most important level. There are some obvious threats against which smart devices must be protected. The most common is loss or theft that could result in corporate data leakage. Another threat is unauthorized use of these smart devices that may lead to corporate data misuse. The third threat is malware specifically designed for these devices.

Identity is at the center of the Force 5 Tornado technologies that are reshaping the enterprise. To reiterate, Gartner has observed that these are forces that are fundamentally changing business. Collaboration has become mainstream with organizations now using social platforms to communicate not only with customers, but internally among employees and with machines as well. Employees everywhere are accessing business applications and data through mobile devices. Information is evolving in tandem, moving beyond a single system, and SaaS applications continue to be widely accessed and adopted.

Digital businesses must now employ identity as a crucial component in managing and securing the changes brought by social, mobile, information, and the cloud. These forces are pushing data and access beyond the firewall, requiring the enterprise to address the resulting security and management issues. Legacy identity and access management (IAM) software is no longer a practical solution for an IT that must deal with cloud applications and remote employees accessing these apps on mobile devices.

Virtual enterprises need identity solutions that are built to manage an environment that extends beyond the traditional network of firewalls. Cloud-based IAM brings visibility to digital businesses internally and control of the shared IT environment throughout their various virtual enterprise partnerships that may span multiple business ecosystems. It is a business management solution that addresses the new identity and security issues in the changed world of enterprise IT. Furthermore, cloud-enabled IAM is scalable and nimble so that a digital business may respond to the adaptive dynamics of diverse identity scenarios.

Business is changing, and the enterprise needs a cloud IAM solution that's up to the task. As enterprises keep moving to the cloud, and as their employees continue going mobile, it just makes sense to solve identity issues from the cloud. IAM is a fundamental element of cloud IaaS for the competitive social and mobile virtual enterprises.

Gartner envisions that half of all enterprises will mandate employee BYOD policies by 2017, introducing potential threats such as:

- Inserting viruses or malware into the virtual enterprise network
- Violation of virtual enterprise data governance rules for access and handling of proprietary data
- Noncompliance with government or industry regulations related to accessing and using restricted data

Gartner further predicts that by 2020, about 70 percent of enterprises will use attribute-based access control (ABAC) as the primary mechanism to protect critical data assets, up from below 5 percent in 2014. There are several technology solutions in the market to ensure safety against these threats, and enterprises need to use careful evaluation and deployment.

An example of this data protection and security technology innovation comes from WidePoint Corporation for a new cloud-based identity-as-a-service (IDaaS) offering. According to WidePoint this service assigns digital certificates to mobile devices for protection of shared data as well as better managing access by laptops, tablets, and smartphones for access to corporate data.

The WidePoint offering leverages cloud-mobile convergence, and may provide big data protection. The IDaaS Certificate-on-Chip service enables:

- Creating a secure VPN connection between the virtual enterprise network and the devices used by mobile or home-based employees—without a proprietary software client
- Ensuring that employees download sensitive data only to authorized, properly configured, and protected devices
- Remotely revoking certificates of devices that were lost or stolen, or belong to an employee who has left the organization
- Implementing a multilevel information security policy that is beyond a discretionary access control-based username and password VPN solution
- Assigning different levels of access to employees, consultants, and trading partners in the virtual enterprise, based on the specific BYOD user device being used to establish connectivity
- Using ABAC to provide the flexibility that digital businesses need to manage their global teams in multiple virtual enterprises throughout multiple business ecosystems

WidePoint CTO Daniel Turissini explained, "Our expertise in building out a federally authorized credentialing infrastructure to a base of over three million users has uniquely qualified us to develop and bring to market a cost-effective, scalable, and easily deployed service that addresses the problems that organizations are presently facing as they extend their IT infrastructures into the cloud." Wide-Point CEO and chairman Steven L. Komar added, "With our long and proven history of expertise in communications life cycle management and identity assurance solutions, WidePoint is uniquely attuned to providing higher-level security as part of its portfolio of managed mobility solutions offerings to commercial and government markets. The IDaaS Certificate-on-Chip service provides customers with additional security in a manner that not only can increase worker productivity, but is also complementary to the organization's unique security policies and related compliance requirements."

Additionally, IDaaS data protection and security technology with ABAC may be the solution to the hybrid cloud multi-tenancy security challenges of big data. This approach involves the use of so-called data lakes as data storage architecture. Peter Guerra, principal at Booz Allen Hamilton, explained, "We have built a series of big data platforms that enable clients to inject any type of data and to secure access to individual elements of data inside the platform. We call that architecture the data lake."

The difference between a traditional data warehouse and the emergent data lake reflects the issues for the system of record (SOR) transformation into the system of engagement (SOE). As a result, the rigid pre-analytical processing data structures of the warehouse are replaced by the fluid metadata tagging of the big data streams being collected and stored as they flow into the lake. The IDaaS-ABAC approach can be applied to securing discrete data elements or the whole lake, depending on security needs and performance considerations.

Mobotory: Business Agility Strategy in Action

Jon Stevenson is CEO of Mobotory, a young high-tech start-up. It is fast growing as a digital business by leveraging relationships with key partners and has formed virtual enterprises with a global reach. This business agility strategy has enabled Mobotory to become a valued member of several business ecosystems in diverse industries around the world.

Mobotory creates mobile enterprise solutions for management of large-scale events that utilize the convergence of the Force 5 Tornado technologies to disrupt its target event market spaces. It is based on a modular architecture with a core app engine that integrates safety, security, operations, engineering, production, and broadcast television logistics management applications.

This is his *creating business agility* story.

Why We Started This Company

While building an informational mobile application for a sports client, we gained access to operational teams of the sporting events and realized that operations were still being run the same way as they had been for decades, and we saw the need to build something to overcome the technical limitations of paper, walkie-talkies, and analog systems. We built the Enterprise Operating System (eOS) to enable seamless real-time simultaneous collaboration, to track flow of information, and to create ease of use for the end user.

What Sets Us Apart

We designed eOS from the ground up for the mobile environment. It is a native application that makes data easy to access, navigate, and interact with right from a handheld device. It's a white-label solution that is easily customizable for different industries with modules that integrate easily.

What the Enterprise Operating System (eOS) Can Do for You

Mobotory delivers easy-to-use mobile platforms with reliable network architectures designed to make your events manageable. Our Enterprise Operating System (eOS) is an integrated mobile software suite that lets you run all aspects of your event in real time from virtually anywhere.

We understand the challenges that you face on a daily basis. Unexpected change, disorder, and confusion are inevitable. Without the right tools, keeping track of staff members, patrons, vendors, and parking, along with stacks of scripts, session schedules, and maps, can quickly become an overwhelming ordeal.

Our eOS is the next evolution in event management. It is a simple and intuitive app that lets you and your team capture, share, and act on information on the fly from wherever you are. Stop problems from unnecessarily complicating your event, and give yourself an edge before, during, and after game day. Its seamless communication and flow of information allow you to proactively manage risks, resolve issues faster, and reduce operating costs.

With eOS, your data is safe and accessible. Behind the scenes, this agile platform is built on secure private cloud technology. Consolidate data centers and deploy workloads on shared infrastructure with built-in security and role-based access control. Our intelligent networks and architectures ensure connectivity you can rely on. Moreover, eOS works with your existing hardware and software investments.

The eOS system's central database puts your historical data to work for you, safeguarding your time, resources, and public image. Textual, photographic, and video data logged by your team with eOS can mitigate, and even prevent, legal exposure stemming from incidents. Understand details of your operations by reviewing key metrics during and after the event with eOS's analytics module, and use this information to improve management going forward.

What Features and Benefits eOS Delivers

Features

- Manage incidents when and where they occur.
- Stay connected with flexible and reliable network infrastructure.
- Capture video, photo, and text.
- Store data securely for future reference.
- Track issues using map and list views.
- Use the virtual command center.
- Receive live event script updates.
- Use the simple and intuitive interface.
- Communicate in the field.
- Act quickly with customized task assignments.
- Paperless general information integrates with existing IT infrastructure.

Benefits

- Better response coordination
- Real-time situational awareness
- Streamlined communication
- More efficient personnel deployment
- Reduced incident frequency and severity
- Lower insurance costs

- Better lawsuit protection
- Reduced negative publicity
- Superior patron and partner event experiences

What the eOS Modular Architecture Includes

The eOS core feature set consists of the following interchangeable modules:

- *Incident reporting.* Create a robust, reliable record of issues as they happen using pictures, video, and text.
- *Security suite.* Maintain situational awareness with an interactive bird's-eye view of your event.
- *Task management.* Assign, track, and document your team's work flow more effectively and comprehensively.
- *Contacts.* Connect at the touch of a button by phone or e-mail.
- *Activity script.* Create your playbook, free from the constraints of paper and updated in real time.
- *Information.* Keep all mission-critical information and documents at your fingertips on any device.
- *Notes.* Record additional on-the-fly observations for real-time and future use.
- *Command center.* Create your operations hub from anywhere.
- *Parking.* This gives you a 360-degree view of your venue's parking, including allocated car space and revenue.
- *Analytics.* Understand how you are doing by evaluating key metrics during and after the event; map your progress event by event.
- *Customization.* Tailor the look and feel of eOS to meet your needs.
- *Secure database.* There is reliable data storage using high-level encryption with built-in security and role-based access control.
- *Live debrief.* Record and share new information as it becomes available.
- *Infrastructure.* We provide the hardware and software necessary to get eOS running.
- *Implementation.* We'll get you up and running as soon as possible.
- *Network architecture.* A secure cloud solution with intelligent networks and technology architectures ensures reliable connectivity that works with your existing hardware and software infrastructure.
- *Fan module.* Fans have one-touch access to event security by phone or SMS, as well as the ability to report incidents directly to the central system.

We listen to your needs and can also custom-tailor additional modules to fit your unique circumstances.

Our Keys to Success

We understand our clients' businesses, and we know how to use mobile technology to address the challenges that they face on a daily basis. We've partnered and codeveloped white-label solutions with companies to license to their clients as well as working directly with event properties. Our team's diverse background in sports, entertainment, engineering, software, and law allows us to sit down with our clients to create reliable, easy-to-use solutions that our partners actually use.

Our Accomplishments

We have launched a full-product version of eOS with its core features to address our partners' and clients' industries, and we have licensing agreements in place with several companies to white label eOS for their clients. In addition, eOS has already been successfully deployed at a number of events in 2011 and 2012, including the Fiesta Bowl, Insight Bowl, and the Summer Olympics in London, as well as the visit of Pope Francis to Brazil in 2013.

The visit of Pope Francis to Rio de Janeiro for the 28th World Youth Day program, July 22–29, 2013, served as a full-scale field test and evaluation of the Mobotory eOS solution for potential nationwide deployment by the Brazilian Federal Police. The Federal Police established a partnership with Mobotory to use eOS for monitoring the big events being produced for the Pope's tour. The objective was to provide a faster response to event problems if they arise, such as evacuation during a fire or to detect and prevent street congestion, accidents, or crime. Mobotory is working with the Federal Police on a proposal that could be adopted for the Summer Olympics in 2016.

In the next chapter, we will elaborate further on the convergence of these Force 5 Tornado technologies and of social media in particular that is enabling digital businesses in many ways by listening to the voices of all the various stakeholders (customers, partners, employees, and independent consultants) in their business ecosystem.

CHAPTER

7

Listening to the Voices

If you are reading this chapter, you may already have started thinking about how these disruptive technology forces are converging to provide all of the resources that you need to transform your business quickly with the right decisions for your sustainable competitive business advantage. We have witnessed some major paradigm shifts toward communication, collaboration, and evolution of new social media in recent years that are forcing all of us to listen to voices and respond accordingly. We also introduced the fourth dimension as trust in terms of "listening to our own conscience" for multi-dimensional scoring of business agility readiness in Chapter 2 besides profile, lifestyle, and relationship engagement in predictive analytics and cognitive intelligence. We recognize the fact that listening to our own inner conscience offers prudence in making the right decisions and surely helps in creating business agility. We also realize that wisdom lies in public voices and, in business terms, voices of the ecosystem (customers, partners, and employees). The shift to social media and the transformation of current business to social business are happening so rapidly that if one has not paid attention one may lose out and quickly be out of business. These changes are sometimes referred to as crowdsourcing, social networking, social business, and Enterprise 2.0. We believe that whatever they are called, they have surely emerged as major forces to transform your business by providing resources to listen to the voices of the ecosystem where you play and run your business.

We shouldn't be surprised at the growing numbers in our well-connected ecosystem and society in general. Here are some recent facts that are revolutionary and that have impacted our sociopolitical, economic, and business landscape:

- June 2012: 2.4 billion global Internet users (except China)—8 percent year-to-year growth, driven by emerging markets
- February 2013: 1 billion tweets a day
- March 2013: Facebook > 1 billion users
- October 2012: Twitter > 500 million users growing @ 150,000 every day
- January 2013: Foursquare—3 billion check-ins
- March 2013: Blogs—WordPress reported 40 million new posts
- December 2012: Pandora Internet Radio users listened to 13 billion hours of music
- July 2012: Netflix reported 1 billion hours of video
- March 2013: YouTube reported > 4 billion hours watched per month.
- LinkedIn recently surpassed 200 million members.
- 50 percent of social network users are connected to brands.

We discussed in Chapter 6 in detail how mobility with smart devices at people's fingertips has accelerated the use of social media to communicate and collaborate. McKinsey & Company has reported that the revenue growth of social businesses is 24 percent higher than less social firms, and data from Frost & Sullivan backs that up across various key performance indicators (KPIs). In this chapter, we focus on various social media, platforms, and technologies that would enable existing businesses to become smarter and new businesses to grow rapidly.

Social Media: A New Disruptive Revolution

Social media is a new disruptive revolution causing rapid change in the mode of business communication. Businesses must explore and evaluate these media to improve their marketing, sales, customer service, and brand reputation. Smart devices (smartphones, iPads, BlackBerries) are becoming a necessity for sales and field service personnel in many organizations; the bring-your-own-device (BYOD) model is supported by many businesses; and access to internal networks and applications are provided on these devices.

These social media have caused a major impact on sociopolitical campaigns in the recent past. Not so long ago, President Barack

Obama used these media for his political campaign that resulted in a resounding victory. We also observed that ordinary people using Facebook and Twitter brought down rulers in Tunisia, Egypt, and Libya and are threatening absolute rule in Syria. And in India, one man's campaign against corruption went viral, bringing thousands of people together globally in Anna Hazare's support for a greater cause.

We have entered the era of a connected society with powerful media and smart devices in people's hands, and businesses need to be vigilant and alert to listen to these voices. In this new work environment, businesses will have to display transparency to earn trust and faith among employees, partners, and customers. Customers who don't like a product can quickly broadcast their disapproval.

We are all familiar with the story about "United Breaks Guitars." When United Airlines baggage handlers in Chicago damaged Dave Carroll's $3,500 guitar a few years back, he tried to get his claims from the airline the old-fashioned way. But after several months of repeated phone calls and faxes with various customer-service representatives, the airline refused to accept his claim. Mr. Carroll, a professional country music singer from Canada, channeled his frustration into a song and a video, which he posted on YouTube. Since it first appeared, "United Breaks Guitars" has been viewed more than 4.4 million times.

Airlines in the United States have been the quickest to embrace social media as a low-cost public relations and marketing tool, in particular to spread the word about fare sales or to make announcements about new routes or services. Carriers like Southwest Airlines, JetBlue, and Alaska Airlines are among the most active users, each with online followings. Even some airports, like Hartsfield-Jackson International in Atlanta and Logan International in Boston, are using dedicated channels on Facebook and YouTube to provide travelers with information like how to use the airport train system or to give updates on construction projects or changes to rental-car facilities.

The social media's astonishing success in less than eight years has attracted more than a billion active users in almost every country and made it the world's most popular tool for communication and collaboration. Facebook provided users with a personal medium to broadcast to its network. Prominent businesses offer their versions of a hybrid Twitter/Facebook for employees. Oracle with its recently announced Oracle Social Network (OSN), Salesforce.com with its product Chatter, IBM with its Connections software, as well as start-ups

Yammer and Jive, offer these collaborative tools for communication. "'Information is power' used to mean that hoarding information gave power. Now we're seeing that sharing information is power. The more we share, the more we can help other people and the more it becomes apparent we're an expert and a valuable employee," says David Sacks, CEO of Yammer.

Many books have been written on social media and social business in the recent past and drawn great attention from key decision makers across all sectors. Sandy Carter in her book *Get Bold* (IBM Press, 2011) outlines AGENDA (align goals, gain trust, engage, network, design, and analyze) for the success of social business and its characteristics with expected business outcomes. She is a great evangelist of the social business transformation and argues passionately in her book about the need of an AGENDA to survive and thrive in the current tornadoes of disruptive forces. It is extremely important to align goals and culture of an organization with changing business needs and with the new mode of a socially connected ecosystem. Businesses need to gain the trust of customers, partners, employees, all stakeholders and their friends, and followers alike. They need to engage with clients and ecosystem partners offering a more delightful experience. She goes on highlighting the need of the process for social network and design for building trust of all stakeholders. More importantly, she concludes, it is vital to analyze the patterns of sentiments building around products and services. Technologies around social media are mere enablers to capture and listen to the voices around your business that provide inputs for the right decisions. It also helps in cognitive intelligence to run and manage the current agile business.

In our view, social business is extremely important in this new business environment, and this new paradigm shift has defined new levels of customer engagement.

The Six Layers of Customer Engagement

1. *The web*. When companies moved to the web, they asked customers to be self-sufficient with regard to product information, customer service, and ordering.
2. *Social media*. The social web opened up possibilities of public, two-way conversation.
3. *Facebook/LinkedIn/Twitter*. These are the Internet for many people, and they handle all of their communication with

friends and companies through the world's largest social network.

4. *Mobile.* With a phone in every pocket, customers are now looking for information that they can consume on their mobile devices.

5. *Augmented reality.* Digital information can now be placed on top of the real world.

6. *The game layer.* This builds on the mobile layer and lets businesses turn the world and their businesses into a game.

Consumerization of information technology (IT) is associated with ease of use, attractive interfaces, intuitive functionality, and low prices. In the corporate IT world, this move to consumerized IT has been described as the penetration of employee-purchased mobile devices like the iPhone, iPad, and Android phones and tablets. This phenomenon is already growing and entering large organizations rapidly. The immense success and proliferation of Facebook, Twitter, LinkedIn, Foursquare, and mobile/smart devices such as iPhones, BlackBerries, and tablet PCs among consumers has created the consumerization of IT and a new paradigm shift seeking a pleasant web experience. Now, consumers have become more powerful than ever before with access to information and social media to communicate to the world at their fingertips.

Social computing and the use of social media are changing the way people interact with each other and with companies online. The majority of shoppers begin their process online, and the most frequent starting point is the retail site itself. These consumers are engaging, connecting, and collaborating. They want to understand what their friends liked, what other options are available, and what people like them ultimately bought.

Most of these consumers consider Facebook recommendations when making decisions about purchasing. Consistent experiences across multiple channels and devices have offered customers more choices for accessing the web in new, engaging, and collaborative ways than before, and they want that ease and diversity to be reflected in their dealings with businesses as well. Consumers change channels and switch devices whenever they need to. They can keep tabs on friends and family on Facebook and follow Twitter regularly. They can find a nearby restaurant with Foursquare geolocation on their phone and then look up reviews of that restaurant on Yelp.

Executive Insights
Kalpesh Desai, CEO of Agile Financial Technologies

Inflection points to businesses brought about by technology are nothing new. However, the emergence of social media platforms has left financial services firms grappling with the fact that not only are potential and existing customers expressing their preferences on this medium, but the medium is instrumental in driving customer behavior.

Financial institutions exist in an extremely competitive environment and need to adapt rapidly to the changes evolving around them to survive, grow, and manage risks. The advent of social media and mobility apps released by financial institutions that permit them to connect with their customers' profiles on these platforms generates voluminous data that not only captures their potential customers' buying preferences, but also enables them to profile their customers accurately. Thus comes the need to filter through this data and generate analytics that could be better used not only to position the right products, but also to identify potential risks and threats that would not be captured through traditional means that financial institutions have adopted today. Hence, social media is still uncharted territory for banks and insurance companies.

The way we communicate has changed, with the advent of social media and community forums becoming the channel of choice for customers to voice their opinions, seek advice, and post feedback. Collaborative tools and content dissemination tools have to adapt to this shift in behavior to equip the institution to better manage its communication process.

How many of us now rely on Twitter, Facebook, or LinkedIn to find out breaking news, pose queries, and even post customer service issues? It is this shift in behavior that is prompting financial institutions to examine how the medium will impact customer relationships. Institutions will have to review their practices and also examine their processes, considering that social media interaction will bring forth a convergence of their technology, customer relationship, and corporate communications teams.

Social media can be leveraged to track how the institution is perceived, and ancillary analytical tools are available to enable it to track trending topics and blogs mentioning the institution. Since the medium is viral in nature, it is imperative for the institution to include the tracking of such perceptions in its overall customer relationship management (CRM) strategy.

Consider this: It is likely that most comments that a consumer would put out there would be negative. Very rarely does a consumer go out of the way to post a positive comment, unless the service experience was exceptional. Either way, the communication process needs to be captured and responded to by either isolating the dissenter by educating the person in a public forum or advocating for a supporter by spreading the good word.

Customers who use the institution's online services will also be more likely to adapt to a new trend that is emerging—where banks and insurance companies are integrating their channels with social media platforms. Take the example of ASB Bank from New Zealand, which is credited with opening the world's first virtual branch on Facebook. You can interface with the bank on Facebook on any topic ranging from your account administration to originating an inquiry for a new loan. Social media platforms that provide you with the capability of building applications that enable interaction are untested waters, but a surefire way of ensuring that you are an interactive click away from your clients.

Interestingly enough, we have also come across insurance companies offering advisory services to their clients and curtailing insurance fraud by simply checking out activities of insurance claimants who may have put in fraudulent claims. Fraud detectives are scouring the social media for evidence as a process of validating claims. A case in point was reported by the *Los Angeles Times* in January 2011 of a disability claim on account of a bad back being refused because the claimant had boasted on Twitter and Facebook about completing a marathon.

Financial institutions have their work cut out for them while they figure out their communication and channel integration strategy for social media platforms. At the very least, security policies and systems will have to be reexamined once channels are extended onto social media platforms.

Financial institutions will soon have to formulate their customer relationship, communication, technology, and channel integration strategies around the functional building blocks of social media platforms—identity, conversations, sharing, presence, relationships, reputation, and groups (Kietzmann's Honeycomb Framework).

Executive Bio: Kalpesh Desai is the CEO of Agile Financial Technologies, a leading global software products company that focuses on the insurance, banking and financial Services sector. He is a serial entrepreneur and has over two decades of experience in servicing the financial services sector.

Mobility: Enable Agile Relationships

We have witnessed a smart revolution of the mobile space (discussed in Chapter 6). This unprecedented growth of connectivity is creating an overwhelming range of new possibilities, and tapping, swiping, locating, pinging, and socializing are quickly becoming part of normal human behavior. Technology is starting to change people, and these people, whether consumers or employees, will change businesses. In this rapid shift, mobility has to be an integral part of the solutions and the framework.

Mobile usage will surpass that of PCs and other wired devices by 2015. Smartphones will outsell traditional cell phones. Tablet sales are booming. Mobile data traffic is expected to increase 26-fold between 2010 and 2015. Businesses must optimize their websites for mobile use and prepare to target customers based on context and location. Mobile access must be fully integrated into the web presence, optimized and synchronized in real time, offering rich media content scaled and targeted to the device in question.

In today's ever-changing and most competitive business environment, consumers are seeking more personalized care and services for any engagement before they enter into a transaction. It is natural that the relationship begins with greetings, smiles, and conversation, and then an understanding of the needs and behavior emerges in the process.

User engagement involves a mixture of quantitative and qualitative analysis. Quantitative analysis offers useful patterns and is generally more scalable and easier to conduct. User engagement also involves contextual study and ethnography. These provide information, including what the users' routines are in daily life, and what their needs are for which they have visited the electronic website, physical store, or workplace.

Social computing is changing the way people interact with each other and with companies online. More than 40 percent of consumers factor in Facebook recommendations when making decisions about purchasing. Customers on the website may want to "Like" a product on Facebook or tweet about something they find. Or the reverse: While on Facebook, Liking the company could make the customer eligible for special offers that appear on the corporate website.

Customers are used to accessing the web in new and engaging ways through multiple channels and devices, and they want that ease and diversity to be reflected in their dealings with businesses. Yet companies need to maintain branding in a consistent way across multiple platforms and keep track of customers' movements from device to device throughout the day. The current multichannel environment makes marketing so complex that creating targeted, personalized, relevant experiences is harder than ever. And when you get it right, the bar is constantly rising. Companies are struggling to find a way to reconcile sentiment analysis, location, channel, demographics, and the many other factors that surround an interaction.

Marketers and line-of-business leaders need to find a way to control the online experience easily and intuitively. Ideally, marketers should be able to identify visitors quickly, follow their history across multiple channels, and, by evaluating real-time activities against historical data, make time-critical point decisions. Marketers should be able to analyze interactions and be empowered to change the experience fast.

The entire spectrum of components and data needed to create a consistent and compelling web experience today is comprised of diverse assets such as websites in multiple languages, user-generated content, micro sites, mobile and multichannel sites, social channels, and more. Meanwhile, companies have made enormous investments in CRM, campaign management, and other enterprise systems that house critical customer data. Often, these are disconnected from online customer engagements, but companies must integrate and manage all of these facilities to create a truly engaging experience for customers across online channels and between online and offline channels.

CITO Research explains the challenges of contemporary web management for enterprises and the business importance of web experience management as the basis of an integrated online strategy. This concept is vital for executives who are concerned about the strategic direction of their companies and who seek to provide an experience that will drive competitive success.

Web interaction has changed a great deal and entered a different wave now. The first wave, referred to as Web 1.0, provided the platform to publish information about products and services to external and internal consumers. The second revolution, referred to as Web 2.0, deals with technologies such as wikis, blogs, tagging, linking, discussions, and Really Simple Syndication (RSS) to provide dramatic efficiencies to people working together with global virtual teams, partners, and customers. Currently, technology is advancing through the evolution of Web 3.0, which focuses on the semantic web and personalization. Web 3.0 is where the computer is generating new information, rather than humans doing so.

In order to deliver a pleasing web experience, one must incorporate social media, tailored through targeting, and deliver it through multiple channels, each with its own form factor and design characteristics. Web experience includes five major dimensions:

1. Social media
2. Multiple channels and devices
3. Targeted and personalized experiences
4. Multiple corporate stakeholders
5. A spectrum of components and data

Social media has evolved as a powerful platform to create a web presence globally and instantly without much investment. In order to take the best advantage of these media, businesses need to offer pleasant and engaging experiences to build community. This includes collaborative tools such as comments, blogs, ratings, and reviews. The various social media offer much more than communication and collaboration. We need to evaluate and address the following questions:

- How can our social media presence be integrated with the rest of the web experience?
- If a customer shows a particular interest on Facebook, how can the company make sure that this interest is acknowledged when the person comes to the corporate website?
- If a customer interacts with the company on Facebook or Twitter, shouldn't their interactions be acknowledged when the same person comes to the main website?
- Shouldn't positive interactions be promoted for others to see or share?
- Shouldn't marketers have the ability to address negative, unwarranted, or critical comments?

It's essential that marketers have the right tools for social channel enablement so that they can moderate and optimize the experience of social media on their site and across the social networking sites important to their customers. In this evolving communication pattern, the company website should be customized for each channel or device, the web browser, Facebook, Android devices, and iPhones. Ideally, a company website should be optimized for commonly used devices, with rich media and interactive panels. Part of this challenge is technical, such as integrating with third-party applications like Facebook, publishing content to diverse mobile devices, or integrating geopositioning. But there are also broader challenges of providing a contextual experience around each customer and allowing the business-to-customer interaction to move between platforms without missing a step. These challenges need to be addressed with a comprehensive strategy and with an integrated user engagement platform.

Customer Engagement: Key Business Challenge

Customer engagement is a key challenge for many businesses and a matter of ongoing optimization. Companies must acknowledge a customer's history of interactions and changes to personal profile details. Marketers need the ability to engage with customers through both explicit criteria (profile of a registered user, purchase history, CRM data, IP address, location, device type) and implicit criteria (behavior on the site, keyword searches, navigation). With this information, companies can begin to develop a customer profile, assign that profile to a customer segment, and target customers with appropriate content. As loyal and repeat customers interact with the website, their experiences can be continuously tailored with panels, messages, and offers. If the customer is volunteering information, reading content, or purchasing, marketers require analytical tools for tracking the effectiveness of online content and adjusting it to optimize its success.

In the current business scenario, most enterprises possess data but lack comprehensive analytics capabilities to make meaningful use of that rich data. Processes for targeting customers effectively need to combine the best of marketer-controlled analysis and automated optimization. Organizations require tools for marketer-controlled customer segmentation and the assignment of content or promotions that will be most effective for those segments. Businesses need data to make decisions, but not just a data dump. They need real-time intelligence on their customers and their behavior across channels focused on the right indicators to directly inform their decisions. And they need these capabilities paired with predictive analytics and automated decision making.

With the evolution of social media, expectations of users and line-of-business managers have changed as well. These users need to be empowered to build websites, design the layouts, make content changes, set up targeting rules, control user-generated content, and enable the mobile web, all from an intuitive and easy-to-use interface. IT remains an important stakeholder because the web is and always will be a critical enterprise software system, but IT people don't want to spend their days supporting the marketing department's content changes; instead they want to focus on more strategic initiatives.

To create a compelling web experience for customers, companies need the ability to organize and access their enterprise data and leverage it in web interactions. For example, a company may use customer relationship management (CRM) to create customer segments for direct mailings. But if CRM cannot talk to the web content management system, the company cannot reuse this intelligence online. If an organization creates a campaign to encourage repeat business, the campaign needs to be effective regardless of whether the customer is in front of a work computer, on the road on an iPhone, visiting a physical store, or calling customer service. And the organization needs to know what happened across the other channels of interaction so that it can make sure the campaign is applied appropriately. How can organizations bring customer data to bear in the web channel? How can organizations ensure that customers have an optimal and consistent experience with the organization, across both online and offline channels?

Executive Insights
Amit Srivastava, Solution Delivery
Manager at NEC

The proliferation of social media, instant messaging, and data warehouses has opened a plethora of opportunities across various industry verticals. This, coupled with innovations in the areas of biometrics, video analytics, and mobility, can provide competitive advantage to airlines, airports, and law enforcement agencies. The vast amount of images, videos, and textual information is being processed every moment and provides a gigantic data mine. It can be leveraged to determine patterns that could be effectively utilized to determine future terrorist attacks, criminal activities, and illegal immigrants.

Public or external data such as Facebook, LinkedIn, Twitter, YouTube, and Gmail, coupled with secured internal data such as passenger, travel, forensic, and biometric information, as well as criminal records, can provide valuable insights into criminal activities and their interactions. Imagery data can be dynamically captured from security cameras installed at public places such as railway stations, shopping malls, sport stadiums, and airports. Movements of suspects carrying mobile devices can easily be tracked globally and their activities contained. The number plate recognition systems, facial recognition software, scar marks, and tattoos assist law enforcement agencies with useful patterns.

Freely available public data on the web combined with data available from reliable internal systems can present interesting patterns. For example, if we search for a suspect, Mr. X, on the web and find his account on Facebook, we can look at his images and connections to find acquaintances and then track everyone's movements to deduce useful information. We can also poll internal systems to link them with fingerprint and biometric data to get interesting findings.

Another example could be tracking illegal immigrants at airports. If we capture the images of passengers while disembarking the aircraft, by the time they arrive at passport control, valuable information can be retrieved and recorded for them. So if someone destroys travel documents at the airport, still the person can be tracked to the aircraft from which one disembarked.

Executive Bio: Amit Srivastava has been involved in the implementation of business solutions in diverse industries such as airlines, airports, utilities, education, and law enforcement, leveraging the latest innovative technologies such as pervasive computing, mobility, biometrics, video, business intelligence, and data analytics.

Today's requirements for web experience management entail a paradigm shift from the way the web was managed five or 10 years ago. Where web content management (WCM) systems several years ago helped IT administrators manage content for static one-size-fits-all websites, today the need has shifted dramatically. As the web has become a critical business and marketing tool, organizations must empower their marketers to manage the online customer experience as a whole. This web experience must provide a targeted and personalized, dynamic, social, interactive, and optimized experience across multiple channels. Organizations today need a web experience management system that is focused on these capabilities and that is capable of deploying a customer experience of this sort across the largest enterprise environments. Web content management capabilities remain the critical foundation of the tool set—but it is no longer enough to simply manage content online.

In order to provide an integrated customer experience, businesses evaluate integrated web content management and front- and back-office systems. This allows the enterprise to be more effective at targeting and customer service. The web experience can no longer remain separate from critical customer-focused systems like CRM and e-commerce.

Given the challenges of personalization, multiple channels, and the need for marketers to monitor, control, and optimize the web experience for customers, a total web experience management solution is needed.

Executive Insights
Christopher Sowa, Vice President,
Customer Strategy and Insight, Oracle

With more information and interactions moving online, the world is becoming more and more like a small town. Information about you is available to those who are geographically distant, and suddenly you have the ability to have "local" interactions with experts or friends across the globe.

Despite the fact that many of the same social rules that apply in person apply online, many IT executives are unsure about the best path forward for managing online social relationships. Commonly, IT executives are on the "hidden in the sand" path. The second path executives are on is the "customer is my prey" path. For these companies, the online domain is viewed as a place where customer interactions are solely equated with sales, and customer information should be sold to the highest bidder. Imagine the repercussions of this mentality in real life—if, whenever I saw employees of my local credit union at the store or a barbeque, they tried to sell me something or sell my banking information to others in the neighborhood. The same is becoming true online. Customers begin to avoid all interactions with organizations that harass them. With people also starting to protest what they see as big brother government and companies abusing their information and privacy, the ramifications of not paying attention to these issues will be severe.

Business executives and IT executives need to spend less time thinking about online social interactions and more time thinking about how to make online interactions consistent with real-life interactions they have with their customers. Executives should think about their cross-channel social interaction platform, including online social networks, e-commerce, mobile, and in-person interactions, by making sure they are covering the following seven key elements:

1. *Listen.* Get to know your online communities and key influencers by leveraging technologies that cut out the noise and can help you hear important customers and influencers across social networks. This will allow you to learn how to better improve your products and more effectively engage your customers.

2. *Protect your company's online reputation.* Just like in real life, if someone is spreading misinformation about a company, executives need to have monitoring capabilities and the ability to quickly react. Executives also need to have the correct infrastructure put in place to foster expert communities to help refute misinformation and to position solutions properly.

3. *Earn the right to an online relationship or any business relationship.* Provide valuable expertise that can help your customers with their problems or decisions when they need it. Respond quickly to complaints or concerns that your customers have about your products.

4. *Treat customers in the same manner whether the setting is online, offline, or across channels.* If you have high-value customers, they expect the same royal treatment whether they interact with you on the phone or post to one of your online forums.

5. *Leverage analytics to integrate structured and unstructured data to help you tier important customer relationships and create consistent rules for interaction.* Much the same way people prioritize among offline relationships, executives need

to decide which types of relationships are going to be most mutually beneficial over the long term and where to invest.

6. *Engage your employees.* Employees are the gateway and the glue to key social relationships. Leveraging online collaboration tools can cement this glue and increase productivity up to 25 percent.

7. *Create and publish a social set of ethics for customers and employees.* This set of ethics should include how you interact online and offline. It should also cover items on how you view customers' personal information and steps you can take to safeguard relationships. A set of ethical guidelines is particularly important because many online social norms are still evolving.

New tools for managing social interactions across channels can help create the same kinds of excellent in-person relationships we experience at our local stores. For this reason, the path forward should be a familiar and mutually beneficial one based on leveraging strong social relationships.

Executive Bio: Christopher Sowa has led the development of customer strategies, financial strategies, analytics strategies, and operational models used successfully by multinational companies in Europe, Asia, Australia, and the United States. He is a subject matter expert in understanding the value of business process reengineering and technology to large corporations.

With recent technology and tools, we can easily build and deploy a virtual web store where consumers may get a near real-term user experience with personalization and personalized care. On an intranet or a business-to-enterprise (B2E) web portal, personalization is often based on user attributes such as department, functional area, or role. (See Figure 7.1.)

Personalization: A Key Tenet of User Engagement in Business

Sometime back, I walked into a bank to carry out a normal banking chore—depositing a check. I was overwhelmed by the warm greetings

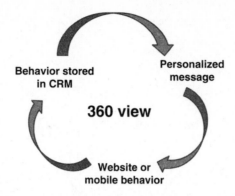

Figure 7.1   Customer Behavior and Categories of Personalization

of the branch manager, and he even offered to fill out the deposit slip while I was waiting in line for the teller. Thinking it might take a while, he then offered assistance to have my check accepted for deposit by a personal banker. He continued to offer the best care he could while I was in the bank.

When I walked into his bank again for another banking transaction, I was pleasantly surprised to receive his personal greetings by name with a smile and again his offer to assist with my transaction. This time, I had an appointment with a loan officer for a refinancing. When he saw that the staff was still busy with another customer, he offered to carry out all necessary photocopying of my documents that might be needed. While he was doing this extended personalized service, he was winning my trust and my heart in the process. By then, the loan officer was free and ready to meet with me with all my documents ready for our meeting. I would categorize the manager's assistance as a clear display of personalization that would go a long way in building trust and gaining, growing, and retaining business for his branch and for the bank in general. In contrast, I receive numerous aggressive and bothersome call center calls from its competitive bank for its services, and I refuse to take those calls. I am sure many of us have faced similar episodes in our lives, and we appreciate the significance of personalization and personalized care in business settings.

Customer services have been widely used and misused, and now businesses need to reevaluate the paradigm shift of customers' needs and expectations. Personalization implies that the changes are based on implicit data, such as items purchased or pages viewed.

There are three categories of personalization:

1. Profile/group based
2. Behavior based
3. Collaboration based

Web personalization models include rules-based filtering, based on "if this, then that" rules processing, and collaborative filtering, which serves relevant material to customers by combining their own personal preferences with the preferences of like-minded others. Collaborative filtering works well for books, music, video, and so on.

There are three broad methods of personalization:

1. Implicit
2. Explicit
3. Hybrid

With implicit personalization, the personalization is performed by the web page based on the different categories mentioned before. With explicit personalization, the web page is changed by the user using the features provided by the system (such as Oracle WebCenter sites). Hybrid personalization combines both approaches to leverage the best of both worlds.

Personalization is also being considered for use in less overtly commercial applications to improve the user experience online. Facebook introduced Instant Personalization recently. This new technology is different from social plug-ins, which many B2B and B2C sites are already using. Social plug-ins include things like Facebook live streams and Like buttons, and are intended to drive user engagement and make a website more social. With Instant Personalization, Facebook shares data with a handful of non-Facebook websites.

Social business is built upon three pillars—people (culture/leadership), process, and technology. Employees, partners, and customers are major constituents of any business. The most effective approach to enabling a social business centers around helping people discover expertise, develop social networks, and capitalize on relationships. It helps groups of people bind together into communities of shared interests and coordinate efforts to deliver better business results faster. An effective social business embodies a culture characterized by sharing, transparency, innovation, and improved decision making. Such a culture enables deeper relationships within the organization and with customers and business partners.

Culture change may be the most challenging component of successfully transforming into a social business. Social tools provide a gateway for information exchanges across geographies and organizational silos. Building trust and encouraging social interactions are essential to driving social change in the workforce. To become a social business, we have to recognize that employees need to be agile, informed, and able to work beyond their specific job descriptions.

Technology is certainly a key factor in the evolution. An organization must adopt tools that work efficiently in order to successfully make this transformation. While social software adoption is on the rise, a growing challenge for global organizations is the ability to manage risk while harnessing insights from a wide variety of social communities and remaining compliant with their own governance policies, including practices dictated by their regulatory requirements. With these new advancements around compliance enablement, a social business can confidently activate networks of people to use a variety of collaborative tools, to improve and accelerate innovation.

Business process optimization is extremely significant for any changes, and an organization must go through the process of identifying market factors that are generating the need for a transformation. It must recognize the social objectives it needs to accomplish, and then establish social outputs that will support the objectives. Finally, executives need to determine which platforms, applications, and features they'll need to meet desired outcomes. These basic principles or processes are vital to the success of a social business.

Sentiment Analytics: A Better Way to Drive Business Focus and Agility

Collaboration between social media and business has given rise to new dimension of sentiment analytics to capture, process, and analyze sentiments and behavior patterns of business stakeholders (customers, partners, and employees). Sentiment is nothing but feelings (attitudes, emotions, and opinions) expressed in informal media. Now, with the abrupt and rampant proliferation of social media in the form of Facebook, Twitter, and LinkedIn, businesses have a great opportunity to capture and analyze feelings in their business context.

Sentiment analysis helps in understanding customers' opinions and experiences from across multiple channels in social media. The explosion of data in all forms from blogs, online forums, Facebook, Twitter, and other social media channels has given consumers a virtual soapbox of unprecedented reach and influence for publicly sharing their thoughts on events, products, and services. Businesses, academics, and journalists are using sentiment analysis to tap into this social media buzz. By applying analytics and natural language processing (NLP) technologies, they gain a better understanding of consumer preferences, market trends, and brand awareness. Natural language processing, statistics, or machine learning methods are used to extract, identify, or otherwise characterize the sentiment content of a text unit (sometimes referred to as opinion mining), although the emphasis in this case is on extraction. Obviously, these expressions constitute big data by their volume, velocity, and value, and need a big data platform to process them and advanced analytics tools to analyze them for predictive analytics for effective decision making (discussed in detail in Chapter 8).

Change Management and Business Agility for Social Media

The following *CMO Insights* are from Ryan Bifulco. Ryan is a travel and digital pioneer with over 20 years of experience. An expert on social media and digital marketing, Ryan has been featured on Business Talk Radio, ABC Radio, MediaPost.com, the *New York Times*, and *USA Today*. Ryan founded Sensei Project which offers social media and digital PR amplification to travel and lifestyle brands. He also founded and leads Travel Spike which is the largest travel media platform offering digital advertising to hundreds of travel and tourism clients.

These social media insights emphasize the critical role that relationship management plays in propagating cultural change within the business ecosystem. He observes that use of social media can be hard for companies to embrace fully since it goes against what most companies are used to doing. Traditional thinking says you need to control your own brand and marketing messages. You need to market your products and services to your customers. Since social media actually involves user-generated content it requires customer-centric thinking with less corporate control. The most successful social media marketing programs allow the user to participate and engage rather than trying to market to the user. You need to let go to get ahead with social media marketing.

To truly execute amazing social media programs, your company must take the handcuffs off of the social media team. It does not matter if that is an internal department or an external ad agency. Of course you can have some basic checks and balances built into your process, but for the most part your social media efforts must happen in real time. Social media also requires speed, as most things happen in minutes rather than days. Your company will not have time to debate internally about how to answer Twitter replies or blog comments. You will need to respond instantly and already have your processes laid out before the social media conversations even begin. Users will not wait for your corporation to engage on your time line, and they will not tolerate canned responses. Part of your social media output must be actual conversations without a script. Some of the best social media marketing centers around a personality or individuals at an organization rather than at a faceless corporation. People like to connect with like-minded people, and tapping into that concept can lead to big wins within social networks.

Many companies are risk averse, and that limitation can stifle creativity and innovation. If you can't try new things, then you can't discover new opportunities and applications to incorporate social or digital media into more aspects of your business. Social media should not be pushed only toward the marketing department. It needs to be at least considered enterprise-wide. Human resources (HR) might benefit from LinkedIn. Sales might benefit from more social leads. Customer service might improve if staff can leverage Twitter rather than only using call centers or e-mail. Big data is the hot buzzword now, and certainly social and mobile media are a part of that arena. Your research department or analytics team should be utilizing social data to enhance their inputs.

One solution to help your company be more agile and more ready to embrace social media is to form a social media task force. This team can help with change management and keep your organization updated with changes. The team should consist of staff from various levels and departments.

Ryan offers the following case study of social media best practices that describes how Accor Hotels use digital relationship channels to engage their customer community.

Goals

Accor Hotels uses Twitter to connect with its global community; inspire travelers about destinations and hotels around the world; invite them to share information; provide timely responses to comments, inquiries, requests, and concerns; as well as help people book their travel. In this way, Accor goes beyond being "just" a hotel group and is instead a trusted advisor, expert, insider, and travel companion.

A secondary goal was to expand their reach and engagement with audiences who are not yet familiar with their brands or hotels. Increasing brand awareness ultimately means increasing sales.

Strategy and Tactics

1. Provide valuable content and make it fun
2. Do direct consumer outreach
3. Respond to consumers in a timely manner
4. Recognize their followers for their engagement

Execution

They developed a very organized editorial calendar throughout the year, highlighting a new destination every week (Destination of the Week). Then each day of the week, they tweet around 12 times per day, with each day adhering to a different theme to keep their content fresh and interesting. Throughout the week, they will focus their content around Pictures and Culture (Monday), Talk (Tuesday), Visiting the Destination (Wednesday), Traveling with Accor (Thursday), and General Fun (Friday). They actively solicit advice from their fans about their highlighted destinations and retweet them, making them part of their valuable network of travel experts. They also participate in #TravelTuesday and #FollowFriday, offering location-specific recommendations to their followers so that these experts can guide them.

In addition, Accor sometimes participates in weekly travel chats (#TNI) to position themselves as experts in the field. They regularly engage their followers with weekly small giveaway contests based on the destination. Accor also offers frequent travel deals and will often help customers who respond to them with discounts specific to their intended destination, thus tailoring their experience.

Every day, the brand also fields customer service inquiries, giving advice where needed and coordinating with global customer service teams. Their persona is light, adaptive, and values their followers.

Evaluation: Success, Results, or ROI

In less than 14 months after launching their new animation and engagement strategy, they increased the number of followers by 330 percent. They increased the number of retweets per month by 285 percent. Even more indicative of their raised community awareness is that they multiplied the number of mentions per month by three! Their overall impressions per month have likewise almost tripled.

The following examples (Figures 7.2 to 7.8) depict some notable interactions.

Examples.

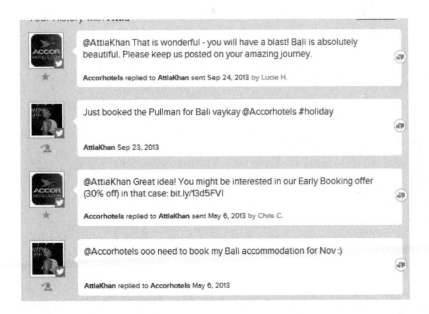

Figure 7.2   Helping a Sale

Figure 7.3   Upselling

Figure 7.4   Recognition to Their Loyal Followers

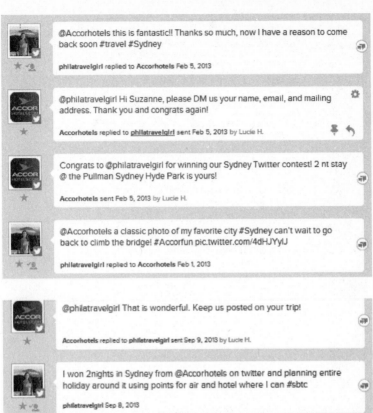

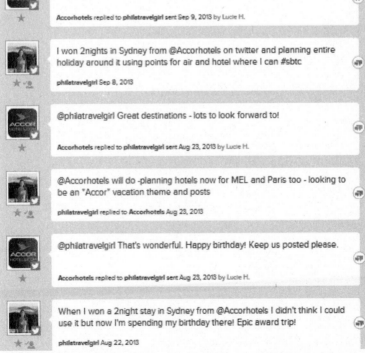

Figure 7.5 Fun Twitter Contests: Being Part of Special Occasions

Figure 7.6   Participating in Twitter Chats

Figure 7.7   Providing Inspiration

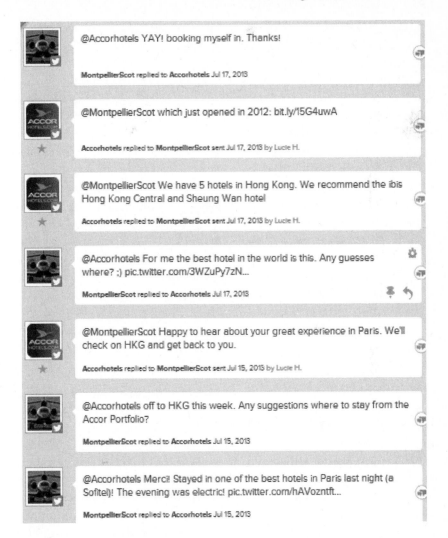

Figure 7.8   Customer Service

Oilstop: Using Big Data to Drive More Intimate Customer Relationships, and Social Media to Enhance Community

Additional CMO insights are contributed by Ross Halleck, CEO of Halleck, Inc. Branding and Marketing, founder of Halleck Vineyard, and one of *BtoB* magazine's Top 100 Most Influential Internet

Marketers. His insights focus on how CMOs may leverage their understanding of these converging technologies to better communicate with their customers through the media they prefer, engage prospective customers through common interests, and utilize information to build stronger, more personal, and more lasting relationships. A great example is his story about the customer engagement strategy initiated by Oilstop.

There probably isn't a more mundane business than performing oil changes and routine maintenance services on motor vehicles. The environment is replete with quick service, no-brainer options for addressing that red light when it pops on in your car, or when you notice your odometer is higher than you expected.

So it was our challenge to identify and execute marketing tactics to increase car count in this regional oil change chain.

Oilstop has been serving guests in the western United States since 1978, beginning with a modest independent car wash in Medford, Oregon. In 1984, an oil change shop was added and the organization has been expanding ever since, establishing presences in southern Oregon; Sonoma County, Central Valley, the South Bay Area, and southern California; and Tucson/Santa Fe.

Currently, Oilstop has 22 stores, both independent franchises and corporate-owned. All share a technology platform, allowing seamless data collection and exchange. This enables deep knowledge of the buying patterns of their guests, as well as a complete history of all maintenance performed based on license plate number. Further, mileage is tracked during each visit, alerting Oilstop of required and recommended maintenance. By presenting this information at each visit, the customer experience is enhanced to a co-creative relationship: no pressure is applied by Oilstop, so customers can make informed decisions about the maintenance of their vehicles. The big data in Oilstop's case is employed to build trust for a more intimate relationship with its guests.

Oilstop's Business Strategy

The Oilstop brand is built on service, hospitality, and honesty. These values pervade every aspect of the organization and extend to every guest, encouraging confidence in their vehicles and trust in Oilstop. By serving guests with integrity, Oilstop is confident that guests will recognize this, return, and refer others.

For people who care about their cars and their community and appreciate being treated with kindness and respect, Oilstop is a service provider that can be trusted. It is *only* by serving the needs of its guests that it will succeed. The company strives to keep the cars of guests running well and for each guest to leave with a smile of confidence. The team is the best trained and the most honorable in the business. Their guests are the best treated and most loyal. So by increasing car count, Oilstop knows that it can achieve overall growth in the long term.

Tactical Game Plan

Although it was clear that social media was becoming pervasive, its use for communicating about car maintenance issues was unclear. Building community around a commodity service such as oil changes seemed counterintuitive; but with Oilstop customers aging, attracting a new generation was critical to ultimate viability for the organization.

All market research was pointing to rapid adoption of social media across *all* demographic sectors. Four questions were to be answered:

1. Which are most relevant?
2. How to best employ them for greatest return on investment?
3. How to employ appropriate social media, yet not dilute or compromise the integrity of the brand?
4. How to best deploy social media to increase car count?

Challenges and Opportunities

Founded on the universal values of kindness, respect, and integrity, the Oilstop philosophy of service is inspirational to guests and employees alike. As a cascading effect of these values, Oilstop was identified by Chevron as among its top retail channels in the United States. Chevron offered to support the company's growth through investment.

Further, the company supported a culture of philanthropy that was deep-set and shared with guests. This seemed like an opportunity on several levels. By extending the reach through social media, Oilstop could engage more participation in its philanthropic efforts. Getting the word out would have a halo effect on the brand, while not intentionally crowing about Oilstop's good work. We hoped to get the community talking about Oilstop. Further, Oilstop could more greatly benefit local charities, rather than the primarily international work that the company was doing, by including the local community to recommend worthy beneficiaries. We were aware that we could seed the conversation, but would not control it.

As a basis for any marketing outreach, Oilstop maintains contact information for more than 80,000 customers/guests, including e-mails, phone numbers, and home addresses. In effect, the company knew who its customers were and where they lived, and could reach them. Being data-centric, Oilstop captures every car and logs its entire service history from the first visit by license plate number. This is attached to the contact information. To make use of this big data, Oilstop has a fully engaged marketing team employing direct mail, advertising (TV, newspaper, radio, Yelp), and e-mail.

Solution

The world of social media not only is dynamic by channel, but channels are multiplying exponentially. Facebook is taking on the characteristics of a large multicultural nation, while across the country and the world new channels are rising to "darling" status. Pinterest, Google+, Twitter, Foursquare, and scores of others are yo-yoing like a "Top 10" chart.

In attempting to determine a productive route, it was apparent that all effort would serve as ongoing research. This view would allow adjustment in approach based on results, rather than making investments on intuition, belief, or information from others.

We began by conducting primary qualitative research in a key market by audience segment to determine drivers of choice and media of preference in selecting oil change service providers. This included recruitment by profile and a series of in-depth focus groups.

Results from this work informed a deeper understanding of our target guests.

Design: Social Graph of Trading Partners and Social Networks

With this greater knowledge, we developed a request for proposal for social media agencies in the region. We identified a selection of providers to Oilstop collected from sales calls made over the course of 24 months. We also researched local agencies online.

In qualifying the agencies, we were consistently bombarded with success stories employing a broad selection of social media, reinforcing each other. We realized that we did not know enough about each of the channels to make informed decisions about a media mix.

We had a preexisting directory relationship with Yelp. This was almost created for us by the social engagement of past guests. We decided to engage more proactively by updating our profiles, linking our profiles to a coupon on the Oilstop website, and exploring a modest advertising relationship to disable other advertisers from a presence on our Yelp listing.

Plan: Gap Analysis to Select Best Partner

We reviewed proposals from the social media agencies that responded to determine the best fit of capabilities to address our issues.

Most social agencies had no orientation to return on investment (ROI), believing social media critical just because of its rising popularity. We were not so inclined. But ROI metrics were not clear in any case, despite some claims to the contrary.

Many of the client companies of these agencies were embarking into social media out of fear of being left behind, reinforcing the lack of necessity by social agencies to be accountable. Many jargon terms were bandied about by all the agencies, heightening confusion and fear. This reinforced our desire for ROI metrics.

Oilstop interviewed all candidates. Then we interviewed all references with a standardized list of questions. Based on this information, one agency rose to the top. Oilstop engaged that organization and worked closely to familiarize the members of the account team with the philosophy and voice of the company.

Despite contrary counsel to employ multiple media simultaneously, Oilstop elected to focus on Facebook, as it was clearly the 800-pound gorilla. Any learning could be extended to other media if we achieved desired results.

Build: Digital Business Social Media Management System

Oilstop reviewed and monitored everything that was posted by both agency and public participants for the first months, guiding agency responses until achieving confidence in the agency to communicate accurately and effectively for Oilstop.

Oilstop coached the agency when the voice did not match corporate culture.

We attempted various tactics to achieve return on investment. While Likes and engagement were tracked weekly, these were only indicators of exposure, not metrics of success.

It was determined at the outset that the tactic of "buying Likes and friends" was not aligned with the values of Oilstop. All Facebook Likes and support would need to be organic. So we began with all Oilstop employees and encouraged their participation and outreach.

Based on agency recommendations, Oilstop offered coupons on its primary website and on Facebook to incite visits to the shops. To increase exposure, we employed retargeting advertising to further increase downloads of coupons. This, in effect, follows someone who has clicked on the Oilstop website or Facebook page and displays an ad somewhere along their path to remind them of their interest and incite a coupon download. This ad could show up on any other site the person visits.

Every week, Oilstop tracked Likes, engagement (posts), click-throughs, and coupon redemption by sources (bar codes were included on every online coupon).

Lessons Learned

Social media is very complex, requiring careful and strategic engagement. It demands consistent and persistent presence and monitoring to get the most out of it, but also to defend against unintended consequences. Social media puts you upfront and personal with your public in ways that can hurt as much as help.

It demands authenticity of voice and intention. Unethical or deceptive tactics can be very self-destructive. Further, like any media, social is highly impacted by creativity with both images and messaging to engage an overcommunicated audience.

With recruitment ads, for instance, we found that by simply swapping out an image, without changing the copy at all, we could impact response rates by a significant percentage. We could garner engagement with the posting of interesting or provocative photographs and comments.

We also learned that social activism compels engagement. Local philanthropy is most effective, but any demonstration of giving is rewarded with loyalty.

But at the end of the day, money talks: Coupons and incentives were highly effective in enticing engagement and increasing car count. No surprise here, but what was surprising was the lack of emphasis those early social media companies placed on this tried-and-proven tactic. Coupons, coupled with retargeting advertising and website integration, allowed us to achieve ROI.

But the ROI did not cover the costs of the agency. This compelled us to ask the agency to coach us for its departure. We ultimately released the agency and brought in individual contributors to perform the most valuable tasks and services. These included weekly posting, creative development and experimentation, retargeting, and monitoring.

So despite its meteoric rise to significance, social is just another medium. Regardless of the biases of all agencies and pundits, we learned that social is effective only if it is an extension of overall marketing strategy and plan, incorporating all relevant media and data. The data are critical and are primarily achieved in actual customer interactions.

Social media is no magic bullet. It simply extends the options and complexity for effective communication. It cannot be ignored or overlooked, but it also must not be overemphasized. It takes a great deal of time to work it.

Like an element in a marketing mix, it needs to be funded in accordance to its benefits.

Next Steps

Oilstop intends to extend and deepen its engagement with philanthropy locally. It intends to continue to leverage its big data and social media more fully to deepen guest relationships and make them even more sticky.

The company will be providing every guest with a tablet computer to use in their car while having the car serviced. Accessible on the tablets will be:

- Service history of the car
- Complete information about all services being offered and administered
- Videos explaining the services being performed
- Access to the guest's Pandora station
- Information about charities being supported
- Customer loyalty program

- Web and e-mail
- Customer satisfaction survey

We learned that younger guests listen to Pandora over 20 hours per week and that 97 percent do not subscribe, so listen to advertising. From our own primary research, we determined that they enjoy humorous ads. Oilstop will blend music with humor in all communications.

Oilstop is engaging with Pandora to develop a highly targeted video, audio, and static visual campaign. One of the marvels of big data is that Pandora guarantees impressions because it knows when people are looking at the screen by actions of their devices. It knows the demographics of each and every Pandora user as well as the geography of the device based on GPS location. This makes advertising on this sophisticated network very compelling. We will be able to measure results.

Oilstop is building a partner network of automotive service providers in each area that share the same values of quality, service, integrity, and humility. The company intends to meet regularly with these groups to share learning, exchange referrals, and build community and trust. Data will be shared across partners.

Oilstop is beginning a customer loyalty and referral program based on its capacity for big data. The company will provide e-mails to people to share with friends with offers off their first oil service. This will be tracked to the originating guest with benefits derived from successful referrals.

Oilstop will continue to track metrics, integrating social and other media, based on market, demographics, big data, and objectives.

The ongoing operative word will be to adapt, adapt, adapt.

In the next chapter, we will try to uncover the secrets, hype, new concepts, and predictive analytics capabilities emerging out of big data. Harnessing collective intelligence with all data sources available to business today provides unparalleled intelligence and predictability about the business. Big data tools and real-time in-memory processing capabilities can be leveraged and exploited to reap greater benefits. It is also said that we need to see the future of the business with reference of current data combined with a rearview mirror of historical data to drive business agility for sustainable competitive advantage.

CHAPTER 8

Role of Collective Intelligence

By now, you may have started receiving the notification e-mails or letters from your utility company regarding your usage and how you may save if you run your laundry or dishwasher after a certain time in the evening during off-peak hours. You may also have come across an advertisement by Progressive Casualty and Insurance Company regarding Snapshot—a sensor that will capture driving patterns of a good driver—and how you may be rewarded with a good driver discount, saving a lot on your policy premium. You shouldn't be surprised to see promotional offers from your favorite retailers on specific merchandise that you care about or frequently shop for based on your buying interests. Have you ever paused and thought about how these vendors or service providers are able to analyze and communicate to you directly to suit your interests and needs? These smart meters used by utility companies, sensor devices used by insurance companies, and web logs analyzed by retailers enable them to capture data at the point of occurrence in real time, store and analyze data to help them understand the behavioral patterns, and guide them as to trends. These data are high in volume, get generated at high velocity, come in a wide variety, and are therefore rightly termed big data.

We are faced with challenges to make decisions every day; some are minor such as paying bills, and some are major such as buying a house, investing in stocks, developing a product, acquiring a company, or growing market share; those major decisions need some relevant information in that context. When we look back many years to when there were no computers or ready access to data, we wonder how people made these major decisions in day-to-day life, businesses, or even administering nations.

In ancient times, rulers based their real-time decision capabilities on intuitive and cognitive intelligence and advice by their council of ministers. They used to visit the street in disguise to gather conversations of citizens in order to get real-time feedback and sentiments to execute effective decisions. In those days, there was no support from technology, and all decisions were based on intuitive judgment. Our brains take in massive streams of sensory data and make the necessary correlations that allow us to make value judgments and decisions, all in real time.

Relating the preceding to our current era, we are given the support of computing power with additional memory and data processing, all on demand when we need it and in the cloud infrastructure (discussed in Chapter 3) to make real-time decisions. Recent technology such as big data analytics helps and supports us with the right information; real-time event messaging provides it at the right time, mobility at the right place anywhere, and social media in the right context to make the right decisions. With computing power and cognitive intelligence, we are in a much better situation to make real-time decisions in the business context.

Big data is a major revolution of the current times and will have a large impact on advanced analytics in the coming years. Big data is becoming relevant in all business cases, and it will help in gaining sustainable competitive advantage. As the technology platform is maturing rapidly, organizations need to give strategic importance to big data sources to gain insights and to offer their products and services based on customer needs. Analytics and business intelligence (BI) based on new big data sources will help business decision makers with greater predictability.

This chapter deals with big data concepts, background, and relevance across industry sectors, and offers some case studies to provide in-depth understanding and many examples of how an organization may deploy and implement big data analytics alongside its existing infrastructure.

Why Should You Care about Big Data?

Big data, one of the most talked-about information technology (IT) solutions, has emerged as a new technology paradigm to create business agility and predictability by analyzing data coming from various sources. The term *big data* was coined in the 1970s and was used to describe large amounts of data generated by oceanography and meteorological experiments. Big data can be understood as a natural evolution of database management techniques that has changed the way data is analyzed. Early implementations of big data solutions can be found during the 1980s—the era of the first generation of software-based parallel database architecture. However, it was not implemented significantly until the maturity of Internet usage, when web search companies faced the challenges of indexing and querying large aggregations of loosely structured data. Existing database technology was not ideal for the challenging task, and neither was it cost effective. Google developed the first wave of big data tools in the early 2000s, which gave birth to several other frameworks and techniques that make the handling, processing, and interpretation of large data sets more economical. By leveraging big data, companies can extract value and meaningful insights from voluminous data beyond what was previously possible using traditional analytical techniques. This also deals with new phenomena of the volume, velocity, and variability of massive data coming from social media, web logs, and sensors combined with transactional systems. Within these heaps of massive data, we have a treasure trove of information that can be extracted to save us from major disasters or accidents and proactively help the growth of businesses.

Big data is characterized primarily by large and rapidly growing data volumes, varied data structures, and new or newly intensified data analysis requirements. This enables us to deliver our customers in context the right offer, message, recommendation, service, or action, tailored and personalized to deliver unequaled value. With a multichannel customer experience platform for true cross-channel decisions that enables consistent operational decisions for the web channel, in the contact center, at the point of sale, and across all lines of business, we have the technology solutions for cross-channel learning and decisions. The automatic insights derived from one channel are seamlessly used both within and across other channels.

A balanced decision management framework that combines both business rules and self-learning predictive models helps in real-time decisions. This also helps in arbitrating rules and predictive model scores in the context of organizational goals/key performance indicators (KPIs) at the moment of a decision's execution.

Executive Insights
Javier Cabrerizo, Vice President, Big Data, Exadata, and Database, Oracle

When one looks back at how businesses were run not so long ago, and compares that with the way they are run today, one of the most striking things to observe is the evolution of how decisions are made inside organizations. One can claim that we have moved from a judgment-based management to a fact-based management model. In other words, today almost every company has a solution to manage its data in a more or less efficient way. This applies to financial data, customers' data, supply chain data, and so on. What has happened is that the bar is higher now for any company that wants to compete in any industry. Companies need to react fast, and in order to do so, they need to be capable of knowing the details of their business performance very rapidly. This triggered a massive adoption of IT in the past 30 years that transformed many industries.

Systems that created the data were the customer relationship management (CRM), enterprise resource planning (ERP), and supply chain management (SCM) systems, and the systems that analyzed the data were the data warehousing (DW) systems.

The parallel to these days is that new systems like web logs, sensors, and networks are generating new data, and we need new systems to be able to analyze and process that data. This is the origin of the big data movement.

Executive Bio: Javier Cabrerizo is responsible for growing Oracle's global business of big data, exadata, and database products.

With the evolution of social media, we started seeing the emergence of nontraditional, less structured data such as web logs, social media feeds, e-mail, sensors, photographs, and YouTube videos that can be analyzed for useful information. With the reduction of cost in both storage and computing power, it is now feasible to store and analyze this data for meaningful purposes. As a result, it is important for existing businesses and for new businesses to understand and evaluate the relevance of big data for their business intelligence and for decision making. Closed-loop real-time learning becomes immediately available for the next prediction to drive adaptive, high-value interactions. We may be able to discover and highlight important correlations in the data automatically by way of user-friendly reports. Automated data discovery leads user to the right and relevant business insights.

Executive Insights
Javier Cabrerizo, Vice President, Big Data, Exadata, and Database, Oracle

What is different in the way data is generated today? Essentially two things: the volume and the velocity. As technology evolves and more interactions move to the digital world, more volume of data is generated all the time. Think of the growth of the e-commerce, e-health, sensor-based monitoring activities, real-time location activities, real-time seismic activities, and real-time network usage. All these interactions are generating constant data flows that are very large in volume and have a high velocity. Maybe companies need to get ready to manage data volumes in the range of petabytes and consider it normal.

What is different in the way data is analyzed? Because of the two characteristics of the data just mentioned, the economics of analytics have changed. New models are needed that can process the vast volumes of data being generated in a cost-effective and scalable manner. This has opened the gates to a very important flow of innovative technologies in the open source community, running in low-cost commodity hardware like MapReduce, column-oriented data stores, and coprocessors.

So, as we have seen in the past, companies competing in any industry see that the bar is rising again. In order to be competitive they have to once again increase their ability to process and analyze new, larger volumes of data.

Big data addresses all types of data coming from various data sources, such as enterprise applications data that generally includes data generated from enterprise resource planning (ERP) systems, customer information from customer relationship management (CRM) systems, supply chain management systems, e-commerce transactions, and human resources (HR) and payroll transactions. It also attributes semantic data that comprise call details records (CDRs) from call centers, web logs, smart meters, manufacturing sensors, equipment logs, and trading systems data generated by machine and computer systems. Social media data that include customer feedback streams, microblogging sites like Twitter, and social media platforms like Facebook add up to big data and help in sentiment analysis.

There are four key characteristics—*volume, velocity, variety*, and *value*—that are commonly used to characterize different aspects of big data and are widely referred to in major conferences. The McKinsey Global Institute estimates that data volume is growing 40 percent per year, and will grow 44 times by 2020.

Executive Insights
Javier Cabrerizo, Vice President, Big Data, Exadata, and Database, Oracle

Importantly, business decisions need reliable systems. And reliable systems need reliable companies supporting them. Some early adopters of big data technologies, like online predictive analytics for the retail or airline industry, or risk management solutions in financial services, are expecting their vendors of choice to bring them these solutions. And they are asking them to provide the support levels that they are used to with other systems they are using to run their businesses.

So the conclusions are clear. Any company, in any industry, is going to be affected by this tide of more data generated rapidly. Those that are capable of efficiently processing it and finding insightful and actionable business conclusions will enjoy an advantage over their peers. Companies should be looking at data streams that they generate and thinking of efficient ways to store and analyze the data. Examples are:

- Web logs that can contain valuable information about customer trends
- Credit card usage patterns that can help identify and prevent fraud
- Real-time analysis of infrastructure equipment like oil rigs that can help optimize operations
- Real-time monitoring of health care information that can enable rapid intervention and prevent criminal activity

What Do Key Characteristics Signal about Big Data?

Big data is characterized by its sheer large volume, high velocity, and variety with low value. All major sources such as web logs, sensors, and social media generate new types of unstructured or semi-structured data that has given rise to a new phenomenon in decision making.

Volume

Social media (Facebook, Twitter, LinkedIn, Foursquare, YouTube, and many more) discussed in Chapter 7 generate a large volume of data that need to be stored and analyzed rapidly in context for the right decision making. The volume of machine-generated data or semantic web data is much larger than the traditional data volume. For instance, a single jet engine can generate 10 TB (terabytes) of data in 30 minutes. With more than 25,000 airline flights per day, the daily volume of just this single data source runs into the petabytes. Smart meters and heavy industrial equipment like oil refineries and drilling rigs generate similar data volumes, compounding the problem. The benefit gained from the ability to process large amounts of information is the main attraction of big data analytics. This volume presents the most immediate challenge to conventional IT structures. It requires scalable storage and a distributed approach to querying.

Velocity

The data comes into the data management system rapidly and often requires quick analysis for decision making. The importance lies in the speed of the feedback loop, taking data from input through to analysis and decision making. The tighter the feedback loop, the greater will be the competitive advantage. It's this need for speed, particularly on the web, that has driven the development of key-value stores and columnar databases, optimized for the fast retrieval of precomputed information. These databases form part of an umbrella category known as NoSQL (not only SQL) used when relational models do not suffice (discussed in detail in the technology platforms section later in this chapter). Social media data streams bring a large input of opinions and relationships that are valuable to customer relationship management. Even at 140 characters per tweet, the high velocity of Twitter data ensures large volumes (over 8 TB per day).

Most of these data received may be of low value, and analytical processing may be required in order to transform the data into a usable form or derive meaningful information.

Variety

Big data brings variety of data types. It varies from text from social networks, to image or video data, to a raw feed directly from a sensor source, to semantic web logs generated by machines. These data are not easily integrated in any applications. A common use of big data processing is to take unstructured data and extract meaningful information for consumption either by humans or as a structured input to an application. Big data brings a lot of data that has patterns, sentiments, and behavioral information that need analysis.

Value

The economic value of different data varies significantly. Generally, there is good information hidden within a larger body of non-traditional data. Big data offers greater value to businesses in bringing real-time market and customer insights, enabling improvement in new products and services. Big data analytics can reveal insights such as peer influence among customers, revealed by analyzing shoppers' transactions and social and geographical data. The past decade's successful web start-ups are prime examples of big data used as an enabler of new products and services. For example, by combining a large number of signals from a user's actions and those of the user's friends, Facebook has been able to craft a highly personalized user experience and create a new kind of advertising business.

Does Size of Data Really Matter?

With the proliferation of cloud computing and commoditization of hardware, software, and storage, the growth in data has been explosive in the recent past. This exponential growth is primarily catalyzed by increased activity by digital devices and proliferation of the Internet. Massive volumes of data are generated by digital transactions between companies, machine-generated data (embedded sensors in industrial applications and automobiles), and consumer devices such as laptops, computers, and smartphones. The International Data Corporation (IDC) estimated that 1.8 zettabytes of information were created and replicated in 2011, the equivalent of 200 billion 60-minute high-definition (HD) movies that would take one person 47 million years to watch.

In the past decade, information generated grew at a 38 percent compound annual growth rate (CAGR) versus the world's storage capacity at a 23 percent CAGR. We believe the gap between information and storage will continue to widen, given increased growth in computational power (58 percent 10-year CAGR) as a result of computers, smartphones, and smart sensors that will drive information generation.

With storage on the cloud infrastructure getting cheaper and more affordable, businesses should be able to take advantage of mixing various data types coming from different data sources and analyze them to make effective decisions to manage their enterprises.

How Complex Is Big Data?

Data has traditionally been stored in a structured format, which makes archiving, querying, and analyzing easier. However, with wide usage of various devices, data has become more unstructured. It is estimated that 80 percent of the world's data is unstructured (i.e., unable to conform to traditional relational database structures), which makes analysis and insights on multiple data sets very challenging. Given the pervasiveness of unstructured data, the growth in file-based storage (unstructured data) has outpaced block-based storage (62 percent five-year CAGR versus 24 percent). The sudden rise and usage of social media, machine-generated data, and smart devices has added complexities in managing big data and deriving greater business value from them. These data have emerged recently that may provide greater intelligence and predictability if we can capture, process, and analyze the data in real time or near real time.

- *Social media.* Increased usage of social networking sites continues to drive storage requirements for unstructured data: More than 300 million photos are uploaded daily to Facebook; Zynga processes 1 petabyte of gaming content on a daily basis; 72 hours of video are uploaded to YouTube every minute; and Twitter receives nearly 250 million tweets daily.

- *Machine-to-machine (M2M).* The increased deployment of M2M devices such as smart meters, telematics, radio frequency identification (RFID) devices, vehicle sensors, and industrial sensors with embedded networking has driven machine-generated data. Data generated from M2M devices is expected to grow at a 35 percent compound annual growth rate (CAGR) by 2015. According to research findings, M2M will create an economic impact of $2.7 trillion to $6.2 trillion annually by 2025. And the World Bank and General Electric are pointing to a $32 trillion opportunity on the premise that a 1 percent improvement from the integration of the industrial Internet into energy, transportation, health care, aviation, and other industries can generate savings of around $200 billion, according to the McKinsey Global Institute (www.netcommwireless .com/information/articles/m2m.-the-numbers-are-big-and-only-getting-bigger).

- *Mobility.* The widespread adoption of mobile devices (smartphones, tablets, etc.) has placed the power of the Internet within the reach of a fingertip. The number of global smartphone users recently crossed the 1 billion mark (i.e., one in seven people owns a smartphone), thus driving the consumption, demand, and generation of mobile data. Mobile data traffic is estimated to grow at a 78 percent CAGR from 2011 to 2016, reaching 10.8 exabytes per month by 2016, according to Cisco.

- *Enterprise data.* Adoption of enterprise software solutions and greater IT sophistication has increased the data exhaust generated by enterprise firms. Unstructured data continues to garner a greater proportion of enterprise data and is expected to represent 80 percent of total enterprise data by 2015, up from 64 percent in 2006. The torrent of unstructured enterprise data places an additional strain on corporate IT systems. In a survey conducted by Avanade, a business technology consulting and solutions provider, 55 percent of respondents reported a slowdown of IT systems and 47 percent cited data security issues resulting from increased data exhaust (www.netcommwireless.com/information/articles/m2m.-the-numbers-are-big-and-only-getting-bigger).

Executive Insights
Jnan R. Dash, Former Executive at Oracle and IBM

The most fundamental technologies are those that disappear. They weave themselves into the fabric of everyday life until they are indistinguishable from it. This is pervasive computing we are witnessing today. With the explosion of devices, the computing has become pervasive. Today's cars are computers on wheels, and airplanes are computers with wings. The rapid growth of Android and iPhone applications brings the power to the mainstream like never before.

Three major forces have come together causing rapid disruption to businesses all around the world. They are: (1) cloud computing (finally we are seeing computing as a utility much like what we saw in the electric power, water distribution, and telecommunication industries), (2) smart devices, and (3) big data. As the devices proliferate, a data explosion is happening. No longer can we claim a 100 TB database as big; now we are seeing the petabyte and exabyte scale. Big data will transform business in the same scale or more just like what IT did to business many decades back. The data deluge came to the world of science long before it is coming to the commercial business world. Therefore, the late Jim Gray (Microsoft Research) called this the fourth paradigm in science (experimental science, theoretical science, and computational science were the first three)—data-intensive science (DIS). The total amount of data in the planet is around 1.27 ZB (1 zettabyte = 1 billion terabytes) and is supposed to grow to 35 ZB by 2020!

Executive Bio: Jnan Dash has worked as senior executive and IBM and Oracle and currently engaged as adviser and board member at many companies like MongoDB, ScaleDB, MobiDough, Graymatics, and Sonata Software.

With the evolution of the cloud deployment model, the majority of big data solutions are offered as software only, an appliance, or cloud-based offerings. As is the case with other applications deployments, big data deployment will also depend on several issues such as data locality, privacy and regulation, human resources, and project requirements. Many organizations are opting for a hybrid solution using on-demand cloud resources to supplement in-house deployments.

The highest value from big data can be achieved by combining data coming from big data sources such as web logs, machine data, and social media data with other transactional data within businesses.

Decision makers get the big picture of their customers' behavior, patterns, and preferences over the others.

Therefore, it is highly important that businesses combine their strategy on big data with their comprehensive data analytics strategy. In order to succeed and remain competitive, organizations need to plan for comprehensive data management and analytics.

How Does Big Data Coexist with Existing Traditional Data?

Big data on its own offers great insights for businesses, but it becomes more powerful when it is combined with an organization's existing transactional data and used for analytics.

Web logs or browsing history for example indicates the customer's buying patterns and helps to determine the value of a customer from his or her purchase history in the past.

How Does Target Know?

Knowing someone is pregnant lies in the data-gathering process. To start, Target assigns each customer a Guest ID number. This ID number is then attached to the customer's known credit cards, full name, and e-mail address. By doing this, Target is then able to store and build out a historical time line of purchases by that customer. By analyzing and reviewing the historical buying data of shoppers who were part of the Target Baby Registry, Target was then able to discover patterns in shopper behavior. For example, many shoppers purchase soap and cotton balls, but when someone suddenly starts buying lots of scent-free soap and extra-big bags of cotton balls, in addition to hand sanitizers and washcloths, it signals they could be getting close to their delivery date.

Target uses data as a way to predict consumer behaviors so that it can market products most relevant to an individual shopper. As a result of Target cornering the expected mothers market, the *New York Times* "suggests that Target's gangbusters revenue growth—$44 billion in 2002 . . . to $67 billion in 2010" can be attributed to its better understanding of consumers using big data analytics.

On a similar note, utility companies have started using smart grid data to track their consumers' behavior. Knowing the historical billing patterns of consumers combined with their transactional data from frequent smart meter data makes the analysis even more powerful in a business context.

TXU Energy: Smart Electric Meters

Smart grid deployments are creating exponentially more data for utilities and giving them access to information they've never had before. Accessing, analyzing, managing, and delivering this information to optimize business operations and enhance customer relationships is helping them to extract optimal business value from this data to better target, engage with, and serve customers.

With the help of smart meters, electricity providers can read the meter once every 15 minutes rather than once a month. This not only eliminates the need to send someone for meter reading, but as the meter is read once every 15 minutes, electricity can be priced differently for peak and off-peak hours. Pricing can be used to shape the demand curve during peak hours, eliminating the need to create additional generating capacity just to meet peak demand, saving electricity providers millions of dollars' worth of investment in generating capacity and plant maintenance costs.

TXU Energy is using the smart meter technology to shape the demand curve by offering "Free electricity. All Night. Every Night. All Year Long" (for more, see https://www.txu.com/residential/promotions/mass/free-nights. aspx). In fact, TXU promotes its service as "Do your laundry or run the dishwasher at night, and pay nothing for your Energy Charges." What TXU Energy is trying to do here is to reshape energy demand using pricing so as to manage peak-time demand, resulting in savings for both TXU and customers. This wouldn't have been possible without smart electric meters.

Big data is messy and requires enormous effort in data cleansing and data quality. The phenomenon of big data is closely tied to the emergence of data science, a discipline that combines math, programming, and scientific instinct. Current data warehousing projects take a long time to offer meaningful analytics to business users.

It depends on extract, transform, and load (ETL) processes from various data sources. Big data analytics, however, can be defined as a process in relationship to or in context to the need to parse large data sets from multiple sources, and to produce information in real time or near real time.

Progressive Snapshot: Auto Sensors in Insurance

Traditionally, insurance companies have priced auto insurance based on a driver's history and have given good drivers a discount on policy premiums. Taking early advantage, Progressive Casualty and Insurance Company has introduced a sensor-based Snapshot to track vehicle condition and driving history to help reduce premiums for good drivers and penalize not-so-good drivers with higher premiums. Now with Snapshot, a revolutionary usage-based insurance program, good drivers are offered savings on their auto insurance.

The Snapshot device plugs easily into a car's diagnostic port (usually below the steering column) and automatically keeps track of good driving. The program offers 30 days' free trial to check projected savings online based on driving patterns (e.g., how often you slam on the brakes, how many miles you drive, and how often you drive between midnight and 4 A.M.).

Source: www.examiner.com/article/snapshot-by-progressive-what-is-it-does-it-work.

Big data analytics represents a big opportunity. Many large businesses are exploring the analytics capabilities to parse web-based data sources and extract value from social media. However, an even larger opportunity, the Internet of Things (IoT), is emerging as a data source. Cisco Systems estimates that there are approximately 35 billion electronic devices that can connect to the Internet. Any electronic device can be connected to the Internet, and even auto-makers are building Internet connectivity into vehicles. Connected cars will become commonplace by 2014 and generate millions of transient data streams.

Operational efficiencies, coupled with developments in the technologies and services that make big data a practical reality, will result in a supercharged CAGR of 58 percent between now and 2017.

Big data is the new definitive source of competitive advantage across all industries.

Executive Insights
Ramasubramanian Vaidyanathaswamy,
Senior Practice Director, Business Intelligence
and Analytics, Wipro

Corporations big and small have already invested heavily in business intelligence (BI)/analytics initiatives for the past several years. As we look at how companies are considering adoption of big data technology to bring forth newer insights into decision making, we could place them into one of three categories: early adopters, explorers, and aspirants. In our experience, there is none in the fourth category of "uninterested or do not need."

The early adopters have already gotten big data infrastructure setups, added horizontal capabilities of acquiring unstructured/semi-structured data into the realm of analytics, and embarked on the journey of building business algorithms iteratively to get insights from this data. Marketing is the earliest adopter of this technology for getting insights, largely in the business-to-consumer (B2C) space of getting to know more about customer buy/postbuy behavior. The striking commonality in all the big data projects has been that they have started with an exploratory mind-set. You begin with a set of hypotheses and iteratively apply statistical algorithms or pattern identification until you get the desired insights. Nearly all the initiatives start as proof of concept (PoC) or proof of value in a sandbox.

The explorer category is really a vast set of corporations that are still at the conceptual stage of exploring: (1) what use cases should be run on big data, (2) where the value lies, and (3) which is the right organization (is it the BI/DW organization or engineering or marketing?) to grow this capability.

As a practitioner in business intelligence for over a decade and having successfully seen large analytics implementation projects through for Fortune 100 clients, I am seeing that the way that BI projects are implemented is fundamentally going to shift with big data adoption. For one, the speed of value in getting big insights is at the speed of the Internet, be it social sentiments or customer feedback on product launch. Most existing BI investments are meant for large-scale data and systems integration to get structured insights and consequently are less agile for this speed. For years, investments have been directed toward data plumbing, data quality, data governance, and data reuse—the expectations from the structured data world. However, unstructured data for decision making still is in its infancy, and speed is clearly the winner against adherence to architectural standards. The ultimate value is really doing large-volume unstructured data processing in the big data world outside of the enterprise data warehouse (EDW) and funneling the insightful data back to the EDW. Both EDW and big data are addressing parts of the same puzzle, and eventually the respective architectures will blend and mutually complement each other in delivering analytic value. Often this question comes up: "What is the right unit in an organization to build big data capabilities?" Most of the big data pilots and PoCs are done by the BI organization itself, even though Java skill sets are not usually resident inside this organization.

As a matter of fact, one of the common technical use cases for big data is in shifting the ETL workloads off high CPU processing databases/appliances to Hadoop, and this trend I believe will increase significantly as big data technique gets mainstream.

Executive Bio: Ramasubramanian Vaidyanathaswamy is an experienced professional engaged in providing consultancy services in the areas of business intelligence, big data, and predictive analytics.

Motorola Solutions: Public Safety

Fast Data Streaming Video Analysis with Big Data

Motorola Solutions collects various unstructured data in the form of video surveillance pictures—images on a regular stream at public places such as airports, parking lots, traffic signals, and the like—and makes it actionable and securely distributes it across mission-critical devices and easy-to-manage networks. It's the technology and expertise that turn noise into information, information into intelligence, and intelligence into safety, thereby actively contributing to building safer communities, cities, counties, and states.

Motorola leverages Oracle event processing (OEP) capability to track incidents based on event triggers such as suspicious vehicle enters airport car park (automatic license plate readers [ALPRs]), driver is loitering in car park (video analytics), driver has a BOLO (be on the lookout) alert (facial recognition), and cross-referencing with database for an alert and action to prevent major incidents.

Source: https://solutions.oracle.com/scwar/sc/Partner/SC2PP-MOTOROLA.html.

Executive Insights
Markus Zirn, Vice President, Splunk

If you are in financial services, telecommunications, or online services, your entire business relies on key applications. In all other industries, including government sectors, key applications are also business-critical. If those applications go down, there are significant ramifications. How well they run and are supported, tested, secured, and adopted by users makes a big difference in whether your enterprise does well. Such applications can be on the web or mobile, and can be offered to customers, partners, or employees. Such business-critical applications can be complex and distributed in their architecture or strung together into larger business processes.

Each business-critical application has a complex machine data footprint. Machine data is the window, the vital signs that tell how well these applications are running. Of course, this machine data footprint includes application logs, error logs, and performance data that support the business-critical application. The reality is that the application's machine data footprint provides invaluable information to keep it up and running, to support it better, to test it more efficiently, to avoid security-related issues, and to better manage service-level agreements, track user behavior, and evaluate its overall effectiveness.

In the competitive business environment, it is critical to harness all the valuable information hidden inside the application's machine data footprint.

Executive Bio: Markus Zirn currently leads all product management for Splunk, a high-growth big data company focused on operational intelligence software. He ran product management for all of Oracle's middleware such as service-oriented architecture (SOA), business process management (BPM), process solutions, complex event processing, and ERP user productivity.

How Big Is the Big Data Market?

The big data market is on the verge of rapid growth to the tune of $50 billion worldwide within the next five years. We already see increased interest in and awareness of the power of big data and related analytic capabilities to gain competitive advantage and to improve business agility.

Of the current market, big data pure-play vendors account for $310 million in revenue. Despite their relatively small percentage of current overall revenue (approximately 5 percent), these vendors such as Vertica, Splunk, and Cloudera are responsible for the vast majority of new innovations and modern approaches to data management and analytics that have emerged over the past several years and made big data the hottest sector in IT.

Executive Insights
Shashi Upadhyay, Founder and CEO, Lattice Engines

We live in a big data world. This shift is setting the stage for numerous advantages for businesses, especially in how they market and sell. Data is pouring in from everywhere—the web, social media, marketing automation, and CRM systems and other third-party sources. But this big data isn't just about the data. It is about the insight that we can draw from it to improve our processes and businesses.

How Businesses Can Learn from Internet Giants

Internet giants have been drawing competitive advantage from the influx of data for more than 10 years. Take Netflix as an example. Netflix tracks unstructured data about viewer preferences and ratings to tee up recommendations for new programs to ensure that its customers have the best experience. The company is also using viewership data to determine the right formula for new content development to produce shows that its customer base can't wait to binge watch. In doing so, Netflix is driving engagement and usage over sustained periods of time.

Amazon is another great example of an Internet giant utilizing insights from big data to provide a better experience for its customers. Amazon tracks what its customers purchase and covet in addition to what's purchased and coveted from different locations. It uses that information to recommend products for future purchases. Consequently, Amazon has been able to produce recommendations that result in closed sales totaling more than $75 million in 2013.

To draw the value from big data and gain a true competitive advantage, companies should try to answer the following questions: Can external data be used in some way? Are structured and unstructured data being analyzed to uncover buyer intent? Is data being used both to analyze past events and to predict future events—such as who will purchase our products and services?

The real key to driving competitive advantage through data is to focus on the predictive and prescriptive qualities of the information and insight that are discovered.

Predictive Analytics in Action

Technology and data are fueling a significant transformation in marketing and sales today. Many successful marketing organizations are using the power of big data to build predictive models and transform their businesses through customer acquisition, retention, and expansion. Amazon and Netflix are leading the charge on the consumer side. Companies like Dell and Citrix are doing it on the B2B side.

Business-to-business (B2B) companies can model their own recommendations after Amazon's engines. The answer is hiding in plain sight in many cases. Oftentimes, companies are using cloud technologies like marketing automation and CRM to store data on customers and prospects. The reality is that these systems hold only about 5 percent of what is knowable about a customer or prospect. Data outside of these systems, like job postings, grants, government contracts, social media, patents, locations, credit rankings, and purchase history, can be incredibly indicative of intent.

How does this translate to the real world? One Lattice Engines customer focused on improving its marketing efforts through big data. Citrix, an enterprise software company, was experiencing a very high lead volume with a low conversion rate. By incorporating big data into its traditional lead scoring approach, the company was able to improve its lead conversion rate by 30 percent. Another customer, Dell, had similar success when implementing predictive analytics to prioritize the best leads for its sales team. By highlighting the leads that were most likely to convert, the marketing organization reduced the number of leads it passed to the sales department by 50 percent, and revenue results increased by nearly double.

Driving Competitive Advantage

With data science, marketing organizations are able to go beyond traditional creative approaches and campaigns to impact revenue growth in a real way. Marketers can use attributes from all the knowable data about their customers and prospects from the web to predict whether someone will buy their product, and use that information to determine which leads are ready for sales engagement and which require additional nurturing. With the help of data science and analytics, marketers can ensure that only the best leads are sent to the sales department, ultimately boosting conversion rates.

Companies can also turn to data science to identify opportunities for growth within their existing customer bases. For most organizations, new customers represent less than 20 percent of total revenue, while existing customers drive the remaining 80 percent. In many cases individual sales representatives do not have the information and tools to be successful at up-selling existing accounts. They tend to gravitate to the content and products with which they are most comfortable. Given the limited capacity of individual sales reps, they must make instinctive bets about which accounts and products to focus on. Many newer products, services, or messaging capabilities get limited attention. By applying data science to information hidden in marketing automation and external cues such as hiring trends, funding announcements, and office openings, companies can pinpoint the customer accounts that are ripe for up-sell and cross-sell opportunities.

Sales professionals can also utilize big data insights to get ahead of the competition. In a sense, big data can democratize the selling excellence by helping all reps get on the same page in answering the question, "How can I find the customers who are most receptive to my product/service at a given time?" The insights gleaned from the data can provide a sixth sense about what is happening and arm sales reps with the right product recommendations and messages to be able to close the sale, just as Amazon does.

Executive Bio: Shashi Upadhyay is the founder and CEO at Lattice Engines, which delivers data-driven business applications to help companies of all sizes sell more intelligently based on data science and predictive big data modeling.

Marketing and sales organizations are ready for the transformation that big data and predictive analytics bring. This approach is making existing businesses smarter and more efficient by focusing the right resources on customers and prospects that are ready to buy—crushing the competition.

How Would You Manage Big Data on Technology Platforms?

The recent cloud-based technologies and cloud operating environment (discussed in detail in Chapter 3) based on a scalable elastic model have allowed support for a new services deployment model that can be consumed globally from anywhere on any device. The cloud platform has enabled big data storage, processing, and analytics as well.

Let us examine big data tools, platforms, and applications that may offer predictive analytics capabilities to enable effective decision making for sustainable competitive advantage.

Big Data Tools, Platforms, and Applications

Cloud-based applications and services are increasingly allowing small and midsize business to take advantage of big data without needing to deploy on-premises hardware or software. Manufacturing companies deploy sensors in their products to return a stream of telemetry. The proliferation of smartphones and other global positioning system (GPS) devices offers advertisers an opportunity to target consumers when they are in close proximity to a store, coffee shop, or restaurant. This opens up new revenue for service providers and offers many businesses a chance to target new customers.

Use of social media and web log files from their e-commerce sites can help retailers understand their customers' buying patterns, behaviors, likes, and dislikes. This can enable much more effective micro customer segmentation and targeted marketing campaigns, as well as improve supply chain efficiencies.

As with data warehousing, web stores, or any IT platform, an infrastructure for big data has unique requirements. In considering all the components of a big data platform, it is important to easily integrate big data with enterprise data to conduct deep analytics on the combined data set.

In order to make the most meaningful use of big data, businesses must evolve their IT infrastructures to handle the rapid rate of delivery of extreme volumes of data, with varying data types, which can then be integrated with an organization's other enterprise data to be analyzed. When big data is captured, optimized, and analyzed in combination with traditional enterprise data, companies can develop a more thorough and insightful understanding of their business, which can lead to enhanced productivity, a stronger competitive position, and greater innovation to have an impact on the bottom line. For example, in the delivery of health care services, management of chronic or long-term conditions is expensive. Use of in-home monitoring devices to measure vital signs and monitor progress is just one way that sensor data can be used to improve patient health care and reduce both office visits and hospital admittance.

The requirements in a big data infrastructure involve data acquisition, data organization, and data analysis. Because big data refers to data streams of higher velocity and higher variety, the infrastructure required to support the acquisition of big data must deliver low, predictable latency in both capturing data and executing short, simple queries; be able to handle very high transaction volumes, often in a distributed environment; and support flexible, dynamic data structures.

In classic data warehousing terms, organizing data is called data integration. Because there is such a high volume of big data, there is a tendency to organize data at its original storage location, thus saving both time and money by not moving around unnecessarily large volumes of data. The infrastructure required for organizing big data must be able to process and manipulate data in the original storage location; support very high throughput (often in batches) to deal with large data processing steps; and handle a large variety of data formats, from unstructured to structured.

Executive Insights
Harbinder Khera, Founder and CEO, Mindmatrix

Big Data: The Biggest Words in Marketing Today

The future belongs to companies that are able to make big data actionable and use it to build a personal relationship with their prospects. Have you noticed how sensitive marketing has become today? It's all around you. You take out an auto loan; the bank follows up with a quote on auto insurance. You Liked the Pittsburgh Steelers' page on Facebook; the next time you log in you see Facebook advertisements about special deals on Steelers' jerseys. You walked into a store but didn't buy anything, and yet the next day you receive an e-mail with a special discount coupon on the product you browsed yesterday in the store. All of this is courtesy of big data. Big data has become the magic phrase in marketing today. It throws wide open a big door into the prospect's world, allowing businesses to be a part of the customer's and prospect's daily lives, inconspicuously. Thanks to big data, companies no longer have to rely on gut instinct and guesses but are instead able to make well-informed marketing decisions.

Businesses are subtly monitoring every prospect's action. Every download, every click, every form sign-up offers an insight into a prospect's interests. Information is being gathered from social media activities, web searches, point-of-sale systems, online shopping cart checkouts and even in-store (physical presence) activities to draw a complete picture of prospect preferences—in real time. In the B2C sphere, big data offers tremendous scope for cross-selling and up-selling.

Successful companies are the ones that are able to make their big data actionable and use it to build personal relationships with their prospects and clients.

Has Hadoop Solved Big Data Problems?

Apache Hadoop is a new technology that allows large data volumes to be organized and processed while keeping the data on the original data storage cluster. Hadoop Distributed File System (HDFS) is the long-term storage system for web logs. These web logs are turned into browsing behavior (sessions) by running MapReduce programs on the cluster and generating aggregated results on the same cluster. These aggregated results are then loaded into a relational DBMS system. Since data is not always moved during the organization phase, the analysis may also be done in a distributed environment, where some data will stay where it was originally stored and be transparently accessed from a data warehouse. The infrastructure required for analyzing big data must be able to support deeper analytics such as statistical analysis and data mining, on a wider variety of data types stored in diverse systems; scale to extreme data volumes; deliver faster response times driven by changes in behavior; and automate decisions based on analytical models. Most important, the infrastructure must be able to integrate analysis on the combination of big data and traditional enterprise data. New insight comes not just from analyzing new data, but from analyzing it within the context of the old to provide new perspectives on old problems. For example, analyzing inventory data from a smart vending machine in combination with the events calendar for the venue in which the vending machine is located will dictate the optimal product mix and replenishment schedule for the vending machine.

Many new technologies have emerged to address the IT infrastructure requirements just outlined. These new systems have created a divided solutions spectrum comprised of NoSQL solutions that are developer-centric specialized systems and SQL solutions that are typically equated with the manageability, security, and trusted nature of relational database management systems (RDBMSs).

A few niche vendors are developing applications and platforms that leverage the underlying Hadoop infrastructure to provide both data scientists and business users with easy-to-use tools for experimenting with big data. These include Datameer, which has developed a Hadoop-based business intelligence platform with a familiar spreadsheet-like interface; Karmasphere, whose platform allows data scientists to perform ad hoc queries on Hadoop-based data via an SQL interface; and Digital Reasoning, whose Synthesis platform sits on top of Hadoop to analyze text-based communication.

Tresata's cloud-based platform, for example, leverages Hadoop to process and analyze large volumes of financial data and returns results via on-demand visualizations for banks, financial data companies, and other financial services companies.

Additionally, 1010data offers a cloud-based application that allows business users and analysts to manipulate data in the familiar spreadsheet format but at big data scale. And the ClickFox platform mines large volumes of customer touch-point data to map the total customer experience with visuals and analytics delivered on demand.

Non-Hadoop Big Data Platforms.   Other non-Hadoop vendors contributing significant innovation to the big data landscape include Splunk, which specializes in processing and analyzing log file data to allow administrators to monitor IT infrastructure performance and identify bottlenecks and other disruptions to service. HPCC (High-Performance Computing Cluster) Systems, a spin-off of LexisNexis, offers a competing big data framework to Hadoop that its engineers built internally over the past 10 years to assist the company in processing and analyzing large volumes of data for its clients in finance, utilities, and government. DataStax offers a commercial version of the open source Apache Cassandra NoSQL database along with related support services bundled with Hadoop.

NoSQL databases are frequently used to acquire and store big data. They are well suited for dynamic data structures and are highly scalable. The data stored in an NoSQL database is typically of a high variety because the systems are intended to simply capture all data without categorizing and parsing the data. For example, NoSQL databases are often used to collect and store social media data. While customer-facing applications frequently change, underlying storage structures are kept simple.

Instead of designing a schema with relationships between entities, these simple structures often just contain a major key to identify the data point and then a content container holding the relevant data. This simple and dynamic structure allows changes to take place without costly reorganizations at the storage layer.

NoSQL systems are designed to capture all data without categorizing and parsing it upon entry into the system, and therefore the data is highly varied. SQL systems, however, typically place data in well-defined structures and impose metadata on the data captured to ensure consistency and validate data types.

Distributed file systems and transaction (key-value) stores are primarily used to capture data and are generally in line with the requirements discussed earlier in this chapter. To interpret and distill information from the data in these solutions, a programming paradigm called MapReduce is used. MapReduce programs are custom-written programs that run in parallel on the distributed data nodes.

The key-value stores or NoSQL databases are the online transaction processing (OLTP) databases of the big data world; they are optimized for very fast data capture and simple query patterns. NoSQL databases are able to provide very fast performance because the data that is captured is quickly stored with a single identifying key rather than being interpreted and cast into a schema. By doing so, NoSQL database can rapidly store large numbers of transactions.

However, due to the changing nature of the data in the NoSQL database, any data organization effort requires programming to interpret the storage logic used. This, combined with the lack of support for complex query patterns, makes it difficult for end users to distill value out of data in an NoSQL database.

To get the most from NoSQL solutions and turn them from specialized, developer-centric solutions into solutions for the enterprise, they must be combined with SQL solutions into a single proven infrastructure that meets the manageability and security requirements of today's enterprises.

How Does Oracle Address Big Data Challenges?

Oracle's big data strategy is centered on current enterprise data architecture to incorporate big data and deliver business value, leveraging the proven reliability, flexibility, and performance of existing systems to address evolving big data requirements.

Oracle offers engineered and integrated systems to meet the big data challenge by including software and hardware into one engineered system. The Oracle Big Data Appliance is an engineered system that combines optimized hardware with the most comprehensive software stack featuring specialized solutions developed by Oracle to deliver a complete, easy-to-deploy solution for acquiring, organizing, and loading big data into Oracle Database 11*g*. It is designed to deliver extreme analytics on all data types, with enterprise-class performance, availability, supportability, and security. With Big Data Connectors, the solution is tightly integrated with Oracle Exadata and Oracle Database, so you can analyze all your data together with extreme performance.

Oracle Big Data Appliance. Oracle Big Data Appliance comes in a full rack configuration with 18 Sun servers for a total storage capacity of 648 TB. Every server in the rack has two CPUs, each with six cores for a total of 216 cores per full rack. Each server has 48 GB of memory for a total of 864 GB of memory per full rack.

Oracle Big Data Appliance includes a combination of open source software and specialized software developed by Oracle to address enterprise big data requirements.

Big Data Appliance contains Cloudera's Distribution including Apache Hadoop (CDH) and Cloudera Manager. CDH is the leading Apache Hadoop-based distribution in commercial and noncommercial environments. CDH consists of 100 percent open source Apache Hadoop plus the comprehensive set of open source software components needed to use Hadoop. Cloudera Manager is an end-to-end management application for CDH. Cloudera Manager gives a cluster-wide, real-time view of nodes and services running; provides a single, central place to enact configuration changes across the cluster; and incorporates a full range of reporting and diagnostic tools to help optimize cluster performance and utilization.

Where Oracle Big Data Appliance makes it easy for organizations to acquire and organize new types of data, Oracle Big Data Connectors enables an integrated data set for analyzing all data. Oracle Big Data Connectors can be installed on an Oracle Big Data Appliance or on a generic Hadoop cluster.

Oracle Loader for Hadoop (OLH) enables users to use Hadoop MapReduce processing to create optimized data sets for efficient loading and analysis in Oracle Database 11*g*. Unlike other Hadoop loaders, it generates Oracle internal formats to load data faster and use fewer database system resources. OLH is added as the last step in the MapReduce transformations as a separate map–partition–reduce step. This last step uses the CPUs in the Hadoop cluster to format the data into Oracle-understood formats, allowing for a lower CPU load on the Oracle cluster and higher data ingest rates because the data is already formatted for Oracle Database. Once loaded, the data is permanently available in the database, providing very fast access to this data for general database users leveraging SQL or business intelligence tools.

Oracle Direct Connector for Hadoop Distributed File System (HDFS) is a high-speed connector for accessing data on HDFS directly from Oracle Database. Oracle Direct Connector for HDFS gives users the flexibility of querying data from HDFS at any time, as needed by their application. It allows the creation of an external table in Oracle Database, enabling direct SQL access on data stored in HDFS. The data stored in HDFS can then be queried via SQL, joined with data stored in Oracle Database, or loaded into the Oracle Database. Access to the data on HDFS is optimized for fast data movement and parallelized, with automatic load balancing. Data on HDFS can be in delimited files or in Oracle data pump files created by Oracle Loader for Hadoop.

Oracle Data Integrator Application Adapter for Hadoop simplifies data integration from Hadoop and an Oracle Database through Oracle Data Integrator's easy-to-use interface. Once the data is accessible in the database, end users can use SQL and Oracle BI Enterprise Edition to access data. Even enterprises that are already using a Hadoop solution, and don't need an integrated offering like Oracle Big Data Appliance, can integrate data from HDFS using Big Data Connectors as a stand-alone software solution.

Oracle R Connector for Hadoop is an R package that provides transparent access to Hadoop and to data stored in HDFS.

R Connector for Hadoop provides users of the open source statistical environment R with the ability to analyze data stored in HDFS, and to run R models at scale against large volumes of data leveraging MapReduce processing—without requiring R users to learn yet another API or language. End users can leverage over 3,500 open source R packages to analyze data stored in HDFS, while administrators do not need to learn R to schedule R MapReduce models in production environments. Connector for Hadoop can optionally be used together with the Oracle Advanced Analytics Option for Oracle Database. The Oracle Advanced Analytics Option enables R users to work transparently with database resident data without having to learn SQL or database concepts but with R computations executing directly in database.

Oracle NoSQL Database is a distributed, highly scalable, key-value database based on Oracle Berkeley DB. It delivers a general-purpose, enterprise-class key-value store adding an intelligent driver on top of distributed Berkeley DB. This intelligent driver keeps track of the underlying storage topology, shards the data, and knows where data can be placed with the lowest latency. Unlike competitive solutions, Oracle NoSQL Database is easy to install, configure, and manage; it supports a broad set of workloads, and delivers enterprise-class reliability backed by enterprise-class Oracle support.

The primary use cases for Oracle NoSQL Database are low latency data capture and fast querying of that data, typically by key lookup. Oracle NoSQL Database comes with an easy-to-use Java API and a management framework.

The product is available in both an open source community edition and in a priced enterprise edition for large distributed data centers. The former version is installed as part of the Big Data Appliance integrated software.

Passoker Optimizes Online Betting

Passoker partners with a sports data provider that archives and distributes historical information, critical to gamers' abilities to instantly assess events. The partner collects, packages, and distributes information on some 60,000 events each year, from more than 30 different sports in approximately 70 countries. The incoming data from this service is used to determine the options available for each of the many events tracked on Passoker's betting platform, enabling bettors to wager on eventualities, such as the next goal, free kick, or penalty in a particular soccer match.

Passoker needed a database technology that could rapidly receive the XML files on which its gaming platform relies, and then quickly process those files for relevance. Also essential were high availability, rapid scaling, and guaranteed ordering of events.

Passoker deployed Oracle NoSQL Database as the new platform supporting the company's gaming solutions, reducing development and implementation times by 75 percent (saving 30 to 50 days) over other database options, due to Oracle NoSQL's built-in, configurable replication capabilities.

Source: www.oracle.com/us/corporate/customers/customersearch/passoker-1-nosql-ss-1863507.html.

In-Database Analytics. Once data has been loaded from Oracle Big Data Appliance into Oracle Database or Oracle Exadata, end users can use one of the following easy-to-use tools for in-database, advanced analytics:

- *Oracle R Enterprise.* Oracle's version of the widely used Project R statistical environment enables statisticians to use R on very large data sets without any modifications to the end user experience. Examples of R usage include predicting airline delays at a particular airport and the submission of clinical trial analysis and results.
- *In-database data mining* is the ability to create complex models and deploy these on very large data volumes to drive predictive analytics. End users can leverage the results of these predictive models in their BI tools without the need to know how to build the models. For example, regression models can be used to predict customer age based on purchasing behavior and demographic data.
- *In-database text mining* is the ability to mine text from microblogs and CRM system comment fields, and to review sites combining Oracle Text and Oracle Data Mining. An example of text mining is sentiment analysis based on comments. Sentiment analysis tries to show how customers feel about certain companies, products, or activities.
- *In-database semantic analysis* is the ability to create graphs and connections between various data points and data sets.

Semantic analysis creates, for example, networks of relationships determining the value of a customer's circle of friends. When looking at customer churn, customer value is based on the value of his or her network, rather than on just the value of the customer.

- *In-database spatial* is the ability to add a spatial dimension to data and show data plotted on a map. This ability enables end users to understand geospatial relationships and trends much more efficiently. For example, spatial data can visualize a network of people and their geographical proximity. Customers who are in close proximity can readily influence each other's purchasing behavior, an opportunity that can be easily missed if spatial visualization is left out.

- *In-database MapReduce* is the ability to write procedural logic and seamlessly leverage Oracle Database parallel execution. In-database MapReduce allows data scientists to create high-performance routines with complex logic. In-database MapReduce can be exposed via SQL. Examples of leveraging in-database MapReduce are sessionization of web logs or organization of call details records (CDRs).

Every one of the analytical components in Oracle Database is valuable. Combining these components creates even more value to the business. Leveraging SQL or a BI tool to expose the results of these analytics to end users gives an organization an edge over others that do not leverage the full potential of analytics in Oracle Database. Connections between Oracle Big Data Appliance and Oracle Exadata are via InfiniBand, enabling high-speed data transfer for batch or query workloads. Oracle Exadata provides outstanding performance in hosting data warehouses and transaction processing databases. Now that the data is in mass-consumption format, Oracle Exalytics can be used to deliver the wealth of information to the business analyst.

Predictive Analytics

Predictive analytics is an area of data mining that deals with extracting information from data and using it to predict trends and behavior patterns. Predictive analytics offers capabilities to analyze and understand the behavior that may lead to the actions in the future. In the current business scenario, it is extremely important to implement predictive modeling, scoring data with predictive models and forecasting for future actions. Predictive analytics is business intelligence technology that produces a predictive score for each customer or other organizational element. Assigning these predictive scores is the job of a predictive model that has, in turn, been trained over data, learning from the experience of the organization. Predictive analytics optimizes marketing campaigns and website behavior to increase customer responses, conversions, and clicks, and to decrease churn. Each customer's predictive score informs actions to be taken with that customer.

Analyzing new and diverse digital data streams can reveal new sources of economic value, provide fresh insights into customer behavior, and identify market trends early on. But this influx of new data creates challenges for IT departments. To derive real business value from big data, businesses need the right tools to capture and organize a wide variety of data types from different sources, and to be able to easily analyze it within the context of all your enterprise data. In this competitive business environment, it will be important for businesses to have a blend of a healthy data-science culture for creating business agility, for staying competitive, and for survivability. Data scientists will play a major role in helping C-level decision makers with the right information based on new big data analytics in the context of the business.

In-Memory Analytics

In-memory analytics is the new revolution in data management and offers greater power to run data business with increased agility and more perfectly. In-memory analytics is a methodology used to solve complex and time-sensitive business scenarios. It works by increasing the speed, performance, and reliability when querying data. In-memory analytics is an approach to querying data when it resides in a computer's random-access memory (RAM), as opposed to querying data that is stored in databases. The software platform is optimized for distributed, in-memory processing, to help run new scenarios or complex analytical computations at a faster pace. Now businesses can instantly explore, visualize, and analyze data and tackle problems that were never considered before due to computing constraints.

In-memory analytics can provide fast access to deeper insights to seize opportunities and mitigate threats in near real time, run more sophisticated queries and models using all data to generate more precise insights that can improve business performance, and get answers to most difficult business questions quickly, with the speed and flexibility to meet business needs today and in the future.

SAP introduced HANA a few years ago to exploit in-memory processing capabilities of database to process large data workloads in order to provide data processing and analytics in real time to help businesses make the right decisions based on critical information. It converges database and application platform capabilities in memory to transform transactions, analytics, text analysis, and predictive and spatial data to enrich decision power in business.

Based on in-memory computing, Oracle has also offered an option to switch the database for in-memory processing, exploiting the memory and caching technology.

Spark cluster computing is yet another revolution exploiting in-memory computing in clusters handling large data sets based on the Hadoop framework. Spark can store data in the memory subsystems of the thousands of servers it pulls together, unlike Hadoop, which stores its data on old-fashioned hard disks. It not only fetches data fast but also provides scale-out deployment on demand based on the large number of nodes in the cluster environment.

The Spark cluster computing framework is an outcome of work by two research scientists, Matei Zaharia, a Romanian-born graduate student who has spent the past few years at Berkeley's AMPLab, a research operation dedicated to software that runs distributed software, and another Romanian, Berkeley professor Ion Stoica.

In the next chapter, we discuss the predictability of your business that drives key decisions and the business wisdom associated with it. When knowledge is power, it is extremely significant for businesses to cultivate a knowledge ecosystem for survival, sustenance, continued growth, and business agility. We have highlighted key elements of building knowledge ecosystems and a knowledge management process that would help a business to harness power for continued growth and leadership.

CHAPTER 9

Cultivating Knowledge Ecosystems

Now, as you have come this far in reading the book, you may have realized that these major key technology drivers can help you transform your businesses rapidly and provide agility that was not possible a few years back. But the most important aspect of all these technology innovations is predictability of your business that drives key decisions and business wisdom to run and manage operations effectively. In the information age, when knowledge is power, it is extremely significant for businesses to cultivate the knowledge ecosystem for survival, sustenance, continued growth, and business agility. We have assessed and evaluated the role of collaborative power (Chapter 5) and the role of collective intelligence (Chapter 8). In this chapter, we endeavor to highlight key elements of building knowledge ecosystems and the knowledge management (KM) process that will help a business to harness power for continued growth and leadership.

In the fiercely competitive business environment, all companies are competing in a complex and challenging context that is being transformed by many factors such as globalization, hypercompetition, technological development, and virtualization. These new technological innovations have forced organizations to think and behave differently in order to survive and prosper. Today, we acknowledge that the foundation of organizational competitiveness has shifted from an emphasis on physical and tangible resources to knowledge-based resources. It is imperative for companies to exploit, apply, and integrate their knowledge management capabilities into the enterprise.

The knowledge ecosystem includes all the intellectual abilities and knowledge possessed by employees, partners, and customers as well as their capacity to learn and acquire more knowledge. Knowledge management capability can be defined as the firm's ability to mobilize and deploy its knowledge-based resources in combination with other resources and capabilities.

Knowledge management is a planned, structured approach to develop knowledge management capabilities and to manage the identification, creation, sharing, and leveraging of knowledge-based resources as organizational assets in order to enhance a company's competitiveness. Knowledge management is the discipline of enabling individuals, teams, and entire organizations to collectively and systematically capture, store, create, share, and apply knowledge, to better achieve their objectives. Knowledge management incorporates ideas and processes from a wide variety of disciplines such as information management, information technology management, communication, human resources management, and others. In order to assess the larger picture of knowledge management in the organization, we analyze and evaluate knowledge management as a system in this chapter.

Knowledge management is a topic of interest today in both the industry world and the information research world. In our daily lives, we deal with a huge amount of data and information. Data and information are not knowledge until we know how to extract the value out of them. This is the reason we need knowledge management, which refers to a multidisciplined approach to achieving organizational objectives by making the best use of knowledge. KM focuses on processes such as acquiring, creating, and sharing knowledge, and the cultural and technical foundations that support those processes.

Knowledge management may be described in terms of:

- *People.* How do you increase the ability of individuals in the organization to influence others with their knowledge?
- *Processes.* The approach of KM varies from organization to organization. There is no limit on the number of processes.
- *Technology.* Technology needs to be chosen only after all the requirements of a knowledge management initiative have been established.

Or it may be looked at differently with these factors:

- *Culture.* The biggest enabler of successful knowledge-driven organizations is the establishment of a knowledge-focused culture.

- *Structure.* The business processes and organizational structures that facilitate knowledge sharing are its structure.
- *Technology.* Technology is a crucial enabler rather than the solution.

In this chapter, we emphasize mostly the technological aspects of knowledge management. This approach involves the collection, codification, storage, and manipulation of knowledge using technical systems. The three main features of the system strategy of knowledge management are:

1. The emphasis on codified knowledge in knowledge management processes
2. The focus on codifying and storing knowledge via information technology
3. The attempt to share knowledge formally

Knowledge Management Disciplines and Technologies

Knowledge management also requires specific attention to the human, organizational, and cultural aspects. It is important to understand that knowledge initiates, propagates, and permeates with people within organization. That is why, in contrast to technological knowledge management, socially based knowledge management emphasizes knowledge that can be acquired and shared via a socially interactive process. As we noted in Chapter 7, the evolution of social media has created a revolution in social interaction, and that renews the focus of knowledge management with new perspectives.

Knowledge management draws from a wide range of disciplines and technologies:

- Cognitive science
- Expert systems, artificial intelligence, and knowledge-based management systems (KBMSs)
- Computer-supported collaborative work (groupware)
- Library and information science
- Technical writing
- Document management
- Decision support systems

- Semantic networks
- Relational and object databases
- Simulation
- Organizational science
- Object-oriented information modeling
- Electronic publishing technology, hypertext, and the World Wide Web
- Help-desk technology
- Full-text search and retrieval
- Performance support systems

The sociotechnical paradigm combines the social and technical aspects, and could be described as the study of the relationships between the social and technical parts of any system. The sociotechnical view of knowledge management focuses on a firm's strategy for harmonizing knowledge management activities with technological drivers and social enablers to achieve its business objectives.

The new knowledge management systems must include databases, intranet, groupware, search engines, social media, big data, and predictive analytics. They may be divided into several major categories such as groupware, including e-mail and wikis; decision support systems; expert systems; document management systems; semantic networks; relational and object-oriented databases; simulation tools; big data; and artificial and predictive intelligence.

In general, a sociotechnical knowledge management system could be defined as a set of technological and social elements that ensures the development of a knowledge management process and the creation of appropriate organizational conditions.

According to the previous analysis, we could stress that a knowledge management system includes three main subsystems:

1. The subsystem of the knowledge management process
2. The subsystem of the technological context
3. The subsystem of the social context

The most obvious components of the sociotechnical knowledge management system are people and their knowledge. Knowledge includes explicit knowledge that is expressed in words and numbers and codified in manuals, databases, and information systems, as well as tacit knowledge that is shared collectively in the firm in the form of routines, culture, and know-how. Individual knowledge is transformed into the organizational knowledge through the process of knowledge management. (See Figure 9.1.) The process of knowledge management includes a set of practices or activities that are initiated in organization in order to identify, acquire, create, store, disseminate, and apply knowledge. These key processes are considered during designing the knowledge management system in the organization:

- Knowledge identification means the determination of all critical knowledge that is possessed by employees and their groups in the organization.
- Knowledge acquisition involves the renewal of employees' knowledge by attaining new information, knowledge, and experience.
- Knowledge creation is the creation of new knowledge that is materialized in new products, services, processes, and concepts.
- Knowledge dissemination means the diffusion of knowledge, experience, and valuable information among individuals and their groups in the organization.
- Knowledge application is the productive use of organizational knowledge in business processes through solving problems, making decisions, and designing new products and services for the benefit of the organization.

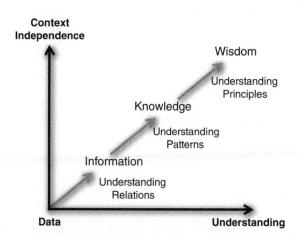

Figure 9.1   Knowledge Management Systems

Knowledge management should be integrated into other organizational processes that create value. The process of knowledge management should also be harmonized with general corporate strategy and maintained by an appropriate culture. This requires the formation of a suitable organizational context (i.e., particular sociotechnical environment), which is created in order to ensure the working of the process of knowledge management. In accordance with the analysis of the main components of the sociotechnical knowledge management system, five major elements of the sociotechnical environment could be identified:

1. *Strategic leadership* means the active interest in knowledge management and its promotion by the leaders and chief officers of the organization.
2. *Organizational infrastructure* includes formal and informal structures that ensure the creation of formal and informal social networks through which knowledge and information flow in the organization.
3. *Technological infrastructure* is designed by technological products (tools) and their systems, which are based on information and communication technologies and used to facilitate the process of knowledge management.
4. *Organizational learning* is an area of knowledge within organizational theory that studies models and theories about the way an organization learns and adapts.
5. *Knowledge culture* deals with the systems of values, beliefs, and norms accepted and supported by all employees in the organization, and based on the acknowledgment of the importance of knowledge and its management.

A collection of data is not information. This implies that a collection of data for which there is no relationship between the pieces of data is not information. Wisdom arises when one understands the foundational principles responsible for the patterns representing knowledge being what they are. And wisdom, even more so than knowledge, tends to create its own context. So, in summary the following associations can reasonably be made:

- *Information* relates to description, definition, or perspective (what, who, when, where). Figure 9.1 illustrates the maturity of information to wisdom with reference to context and understanding.

- *Knowledge* comprises strategy, practice, method, or approach (how).
- *Wisdom* embodies principle, insight, moral, or archetype (why).

The following example with reference to a bank savings account illustrates how data, information, knowledge, understanding, and wisdom relate to interest, principal, and interest rate.

Data: The numbers 100 or 5 percent, completely out of context, are just pieces of data. Interest, principal, and interest rate, out of context, are not much more than data, as each has multiple meanings that are context dependent.

Information: If we establish a bank savings account as the basis for context, then interest, principal, and interest rate become meaningful in that context with specific interpretations.

- Principal is the amount of money, $100, in the savings account.
- Interest rate, 5 percent, is the factor used by the bank to compute interest on the principal.

Knowledge: If I put $100 in my savings account, and the bank pays 5 percent interest yearly, then at the end of one year the bank will compute the interest of $5 and add it to my principal and I will have $105 in the bank. This pattern represents knowledge that allows understanding of how the pattern will evolve over time and the results it will produce.

Understanding: Understanding is a cognitive and analytical process that takes knowledge and synthesizes new knowledge from the previously held knowledge. The difference between understanding and knowledge is the difference between learning and memorizing. Understanding can build upon currently held information, knowledge, and understanding itself. In computer parlance, artificial intelligence (AI) systems possess understanding in the sense that they are able to synthesize new knowledge from previously stored information and knowledge.

Wisdom: Wisdom is an extrapolative and nondeterministic, nonprobabilistic process. It calls upon all the previous levels of consciousness, and specifically upon special types of human programming (morality, ethical codes, etc.). Wisdom is the process by which we also discern, or judge, between right and wrong, good and bad. Wisdom is a uniquely human state that requires one to have the capability to make an intellectual judgment.

Some benefits of knowledge management correlate directly to bottom-line savings, while others are more difficult to quantify. In today's information-driven economy, knowledge resources are proven as an important asset to provide business agility. To get the most value from a company's intellectual assets, it is highly important that knowledge be shared and served as the foundation for collaboration. An effective knowledge ecosystem should help businesses do one or more of the following:

- Foster innovation by encouraging the free flow of ideas.
- Improve decision making.
- Improve customer service by streamlining response time.
- Boost revenues by getting products and services to market faster.
- Enhance employee retention rates by recognizing the value of employees' knowledge and rewarding them for it.
- Streamline operations and reduce costs by eliminating redundant or unnecessary processes.

Figure 9.2 reflects the main technologies that currently support knowledge management systems.

These technologies are well represented by four main stages of the KM life cycle:

1. Knowledge is acquired or captured using intranets, extranets, groupware, web conferencing, and document management systems.
2. An organizational memory is formed by refining, organizing, and storing knowledge using structured repositories such as data warehouses.
3. Knowledge is distributed through education, training programs, automated knowledge-based systems, and expert networks.
4. Knowledge is applied or leveraged for further learning and innovation via mining of the organizational memory and the application of expert systems such as decision support systems.

All of these stages are enhanced by effective work flow and project management.

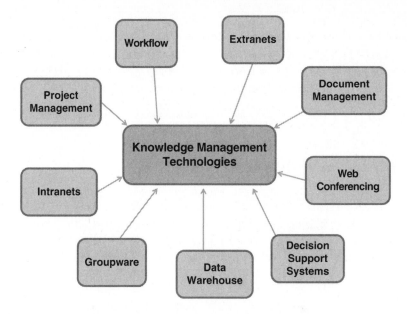

Figure 9.2   Knowledge Management Systems

Leveraging Knowledge Management in Customer Service

Seeking to improve the efficiency and effectiveness of customer service, leading enterprises have turned to knowledge management and realized significant, quantifiable results. Knowledge management enables the following key benefits via customer service improvements:

- Reduced research time
- Increased resolution accuracy
- Reduced training time
- Management of increasing service volumes
- Creation of service insight

As companies support more complex products and broader product portfolios, the challenges of quickly and efficiently resolving customer issues multiply. Contact center investments have focused on telephony improvements, skills-based routing, workforce management, and customer relationship management (CRM) applications, but the key area that has been woefully underfunded is knowledge management. These other investments, while important, address only 20 percent of service call times. Most of the time agents spend on the phone is engaged in research, discovery, and communication of their search results to the customer.

Reducing Research Time

By implementing knowledge management solutions for call center agents and customers seeking self-service, companies can increase their service efficiency and delivery. By understanding the customer's true intent and delivering accurate and consistent answers to the contact center desktop, you can cut costs, reduce average call-handling time, and improve the overall customer experience. This is easier said than done, however. Agents typically must find answers to service issues hidden in a multitude of sources, including product manuals, marketing collateral, corporate policies, bug databases, and case notes. Requiring agents to sift through multiple applications and thousands of irrelevant and outdated documents takes time and leads to an expensive support call as well as frustrated customers.

A knowledge management system equipped with a powerful search capability that scans the enterprise to bring back only the snippets of knowledge relevant to solving the issue is crucial to reducing research time. Furthermore, an agent should never have to research a query that has already been answered. Through case linking and rapid online creation of knowledge, enterprise-wide searches can be reduced as the system becomes smarter and more efficient. As an example, by arming their frontline agents with fast, convenient access to the most relevant information, one customer of Oracle Knowledge for Contact Center has increased its first-contact resolution rates from 40 percent to more than 65 percent. In addition, these tier-one agents can now handle more calls because their research time has been reduced by 55 percent. Plus, they're far less likely to escalate calls to more technical personnel.

Increasing Resolution Accuracy

Most questions can be asked in a multitude of ways, such as "Upgrade service?" "How do I upgrade?" "What are my upgrade options?" and so on. But traditional search and content management engines interpret each word in these questions separately, bringing back hundreds if not thousands of irrelevant results. A knowledge management solution that understands a customer's true intent—including special terms such as product names and industry jargon—and maps the inquiry to predefined results, or that uses true intent to intelligently navigate enterprise content, is the only way to guarantee a high degree of accuracy.

When the success of your insurance business demands that accurate answers be delivered to more than 70,000 independent agents as they write new policies, there is truly only one viable solution to ensure success: knowledge management.

A well-respected specialty insurer discovered that its contact center representatives were struggling, achieving a dismal 28 percent accuracy rate in their responses to agent inquiries as they scoured PDF documents and regulations that were stored in multiple databases.

Managing Increasing Service Volumes

As industry consolidation and acquisitions build the customer base for many survivors of the recent economic downturn, the need for more efficient customer support is rapidly surfacing. Following a key acquisition of one of its competitors, a company saw its call volume triple, while agents struggled to access information stored in isolated support resources. Knowledge management in this case of a merger can help scale existing agent resources to handle increasing volume by helping them work more efficiently. Through the knowledge management platform, inexperienced agents learn from institutional knowledge. It can help reduce the time it takes even top agents to do research while improving their accuracy and their access to distributed knowledge sources.

One year after implementing Oracle Knowledge for Web Self Service, this organization's customer support website was named one of the "Ten Best Web Support Sites" by the Association of Support Professionals. In addition, by allowing customers to effectively search for consistent and accurate answers via the web channel, the company saved $5.8 million in the first year.

Creating Service Insight

The key advantage that a comprehensive knowledge management platform can provide is insight. This type of service insight can be used to push more interactions to the web channel by improving answer delivery and consistency. It can help pinpoint where online-to-assisted-channel escalations are coming from and how to prevent them. It can show the knowledge gaps to take corrective action. And it can show emerging service issues through the moderation of discussion forums.

By harnessing the capabilities of knowledge-infused customer relationship management (CRM) and intelligent integration of CRM and KM, businesses become intelligent and informed to address customers' needs more effectively. With the addition of KM, organizations gain the centralized intelligence they need for delivering fast, accurate, relevant answers. Providing this centralized intelligence is the best way to foster the knowledge and confidence that agents desire. Here are a few ways knowledge-infused CRM can benefit today's support organizations:

- Enhance agent efficiency and effectiveness.

    After downsizing, customer service organizations often lose some of their more experienced support agents. Therefore it is vital to move from a support model in which knowledge and expertise walk out the door when seasoned employees leave to a more collaborative support model in which solutions are developed, managed, and shared as part of the daily resolution process. This not only helps with overall morale and confidence but also empowers new agents to become more proficient faster. Knowledge-infused CRM systems can provide answers in real time with minimal agent involvement. For example, as a service agent is working on the case resolution screen, an integrated KM solution can automatically leverage the context of the interaction and provide immediate advice to assist with the resolution process.
- Minimize training time.

    In the wake of reorganization, a reduction in staff, and turnover, new as well as existing employees need to be trained. Knowledge solutions coupled with CRM can have a dramatic impact on reducing employee training schedules. Instead of investing in training programs that take agents away from servicing customers, management can focus on developing the essential content required for basic problem resolution and knowledge retrieval. Ultimately, organizations can shorten training schedules. Plus, with the KM system accessible through the CRM interface on each agent's desktop, agents can work to get the answers they need in a single application.
- Minimize call resolution times.

    To reduce costs, many organizations have been forced to consolidate call centers or business units, which can mean longer call times, increased escalations, and decreased first-call resolution rates. By arming agents with one-click access to better information, knowledge-infused CRM can help organizations avoid these negative trends. With access to knowledge through their existing CRM interface, problem resolution becomes faster and more seamless for agents.

- Improve consistency.

    When KM and CRM are fully integrated with all support channels, the playing field for agent competencies is leveled and every agent can more quickly and intuitively deliver consistent answers.

Knowledge-infused CRM can be fully leveraged in agent-assisted channels as well as in web self-service. Powering knowledge-infused CRM with a centralized knowledge platform means that customers get the same correct answers, regardless of the channel they use.

Knowledge culminates in wisdom, and collective knowledge captured and delivered within an enterprise helps in managing the business effectively for sustainable competitive advantage.

Force 5 Tornado Convergence Creates Business Agility

Cultivating a knowledge ecosystem is all about culture. A great example is the San Francisco Giants story of how the team parlayed an integrated big data analytics strategy into a World Series Championship in 2010 and again in 2012. The secret to the Giants chemistry is trust, and the master chemist is CIO Bill Schlough, who keeps his team ahead of the game with a world championship culture. After reading the December 17, 2012, article in *Information Week* titled "Chief of the Year" by Fritz Nelson describing his CIO of the Year award, it is clear that if you want to see the convergence of the Force 5 Tornado technologies in action, then you could go see a San Francisco Giants ballgame at AT&T Park.

The story that Bill Schlough tells is about the holistic business value of ubiquitous IT that has transformed the Giants organization in terms of customer experience in the park and online, as well as enabled world championship player performance on the field and reengineered the business of baseball in the front office. Such results are no coincidence; rather they reflect the San Francisco Giants official mission statement as their dedication "to enriching our community through innovation and excellence on and off the field." They embrace the spirit and letter of the strategies and tactics that we have described in *Creating Business Agility*. The following examples are only some of the innovations:

- *Dynamic ticket pricing* . . . The Giants were a pioneer in this area. In 2000, when AT&T Park opened, the Giants' ticketing team, working with Schlough and the IT team, rolled out dynamic ticket pricing, where competitive forces drive the cost of attending a ballgame.
- *One giant Wi-Fi hotspot* . . . The Giants have also become the bellwether for enabling a digital fan experience at the ballpark . . . fans update their social networks and check scores and video highlights from around the league.
- *Big data* . . . teams evaluate factors such as player performance and optimal positioning on the field by analyzing thousands of slivers of data, beginning to let a handful of teams—the Giants among them—take the concept further with Sportvision's FIELDf/x, a video system that helps teams analyze player reaction times—biomechanics.
- *Scouting* . . . beyond picking players, the IT organization's data and video analyses extend to advanced scouting, like figuring out how to pitch and who to trade.
- *High-definition video* . . . The Giants were the third Major League Baseball (MLB) team to introduce an HD video scoreboard . . . replacing all of the stadium's TVs with HD sets transformed the fan experience.

Enterprise systems integration examples include: "replacing the homegrown CRM system the team has used for years, containing information on 700,000 customers, with Salesforce.com, and a new ticketing platform, these two systems (ticketing and CRM) will come together at a few points. The team is testing mobile point-of-sale systems in stores. . . . The goal is to integrate all customer data, from ticket purchasers to callers, into the Giants' ShoreTel VoIP system, and to 'track the value of every customer and accurately assess the likelihood of losing that customer, or how to retain that customer,' Schlough says. The organization wants to cater to each customer based on past behavior and interaction."

As an example of his customer engagement thinking, Schlough wants to install mobile device charging stations around the ballpark in order to deliver apps with a "whole product" digital experience to Giants fans throughout the complete MLB ecosystem.

Another use case describing the role that knowledge ecosystems play in creating business agility is demonstrated by Oracle in winning the greatest comeback in sports history.

How Team Oracle Wins AC34 with Big Data Analytics for Adaptive Decision Making

The story, titled "Faster" by Carol Hildebrand, of how ORACLE TEAM USA has used IT as a strategic tool for defending the 34th America's Cup in San Francisco Bay was published in the September/ October 2013 edition of *Oracle Magazine*. It provides a fascinating look at the ORACLE TEAM USA culture that leveraged a multipronged technology strategy for big data:

1. Real-time analytics
2. Onshore Analytics
3. Race Cutter App
4. Database Management

The AC72s are twenty-first-century sailboats. They are data-driven boats that can fly across the water at a speed faster than the wind that powers them. There are over 300 sensors throughout the boat that collect real-time performance data that is transmitted to a server in the hull. "Sensors measure the strain on the mast, hull, and wing; monitor the load generated on components ranging from the jib to the winches; and monitor the effectiveness of each change made by the trimmers, who constantly adjust the sail wing to fully exploit wind conditions." The raw data consists of over 3,000 variables generated 10 times a second during sailing runs. ORACLE TEAM USA also produces several video feeds and still images of the sails every second.

A typical training run creates about a gigabyte of raw performance data as well as 150 to 200 gigabytes of video, adding it to about 80 gigabytes of weather and boat data, plus performance metadata from the current 2013 America's Cup campaign as well as a cache of historical race data. ORACLE TEAM USA uses this raw performance data, coupled with the videos and still images, tailored for diverse analytics scenarios.

Real-Time Analytics

The AC72s always sail with a chase boat that serves as the real-time analytical hub. The performance team manages a set of 150 variables that are transmitted in real time to the Oracle Database operating on the performance chase boat. The team performs a variety of analyses to optimize boat performance, and sends that information to the ORACLE TEAM USA sailors by a wireless network. Real-time analytics usage extends to the ORACLE TEAM USA sailors who wear "rugged-ized" PDAs on their arms and receive customized information in real-time drive sailing performance. There are also several tablet devices in located on the boat that display general nautical data such as wind speed.

Onshore Analytics

When the boats dock, their servers and the database on the perform-ance boat, are synced with the Oracle Database instance on the team's Exadata Database Machine X3-2. The Oracle Database is the core of the operation. It is used as a centralized race management hub that can support a wide variety of access mechanisms and devices, from traditional queries and custom-built tools to Oracle Application Express–based web pages and mobile apps.

Race Cutter

"The most widely used tool is Race Cutter, a custom application that pulls sensor data from the Exadata Database Machine X3-2, with added metadata markers that synchronize the video, photos, and audio streams with the raw numbers. Team members can click to a certain moment and view all the pertinent information from that time stamp."

Database Management

"The performance team builds reports to help designers and sailors solve the challenges of one-boat testing. Instead of comparing data from two boats under sail, the performance analysis has to be done numerically by comparing data sets. One estimate is that with one-boat testing, you need to collect 40 times as much data to get good results."

Oracle Application Express is used for making information easier to collect and distribute. An example is an application that simplifies performance test data quality control. It also automates the second level of quality control, creating web pages that crew members use to check and correct a lot of what he calls the metadata. Sailors also have access to an Oracle Application Express–based mobile app that automates the 250-item checklist necessary to prep the boat for sailing.

Sailing the AC72s has produced a data-driven racing culture that may serve the America's Cup ecosystem with a new basis of competitive advantage. ORACLE TEAM USA has already demonstrated the ability to improve the pure boat speed around the course over multiple days and sailing conditions by 20 to 30 percent. Clearly the synergy of big data analytics technology and culture may create the business agility needed for sustaining the competitive advantage to defend the future championship.

Although in this dynamic and rapidly changing time it is difficult to foresee the future for more than a few years, we will try to see and highlight the business and technology landscape beyond 2020 in the next and final chapter. We have witnessed these innovations and the game-changing revolution in the past few years impacting our businesses and economy, leaving many wondering what comes next and what the environment will look like in the next few years. We can only say that due to the way technology is converging in all areas and influencing our lifestyles and work environments, it is not going to be the same. Technology has a lot to offer and has great potential to help us run our businesses with greater agility and (most of all) lead our lives in a way that was unthinkable and inconceivable just a few years back.

CHAPTER 10

2020 Foresight

By now, you all must have started speculating about our future and what comes next to disrupt our existing businesses and society in general. We can safely argue that change is constant and we need to be flexible to embrace change and adopt new innovations rapidly that enable business agility. The past decade has been extremely disruptive as a result of the five major information technologies which we have labeled as the Force 5 Tornado as discussed in detail in previous chapters. These trends evolved almost at the same time, and now the convergence of these technologies is maturing and going past the hype curve to offer greater values in business transformation. We have witnessed these innovations and the game-changing revolution in the past few years impacting our businesses and economy, leaving many wondering what will come next and what the environment will look like by 2020. The cloud, social, mobile, video, and big data (discussed in previous chapters) will keep innovating and bringing new business solutions in the next few years. Gartner analysts forecast that the personal cloud will begin a new era that will provide users with a new level of flexibility with the devices they use for daily activities. While leveraging the strengths of each device, this will ultimately offer new levels of user satisfaction and productivity. However, businesses are at the crossroads, and they need to rethink the usage and deployment of these technologies rapidly and favorably to their advantage.

According to Gartner, private cloud computing has reached the peak level of hype, and cloud/web platforms are slipping into the "trough of disillusionment" in the face of platform as a service (PaaS). Gartner tracks technologies through a life cycle that begins with a technology trigger through the plateau of productivity.

According to Gartner, a technology that is in the trough of disillusionment is still sparsely adopted—less than 5 percent of the audience has fully adopted a technology at that point. Once 20 percent to 30 percent of the audience has adopted a technology, Gartner considers it at the plateau of productivity.

"Major trends in client computing have shifted the market away from a focus on personal computers to a broader device perspective that includes smartphones, tablets, and other consumer devices," says Steve Kleynhans, research vice president at Gartner. "Emerging cloud services will become the glue that connects the web of devices that users choose to access during the different aspects of their daily life." The reign of the personal computer as the sole corporate access device is coming to a close, and by 2014, the personal cloud is replacing the personal computer at the center of users' digital lives. Many call this era the post-PC era, a new style of personal computing that frees individuals to use computing in fundamentally new ways to improve multiple aspects of their work and personal lives."

Clearly there has been a disruption in the technology diffusion cycle, which traditionally follows the five-stage pattern of development:

1. Hardware
2. Software
3. Processes
4. Business culture
5. Social culture

The combination of the bring your own device (BYOD) phenomenon and best practices of aligning customer-centric strategies executed using customer-focused processes that interact with customer-facing apps has accelerated technology adoption. Social culture facilitated by social media has promoted social business expectations and digital customer experiences. The result is a hardware–software–social culture loop that shortcuts business process and culture stages. This produces faster tech diffusion within the business ecosystem.

Ecosystemism

There are several other driving forces in conjunction with the Force 5 Tornado technologies that are disrupting conventional business models to create this new era. Recall how the Force 5 Tornado convergence works in terms of the data model shown in Chapter 2. It is a picture of business ecosystem synergy where value is delivered as customer experience at a series of touch points along the customer decision journey, such as the travel life cycle model. It is delivered in real time, based on customers' personalized digital relationships, anywhere and anytime.

The Internet of Things (IoT) is a game changer for the upcoming decade when parlayed with big data analytics creating a "silicon crystal ball" that will form the core of decision process reengineering (DPR). Digital businesses, with innovation as a goal and collaboration as a culture, will outperform competitors. The virtual enterprises formed in the business ecosystem will be stronger and more agile as a result of ecosystem-wide DPR initiatives that optimize the customer decision journey. This enables a sustainable competitive advantage for all partner businesses and their collaborative enterprises, as well as the ecosystem as a whole. By the year 2020 *Ecosystemism* as a cultural imperative will grow. This integrated c-commerce strategy will have gained traction by creating examples of the business agility that market leaders will deploy as a mainstream business model.

Consumerization of Information Technology

Gartner foresees the consumerization of information technology (IT) as having a major impact across various aspects of the corporate IT world. Large enterprises will have to rethink the way they procure and manage IT equipment and services. Provision of computing devices, applications, and services with businesses was controlled by a central department in the very recent past, but with consumerization today, employees are becoming increasing self-sufficient in meeting their IT needs. Products have become easier to use, and cloud-based software-as-a-service (SaaS) offerings are addressing an ever-widening range of business needs in areas such as videoconferencing, digital imaging, business collaboration, sales force support, systems backup, back-office operations, financial, payroll, human resources (HR), supply chain, business analytics applications, and many more.

Businesses have to be flexible in bring your own device (BYOD) strategies, where individual employees can choose and often own the computers and/or smart devices (phones and tablets) they use at work. The Apple iPhone and iPad and other smart devices were designed for individual consumers, but their appeal and usage in the workplace has gone far beyond what was imagined. These devices have created a revolution, and we will see many innovative usages and applications in the near future.

Businesses have increasingly adopted consumerized services such as search, mapping, and social media. The capabilities of firms such as Google, Facebook, and Twitter are now essential components of many firms' marketing strategies. One of the more serious negative implications of consumerization is that security controls have been slower to be adopted in the consumer space, and as a result one of the implications of consumerization is an increased risk to the information assets accessed through less trustworthy consumerized devices. However, this shortcoming may soon be remedied by the chip manufacturers with technologies such as Intel's Trusted Execution Technology and the ARM (Advanced RISC Machines) TrustZone; these technologies are being designed to increase the trustworthiness of both enterprise and consumer devices. However, much of this has simply been a precursor to the major wave that is starting to take hold across all aspects of information technology as several key factors come together:

- Users are more technologically savvy and have very different expectations of technology.
- The Internet and social media have empowered and emboldened users.
- The rise of powerful, affordable mobile devices changes the equation for users.
- Users have become innovators.
- Through the democratization of technology, users of all types and any status within organizations can now have similar technology available to them.

The Internet of Things

The Internet of Things (IoT) refers to uniquely identifiable objects and their virtual representations in an Internet-like structure. In our business environment, more objects are becoming embedded with sensors and gaining the ability to communicate. The resulting information networks promise to create new business models, improve business processes, and reduce costs and risks.

According to McKinsey & Company, in most organizations, information management has a more or less consistent life cycle. Proprietary information is lodged in databases and analyzed in reports, and then rises up the management chain. Information also originates externally, gathered from public sources, harvested from the Internet, or purchased from information suppliers. But the predictable pathways of information are changing. The physical world itself is becoming a type of information system. In the IoT, sensors and actuators embedded in physical objects—from roadways to pacemakers—are linked through wired and wireless networks, often using the same Internet protocol (IP) that connects the Internet. These networks churn out huge volumes of data that flow to computers for analysis. When objects can both sense the environment and communicate, they become tools for understanding complexity and responding to it swiftly. What is revolutionary in all this is that these physical information systems are now beginning to be deployed, and some of them even work largely without human intervention.

Pill-shaped micro cameras already traverse the human digestive tract and send back thousands of images to pinpoint sources of illness. Precision farming equipment with wireless links to data collected from remote satellites and ground sensors can take into account crop conditions and adjust the way each individual part of a field is farmed—for instance, by spreading extra fertilizer on areas that need more nutrients. Billboards in Japan peer back at passersby, assessing how they fit consumer profiles, and instantly change displayed messages based on those assessments. Manufacturing processes studded with a multitude of sensors can be controlled more precisely, raising efficiency. And when operating environments are monitored continuously for hazards or when objects can take corrective action to avoid damage, risks and costs diminish. Companies that take advantage of these capabilities stand to gain against competitors that don't.

The widespread adoption of the Internet of Things will take time, but the time line is advancing thanks to improvements in underlying technologies. Advances in wireless networking technology and the greater standardization of communications protocols make it possible to collect data from these sensors almost anywhere at any time. Ever-smaller silicon chips for this purpose are gaining new capabilities, while costs, following the pattern of Moore's law, are falling. Massive increases in storage and computing power, some of it available via cloud computing, make number crunching possible at a very large scale and at declining cost.

The Internet of Things has great promise, yet business, policy, and technical challenges must be tackled before these systems are widely embraced. Early adopters will need to prove that the new sensor-driven business models create superior value. Industry groups and government regulators should study rules on data privacy and data security, particularly for uses that touch on sensitive consumer information. Legal liability frameworks for the bad decisions of automated systems will have to be established by governments, companies, and risk analysts, in consort with insurers. On the technology side, the cost of sensors and actuators must fall to levels that will spark widespread use. Networking technologies and the standards that support them must evolve to the point where data can flow freely among sensors, computers, and actuators. Software to aggregate and analyze data, as well as graphic display techniques, must improve to the point where huge volumes of data can be absorbed by human decision makers or synthesized to guide automated systems more appropriately.

Within companies, big changes in information patterns will have implications for organizational structures, as well as for the way decisions are made, operations are managed, and processes are conceived. Product development, for example, will need to reflect far greater possibilities for capturing and analyzing information.

Companies can begin taking steps now to position themselves for these changes by using the new technologies to optimize business processes in which traditional approaches have not brought satisfactory returns. Energy consumption efficiency and process optimization are good early targets. Experiments with the emerging technologies should be conducted in development labs and in small-scale pilot trials, and established companies can seek partnerships with innovative technology suppliers creating Internet of Things capabilities for target industries.

The explosion of mobile devices and rapid growth in the Internet of Things is driving transformation of the network infrastructure to meet increasing demand for more connectivity and real-time data. Intel is enabling this transformation by delivering standardized hardware and software that apply open standards and high-volume economics to help reduce costs, while accelerating the delivery of new services, capabilities, and revenue models for service providers.

Industrial Internet

The world is on the threshold of a new era of innovation and change with the rise of the industrial Internet. It is taking place through the convergence of the global industrial system with the power of advanced computing, analytics, low-cost sensing, and new levels of connectivity permitted by the Internet. The deeper meshing of the digital world with the world of machines holds the potential to bring about profound transformation to global industry, and in turn to many aspects of daily life, including the way many of us do our jobs. These innovations promise to bring greater speed and efficiency to industries as diverse as aviation, rail transportation, power generation, oil and gas development, and health care delivery. It holds the promise of stronger economic growth, better and more jobs, and rising living standards, whether in the United States or in China, in a megacity in Africa, or in a rural area in Kazakhstan.

With better health outcomes at lower cost, substantial savings in fuel and energy, and better-performing and longer-lived physical assets, the industrial Internet will deliver new efficiency gains, accelerating productivity growth the way that the industrial revolution and the Internet revolution did. And increased productivity means faster improvement in income and living standards. In the United States, if the industrial Internet could boost annual productivity growth by 1 to 1.5 percentage points, bringing it back to its Internet revolution peaks, then over the next 20 years through the power of compounding it could raise average incomes by an impressive 25 to 40 percent of today's level over and above the current trend. And as innovation spreads globally, if the rest of the world could secure half of the U.S. productivity gains, the industrial Internet could add to global gross domestic product (GDP) a sizable $10 trillion to $15 trillion—the size of today's U.S. economy—over the same horizon. In today's challenging economic environment, securing even part of these productivity gains could bring great benefits at both the individual level and economy-wide.

Wireless Electricity

Wireless transmission of electricity has been a dream for nearly a century, dating back to Nikola Tesla's vision of a wireless world energy grid. Although Tesla's visions never materialized, recent technology innovations have demonstrated the feasibility of efficiently powering devices wirelessly. This chapter offers a technology foresight brief that explores the state of wireless power technology and its future potential.

Interface Innovation

The analog controls that accompanied the rise of the personal computer (buttons, switches, keyboard, joystick, and mouse) allowed consumers to interact with their devices in a variety of ways. But as personal computing devices have grown smaller, smarter, and more mobile, and as they are used for a wider variety of applications, new needs are arising. This brief explores the state of interface technology, emerging tools and applications, and the directions in which interfaces may move.

Internet of Everything: Cisco

Today, the Internet of Everything (IoE)—the ongoing explosion in networked connectivity among people, process, data, and things—is Cisco's IoT vision for transforming manufacturing in startling ways, just as it is changing so many other industries.

IoE delivers seamless, intelligent connections to *every* corner of the manufacturing value chain, optimizing the flow of products, information, and payments in real time.

IoE is driving connections beyond just data. The convergence of connecting people, things, data, and processes is transforming organizations, industries, and our lives. The growth of mobility and cloud computing is further driving innovation and an increase in the number and kinds of connections.

The broad-based adoption of information technology (IT)—and, in particular, the advent of cloud-based capabilities—has leveled the playing field for firms around the world. Market incumbents are increasingly pressured by disruptive innovators and nontraditional rivals bent on attacking revenue franchises and gaining market share through the innovative application of technology.

In nearly all industries, an accelerating innovation curve, in which market discontinuities arising from video, social, mobile, and cloud-based capabilities unlock new competitive dynamics, is reshaping the business landscape. In this environment, barriers to market entry are falling, customers are demanding new ways of interacting, and margins are compressing. In a world characterized by technology-driven parity and fleeting competitive advantages, many business leaders are asking, "Where will the next wave of value come from for our company?"

In February 2013, Cisco Systems released a study (www.cisco.com/web/about/ac79/docs/innov/IoE_Economy.pdf) predicting that $14.4 trillion of value (net profit) will be at stake globally over the next decade, driven by connecting the unconnected—people-to-people (P2P), machine-to-people (M2P), and machine-to-machine (M2M)—via the Internet of Everything (IoE).

Cisco defines the Internet of Everything as the networked connection of people, processes, data, and things. The benefit of IoE is derived from the compound impact of connecting people, processes, data, and things, and from the value this increased connectedness creates as everything comes online. In this respect, IoE provides a clear answer to the question of future sources of value.

The $14.4 trillion in IoE value at stake—the potential bottom-line value that can be created, or that will migrate among private-sector companies and industries based on their ability to harness IoE over the next decade—is being driven by five key areas:

1. *Asset utilization ($2.5 trillion).* IoE reduces selling, general, and administrative (SG&A) expenses and cost of goods sold (COGS) by improving business process execution and capital efficiency.
2. *Employee productivity ($2.5 trillion).* IoE creates labor efficiencies that result in fewer or more productive person-hours.
3. *Supply chain and logistics ($2.7 trillion).* IoE eliminates waste and improves process efficiencies.
4. *Customer experience ($3.7 trillion).* IoE increases customer life-time value and grows market share by adding more customers.
5. *Innovation, including reducing time to market ($3.0 trillion).* IoE increases the return on R&D investments, reduces time to market, and creates additional revenue streams from new business models and opportunities.

IoT Examples, Patterns, and Trends

Since everything is connected, a list of networked devices is beyond the scope of this book. Even delineating all the possible categories would be a daunting ontological task. So the following examples represent our presentation of notable "Things" that we have observed from our information technology outpost located here in Silicon Valley: wearables such as Google Glass, self-driving cars, smart homes, and bionics in health care.

Google Glass: Next-Generation Device

Smart devices have already created a habitual practice to reach frequently for accessing e-mails, to browse the web for social networks, or to conduct an Internet search for some information. Very soon we will have another option, a pair of Google-made glasses that are able to stream information to the wearer's eyeballs in real time. Sources from Google reveal that Google Glass is Android-based, and includes a small screen fitted in eyeglass frames. It also has a 3G or 4G data connection and a number of sensors, including motion and GPS. Glass has a low-resolution built-in camera that is able to monitor the world in real time and overlay information about locations, surrounding buildings, and friends who might be nearby, according to the Google employees. Google Glass is not designed to be worn constantly but will be more like a smartphone, used when needed. Glass will send data to the cloud and then use things like Google Latitude to share location.

Executive Insights Devesh Srivastava, Mobility Architect, Tata Consultancy Services

Google Glass is a wearable computing device that includes hardware features like a 5 MP camera, 16 GB flash memory, Wi-Fi and Bluetooth, bone-conduction audio, a touchpad, and minimal GPS. Its display provides a user experience similar to watching a 25-inch TV at a distance of 8 feet. The device operates on Android 4.0 software.

Outside of Google, it is believed that currently there are only 10,000 Glass devices available; 2,000 of those were given to attendees of the Google I/O 2012 conference, and the other 8,000 devices were procured by people from various walks of life as part of the Explorer program where they earned the Glass device by submitting use cases of how they would use Glass (#ifihadglass).

There is no intrinsic development environment for Glass yet, until Google releases the Glass Development Kit (GDK). Currently there are two ways of developing applications on Glass:

1. *Using Google Mirror APIs.* The platform architecture involves communication between your Glass and the service (also called Glassware); however, due to lack of availability of GDK, the communication needs to go over REST/HTTP using Google Mirror APIs. Although Mirror APIs provide functionality of authentication, keep-alive sessions, and content rendering, this is also a bottleneck, providing inconsistent and sometimes significant delay in content rendering and a frustrating user experience.
2. *Android 4.0 SDK.* Since the underlying Glass OS is Android 4.0, existing Android applications developed using the Ice Cream Sandwich SDK can be ported on Glass. However, the user experience of Android applications on handsets cannot be used or duplicated on Glass devices, with the exception of voice commands.

This leads to an interesting discussion of how Glass can be used. Certainly, it cannot replace existing prevalent mobile devices like smartphones or tablets. Glass can augment these devices, however.

So, consider a scenario where you are watching an event like a football game or a musical concert, and your event attendance as a Glass user is enriched by consuming relevant, contextual, time-sensitive content on your Glass device. For instance, the football game Glassware can provide a short video of the touchdown that just happened, or the musical concert Glassware can provide information about the performer(s) or the surroundings.

It is important that Glassware should serve content to the Glass user that is helpful to the user during that time window of the event; otherwise the user would opt out of that service.

On the enterprise side, Glass could be used in different verticals like manufacturing, health care, or insurance, where the user's activities are enriched using voice commands interaction with Glass.

Glass is not an augmented reality device. However, applications will add more value to Glass users if they provide both augmented reality and artificial intelligence features. For instance, in the insurance domain, a claims adjuster visiting a natural disaster site could be served the structure of the house and how the house appeared before the disaster took place, based on the GPS coordinates.

Self-Driving Cars

Google has made the autonomous vehicle a reality that we may have seen only in a science-fiction movie. Google's self-driving car initiative is moving into a new phase of reality. Three years after first showing the world what it was up to—rolling out a Toyota Prius with laser scanning hardware placed on its roof—Google is moving its big idea out of the lab and into the real world. Its autonomous cars have already driven half a million miles on California roads without a single accident and will soon transform transportation in cities all over the world.

Google talks about making the roads safer, but the company's core business has plenty to gain from freeing up drivers from that task of, well, driving. Americans on average spend 18.5 hours a week in a car, which adds up to a lot of time they could be checking Gmail, editing Google Docs, watching YouTube videos, and clicking ads.

Motivation aside, a big change is under way, and it requires us to start thinking of cars very differently. Vehicles that drive themselves are good example of what happens when cars transform into full-scale, general-purpose computing systems. Self-driving and connected cars will bristle with sensors, negotiate with traffic lights, talk to each other about safety conditions, join into trainlike platoons, and become members of intelligent urban transit networks. Historically, the car industry has focused on passive safety items like seat belts and air bags. With the arrival of active safety technology that lets vehicles take preemptive action, cars will use data to help them decide what to do when drivers aren't paying attention or don't know what to do.

Saving Costs in Home Utilities

Utilities run big, expensive, and complicated systems to generate power. Each grid now includes sophisticated sensors that monitor voltage, current, frequency, and other important operating characteristics. Efficiency now means paying careful attention to all of the data streaming off the sensors. Utilities are now leveraging big data/Hadoop clusters to analyze generation (supply) and consumption (demand) data via smart meters. The rollout of smart meters as part of the smart grid adoption by utilities everywhere has resulted in a deluge of data flowing at unprecedented levels and predictive analytics to help reduce costs at all levels. We foresee greater innovation in this area, with utilities smart meters using powerful predictive consumer behavior analysis and based on a big data model captured by these devices.

Bionics: Wearable Contact Lenses

One step ahead of Google Glass, we foresee the innovation and research toward bionics that will offer wearable bionic contact lenses. This technology could allow wearers to read floating texts and e-mails or augment their sight with computer-generated images. Early tests show the device is safe and feasible, say researchers at the University of Washington in Seattle. Currently, the crude prototype device can work only if it is within centimeters of the wireless battery.

But now that initial safety tests in rabbits have gone well, with no obvious adverse effects, the researchers have renewed faith about the device's possibilities. They envisage that hundreds more pixels could be embedded in the flexible lens to produce complex holographic images. For example, drivers could wear them to see journey directions or their vehicle's speed projected onto the windscreen. Similarly, the lenses could take the virtual world of video gaming to a new level. They could also provide up-to-date medical information like blood sugar levels by linking to biosensors in the wearer's body.

A Swiss company called Sensimed has already brought to market a smart contact lens that uses built-in computer technology to monitor pressure inside the eye to keep tabs on the eye condition glaucoma.

There are many possible uses for virtual displays. Video-game companies could use the contact lenses to completely immerse players in a virtual world without restricting their range of motion. And for communications, people on the go could surf the Internet on a midair virtual display screen that only they would be able to see. "People may find all sorts of applications for it that we have not thought about. Our goal is to demonstrate the basic technology and make sure it works and that it's safe," says Babak Parviz, who heads a multidisciplinary University of Washington group that is developing electronics for contact lenses.

Bionic Contact Lenses of the Future

Ideally, installing or removing the bionic contact lens would be as easy as popping a regular contact lens in or out, and once installed the wearer would barely know the gadget was there, Parviz says. Building the lenses was a challenge because materials that are safe for use in the body, such as the flexible organic materials used in contact lenses, are delicate. Manufacturing electrical circuits, however, involves inorganic materials, scorching temperatures, and toxic chemicals. Researchers built the circuits from layers of metal only a few nanometers thick, about one-thousandth the width of a human hair, and constructed light-emitting diodes one-third of a millimeter across. They then sprinkled the grayish powder of electrical components onto a sheet of flexible plastic. The shape of each tiny component dictates which piece it can attach to, a microfabrication technique known as self-assembly. The prototype contact lens does not correct the wearer's vision, but the technique could be used on a corrective lens, Parviz says. And all the gadgetry won't obstruct a person's view.

"There is a large area outside of the transparent part of the eye that we can use for placing instrumentation," Parviz says. Future improvements will add wireless communication to and from the lens. The researchers hope to power the whole system using a combination of radio-frequency power and solar cells placed on the lens.

What to Expect with a Customer-Centric Business in 2020

The Force 5 Tornado will continue to power business transformation and increasingly become an integral fabric of our lives. Convergence yielding big data analytics will embed intelligence into that technological weave by creating a network of intelligent business ecosystems to enable us to live and work in a smart environment, the Internet of Things.

Imagine what the world would be like if computers were so small, so powerful, and so cheap that they could be built into everything and interconnected to share data all around the world. Well, look around; the precursors of IoT are already in place. Marketing 2020 is envisioned by McKinsey & Company in "The Coming Era of 'On-Demand' Marketing" by Peter Dahlström and David Edelman (*McKinsey Quarterly*, April 2013):

> Digital marketing is about to enter more challenging territory. Building on the vast increase in consumer power brought on by the digital age, marketing is headed toward being on demand— not just always "on," but also always relevant, responsive to the

consumer's desire for marketing that cuts through the noise with pinpoint delivery.

What's fueling on-demand marketing is the continued, symbiotic evolution of technology and consumer expectations. Already, search technologies have made product information ubiquitous; social media encourages consumers to share, compare, and rate experiences; and mobile devices add a "wherever" dimension to the digital environment. Executives encounter this empowerment daily when, for example, cable customers push for video programming on any device at any time or travelers expect a few taps on a smartphone app to deliver a full complement of airline services.

Going forward to the year 2020 and beyond, we will see the digital business model as the mainstream means to deliver customer experience as an integrated relationship management practice across the physical and digital touchpoints in the business ecosystem. The Force 5 Tornado technologies using IoT enable devices, such as near-field communication (NFC) chips, will create an information rich environment. McKinsey envisions that these innovations coupled with ubiquitous global mobility, HTML5 web interactive workspaces, and advanced big data handling engines will transform customer experience:

Consumers may soon be able to search by image, voice, and gesture; automatically participate with others by taking pictures or making transactions; and discover new opportunities with devices that augment reality in their field of vision (think Google Glass).

As these digital capabilities multiply, consumer demands will rise in four areas:

1. *Now.* Consumers will want to interact anywhere and at any time.
2. *Can I?* They will want to do truly new things as disparate kinds of information (from financial accounts to data on physical activity) are deployed more effectively in ways that create value for them.
3. *For me.* They will expect all data stored about them to be targeted precisely to their needs or used to personalize what they experience.
4. *Simply.* They will expect all interactions to be easy.

This is the new world and its implications for leaders across the virtual enterprise. One thing is clear: The consumer's experiences with brands and categories are set to become even more intense and defining. To mobilize for the on-demand challenges ahead, digital businesses must:

- Bring managers together from across the business to understand consumers' decision journeys, to speculate about where they may lead, and to design experiences that will meet their demands (*Now, Can I?, For me,* and *Simply*).
- Align the executive team around an explicit end-to-end data strategy across trends, performance, and people.
- Challenge the delivery processes behind every touch point—are the processes making the best use of your data and interaction opportunities, and are they appropriately tailored to the speed required and to expectations about your brand?

After writing this far, we realize that we are extremely vulnerable and must always be alert, agile, and adaptable to the changing environment that we are living in today. Despite our attempt to provide you with some details about the foreseeable future, we submit that this chapter may not have covered many areas and innovations taking place globally in all business areas at almost the same time. For example we have barely touched on the next generation of big data analytics that provides the foundation for the burgeoning field of artificial intelligence that is driving cognitive computing. Yet that is "grist for the writers mill" in order to update the next version of the *Creating Business Agility* story.

We would be remiss to close this book without a cautionary tale that has an upbeat note on the value of business agility in the context of the dual challenges of cybersecurity and digital privacy. These futures in 2020 are two sides of the same IoT coin in terms of the business value of IT. On one hand, this Force 5 Tornado drives us to change our digital business practices and transform our business ecosystem culture to create the business agility that enables a sustainable competitive advantage, while on the other hand it threatens us with extinction if this technology convergence not embraced and harnessed.

Remember that one of the central themes of *Creating Business Agility* is to adapt management decision making in real-time to balance the strategic goals: decrease costs, increase revenue, and manage risk. While managing cost and revenue are fundamental to business success, risk is the threat that keeps senior executives awake at night. One of the paramount business risks today is associated with managing enterprise information as an asset in the context of the business value of IT as a strategic initiative. Executives want to avoid the "C-change" that disrupted the careers of the CIO and CEO of Target when inadequate policies and practices for cybersecurity management caused highly visible threats to the financial privacy of over 100 million customers. Today the risk management challenge is to manage the unavoidable and avoid the unmanageable—this is what business agility is all about!

Epilogue:
Selling Sonoma County
Wine Country

SNEAKAWAY MARKETING CAMPAIGN
KEYSTONE SCENARIO USE CASE

Business Agility Readiness Case Study

Introduction

As the Epilogue to this book, this is intended to bring closure to *Creating Business Agility* by wrapping up the key concepts fundamental to our business agility readiness theme with an illustrative case study featuring Sonoma County Tourism (SCT). The keystone scenario for the story *of Selling Sonoma County Wine Country* is built on a collaborative marketing campaign management use case—Sonoma Sneakaway.

As a digital business, the SCT vision and leadership has created a vibrant business ecosystem that has resulted in the TripAdvisor 2012 Travelers' Choice award for the "#1 Wine Destination in the United States." Furthermore, the SCT culture of innovation and collaboration has produced best practices recognized by Hospitality Sales and Marketing Association International (HSMAI) for 2013 achievements in marketing and public relations in the travel industry via gold, silver, and bronze Adrian awards.

The virtual enterprise formed to execute the Sonoma Sneakaway marketing campaign strategy was powered by an Ecosystem Hub cloud platform provided by the Simpleview customer relationship management (CRM) system using the Partner Extranet services. This use case focuses on how the platform works as the SCT Sneakaway system of record (SOR) in terms of resulting gold and silver HSMAI

Adrian awards respectively for Sneakaway campaign best practices and associated SCT mobile-responsive website, as well as how it can evolve as the system of engagement (SOE) in accordance with the vVIC architecture.

Key takeaways for this case study are:

- Sonoma Sneakaway as a collaborative marketing campaign for SCT business ecosystem
- Balanced scorecard for alliance strategy management of Sonoma Sneakaway virtual enterprise
- Simpleview as enabling technology for ecosystem hub to engage social CRM processes for delivery of great wine country experiences
- Establish a center of excellence (CoE) for business agility readiness (BAR) as a critical success factor for enabling culture to sustain competitive advantage in business ecosystem value chains

The Sneakaway scenario provides the context for understanding how SCT has created a sustainable competitive advantage. We hope you will enjoy learning about their business agility readiness story and take away what you need for your success.

Overview

The multibillion-dollar travel industry in California is a vital part of the state and local economies. The industry is represented primarily by retail and service firms, including lodging establishments, restaurants, retail stores, gasoline service stations, and other types of businesses that sell their products and services to travelers. The money that visitors spend on various goods and services while in California produces business receipts at these firms, which in turn employ California residents and pay their wages and salaries. State and local government units benefit from travel as well. The state government collects taxes on the gross receipts of businesses operating in the state, as well as sales and use taxes levied on the sale of goods and services to travelers. Local governments also collect sales and use taxes generated from traveler purchases.

Sonoma County Tourism is the official destination marketing organization for California's Sonoma County. SCT is a private, nonprofit marketing and sales organization dedicated to increasing overnight stays in Sonoma County, California. Located 45 minutes from San Francisco, Sonoma County provides a genuine and adventurous wine country experience. Tourism and wine are big business in Sonoma County. More than seven million visitors come to Sonoma County annually, and overnight visitors spend $292 per day, less than half of which is spent on lodging.

SCT is a customer-centric tourism business ecosystem that consists of an environment including a regional tourism board and county council, local governing authorities, as well as local nonprofit organizations, businesses, and residences. SCT has partner relationships with all the stakeholders who are direct and indirect suppliers or providers for the "customer experience" that visitors purchase.

In order to sustain business ecosystem leadership, digital businesses need to develop and execute a customer experience management strategy enabled by the relevant social business technology that will drive a customer-centric value chain as a virtual enterprise. The ecosystem hub architecture will be described in terms of the travel, tourism, and hospitality industry business ecosystems. Such familiar keystone scenarios utilize a virtual enterprise integration methodology that builds on a virtual visitor information center (vVIC) platform as an example of ecosystem hubs developed using an iterative incremental implementation road map.

The key for building next-generation digital businesses is integrating the business ecosystem with customer engagement solutions. Remember, this approach utilizes two fundamental elements of enterprise information systems engineering:

- Ecosystem hub architecture that employs the Force 5 Tornado technologies using collaborative commerce principles
- Ecosystem hub implementation road map that is an extensible, robust, scalable model for digital business transformation in accordance with business agility readiness gap analysis concepts.

These elements provide the foundation of our strategic framework to build systems of engagement (SOE) for creating business agility.

Selling Sonoma County Wine Country scenario features an integrated case study of the SCT Sonoma Sneakaway marketing campaign to illustrate key concepts of business agility readiness described throughout the book. Industry insights into travel, tourism, and hospitality businesses offer a model for modern collaboration on a global scale—literally, as both internal and external enterprise activities, as well as figuratively as business "coopetition" within their ecosystems. The nature of destination and event marketing may be viewed as a microcosm of the global marketplace in terms of to-destination and in-destination business development strategies being simultaneously executed. In these scenarios, the to-destination marketing campaigns are truly collaborative where all ecosystem partners benefit from a larger traveler spend; yet once the traveler is in-destination the competitive battle occurs for "share of wallet"—a zero-sum game.

Digital Business Insights are led by Ken Fischang, CEO; Tim Zahner, CMO; and Jill Vanden Heuvel, Director of Advertising and Industry Relations for Sonoma County Tourism. These insights focus on how CXO teams may leverage their understanding of these converging technologies to create business agility in terms of innovation via a collaborative culture that mitigates risk by celebrating failure as lessons learned in order to drive future success.

Problem

Travel Industry Disruption by Force 5 Tornado

Travel industry has history of IT innovation disruption and now digital video is disrupting the marketing of destinations in the tourism industry:

- First, the global distribution system changes airlines reservations
- Then disruption via Internet disintermediation of travel agent in 1990s
- Now DMAI *Futures Study* cites destination marketing organization disruption via "Googling"

This use case describes a destination marketing industry scenario that illustrates how the ecosystem hub implementation road map can be employed for evaluating business agility readiness. The example used is for the Sonoma County Tourism (SCT) Ecosystem, as depicted in the keystone scenario shown in Figure E.4 for food and wine events, with a concept of operation for the "to-be" SOE as deployed in a future Sneakaway campaign.

This Epilogue outlines the keystone scenario assessment of business agility readiness for the SCT Sneakaway campaign. This use case features an overview of the development of the ecosystem hub via the cloud-based *Simpleview* Social CRM Partner Extranet to describe in more detail how the SCT Ecosystem leverages the Force 5 Tornado technologies to create the business agility needed to gain and sustain their competitive advantage as the leading wine country destination in the USA.

Destination Marketing Industry Trends.   A comprehensive study of the state of the industry was completed by the Destination Marketing Association International (DMAI) in 2008. The core findings were published in the report "The Future of Destination Marketing: Tradition, Transition, and Transformation." According to the objectives of this "Future" study, it has been used to provide a framework and guidance for destination marketing organizations (DMOs) to conduct scenario-based strategic planning exercises in order to better navigate these turbulent economic times.

Strategic Conclusions   Two significant conclusions may be drawn from the study that directly impact a DMO's ability to sustain a competitive advantage as the voice of the customer within the larger travel and tourism industry. This voice is expressed in terms of the three strategic themes—*relevance, value proposition,* and *visibility*—that are reflected in the DMO strategic conversation. It refers to both the internal customer (the destination ecosystem stakeholders) and the external customer (the destination location visitors). The resulting conclusions are summarized as:

- DMOs collaborate with their stakeholders as a virtual enterprise.
- Information technology is an enabler to improve enterprise performance.

These conclusions form the basis of a visitor-centric strategy for a collaborative commerce solution that increases the effectiveness of integrated destination marketing campaigns. Such campaigns need to be targeted to attract inbound destination visitors during their travel planning and also to support at-destination visitors during their stay.

Collaborative commerce (c-commerce) is a strategy for mainstream electronic business (e-business) evolution. C-commerce business practices enable trading partners to create, manage, and use data in a shared environment to design, build, and support products throughout their life cycles, working separately to leverage their core competencies together in a value chain that forms a virtual enterprise (Heisterberg 2003). This definition of c-commerce is made actionable by blending the elements of operations management, performance management, and information technology in order to realize virtual enterprise integration.

Note that value chain refers to the trading partner community with mutually beneficial interests spanning the complete business ecosystem of destinational stakeholders. As a virtual enterprise, this ecosystem operates as a strategic alliance of organizations that collaborate to share core competencies and resources in a manner that improves their ability to do business. Ecosystem synergy is achieved by means of virtual enterprise integration. This enables stakeholders to perform more effectively as a collective whole through their use of information technology and collaborative business practices.

Ecosystem Hub Platforms   The hallmark of a c-commerce ecosystem is a network of ecosystem hubs, based on a service-oriented architecture (SOA), which are e-business platforms that facilitate the sharing of information between trading partners. They utilize Web 2.0 technologies and, in general, are deployed as either a private trading exchange operating as a hybrid cloud with integrated private and community cloud platforms, such as the password-protected members-only partition of a DMO website for stakeholders, or a public e-marketplace, such as a commercial travel portal operated in the travel, tourism, and hospitality industry providing travel planning and/or online travel agency services.

As illustrated in Figure E.1, core platform data management services, based on an SOA embracing open source software concepts, are hosted on a web server with firewalls and secure tunneling capable of handling public key encryption transactions. Layered web services extend outward to support the following generic ecosystem hub functions: directory and middleware, including interoperable data management services for enterprise content management, project portfolio management, and business process management; generic business collaboration tools and messaging services; trading partner profile and catalog services to facilitate virtual enterprise partnering; and customizable vertical industry specific tools and application services.

Ecosystem Hub
Services-Oriented Architecture

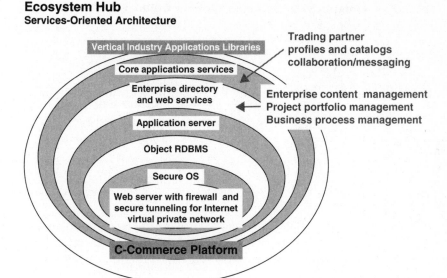

Figure E.1   Ecosystem Hub Data Management Services

As a general business trend, c-commerce strategies are being built around distinct value chain management business models, which facilitate mass customization scenarios via demand chain integration and mass production scenarios via supply chain integration in most industries today. Both types of value chain scenarios are being enabled by software-as-a-service (SaaS) application deployment. As c-commerce evolves as the mainstream e-business strategy for effective value chain management, reengineering of management decision-making processes becomes the critical success factor for enterprise profitability and growth in the twenty-first century.

Challenges and Opportunities

IT needs strategic responses to unprecedented market disruptions, and changing trends with new business challenges and opportunities. Now the cloud can relieve the burden of maintaining the current capital-intensive infrastructure that makes it possible for IT to meet those competitive challenges and take advantage of the disruptive opportunities.

Destination Marketing Organization Leadership Roles and Responsibilities

Destination marketing organizations (DMOs) may operate a central ecosystem hub, serving as the travel business ecosystem leader, in the virtual enterprise associated with delivery of travel and hospitality services to visitors in a destination location. This strategic positioning of a DMO is articulated in terms of fulfilling four key roles from a visitor-centric strategy for destination stakeholders (DMAIF 2008):

1. *Informing, educating, and advising the visitor.* The DMO's key contribution in this dimension is *message integrity*—serving as the official face and voice of the destination.
2. *Advising and supporting marketers.* The DMO's key contribution in this dimension is *matchmaking*—finding or creating opportunities for those who buy and sell visitor-related services to do business with one another.
3. *Advocating the total visitor experience.* The DMO's key contribution in this dimension is *visitor focus*—drawing the attention of all stakeholders to the challenge of delivering a high-value visitor experience from end to end, start to finish.
4. *Supporting destination development.* The DMO's key contribution in this dimension is *strategic perspective*—advocating a master-planned approach to development that recognizes the value of the visitor industry, and providing policy leadership for key developments and initiatives.

Savvy DMOs are using interactive marketing practices as travel content aggregators by leveraging this leadership position to become the central destination information hub for travelers making trip-planning decisions. This strategy is supported from the perspective of several of the "Future" study super-trends—The Battle for Attention, Smart and Friendly Websites, The Electronic Culture, and The Quest for Relevance—and *visibility* is arguably one of the fundamental critical success factors for DMOs:

> Before our prospective visitors actually travel *physically*, they typically travel "virtually." They undertake a journey of knowledge, however brief or extensive, that enables them to make a whole range of choices about what to buy and how. This journey of knowledge

might meander down any number of pathways, including talking
with friends, reading news articles and travel guides, watching TV
shows, and—more commonly these days—exploring what the
Internet has to offer. (DMAIF 2008)

Creating a strategic concept for a virtual visitor information
center (vVIC) architecture is an actionable means to achieve the
ends expressed in the context of the "Future" study. The term *virtual*
has a dual meaning in the definition of a vVIC. First, although it may
exist as a bricks-and-mortar facility, a vVIC is more importantly a
facility that exists in cyberspace and can be accessed from anywhere in
the world. Second, the vVIC uses digital media to provide visitors with
a rich, high-fidelity experience of the destination location, venues,
and activities before, during, and after their trip. Furthermore, it is
important to recognize that a vVIC is both a technology platform and
an advertising content library featuring rich Internet applications
(Heisterberg 2009).

Development of a vVIC requires that a DMO establish integrated
policies, practices, and processes for coordinated acquisition of
technology and content. Operation of a vVIC can be used to create
a visitor experience that differentiates from commercial travel planning portals. Such a visitor experience, created with compelling
content and delivered throughout the travel life cycle, can provide
a DMO with a sustainable competitive advantage that is aligned with
its enterprise business strategy. This may be accomplished using the
three strategic themes, the four roles of a strategic map, and the five
key results areas to provide the framework for DMO strategic planning of a c-commerce solution for improved destination marketing.
In order to provide a more actionable description of the strategic
architecture for a vVIC, Sonoma County Tourism (SCT) is an example of a representative DMO.

DMO Challenges and Opportunities

The past decade has seen the growth of the Internet dominate the
technology market space across all industries, and e-business has
become mainstream business. With this phenomenon has come a
proliferation of the enterprise information portal (EIP), which is a
commercial software product that serves as an ecosystem hub platform to support targeted users in a community of interest that

represents an ecosystem for common business or leisure activities (Heisterberg 2001).

An EIP provides access to relevant structured transactional information, aggregated business intelligence data and trends, unstructured documents and content sources, digital media, and web services. Such an ecosystem hub offers members interaction with rich Internet applications—integrated graphics, animation, audio, video, and collaborative processes for personalized communications between enterprise trading partners.

In the travel and tourism industry, such websites serve as content aggregators and navigation guides to the Internet—aimed at travel customers. Quite apart from the interactive sites of the travel resellers, more and more hotels, visitor attractions, city governments, city-centered magazines, travel publishers, hotel rating agencies, and a host of other specialized sites are siphoning off visitor attention that might otherwise go to DMOs. Becoming a preferred "infomediary"—the go-to source that's positioned as far up the road as possible in the customer's journey of knowledge—will increasingly define competitive advantage in many sectors of business (DMAIF 2008).

Travel Life Cycle Management Scenarios

Primary and secondary research conducted by Rod Heisterberg Associates for a travel and tourism technology client during 2007 and 2008 resulted in the documentation of the travel customer decision journey as a generic travel life cycle model. It describes visitor decision making associated with behavior for the planning, coordination, and management of the travel itinerary. The life cycle model is applicable to convention/meeting, travel trade, and leisure travel scenarios. The development of this model, which drives a series of visitor experience use cases, continued throughout 2009.

The following use case definitions are provided in the context of development and operation of a vVIC using ecosystem hub architecture with Web 2.0 product features and functions. The required enabling technologies for a vVIC can be expressed as a set of fully developed use cases. These system requirements incorporate Web 2.0 functionality, including user-generated content (UGC)—reviews, ratings, photos, and videos; blogs, wikis, and really simple syndication (RSS) feeds, as well as rich Internet applications. Expert concierge

Figure E.2 Visitor Experience Management Defined

services that build and manage the travel itinerary are also described in the use cases.

Visitor experience management principles and practices, shown in Figure E.2, are leveraged to build the vVIC with the Web 2.0 capabilities that facilitate operating as a virtual focus group for evaluating collaborative destination marketing strategies and tactics across the travel life cycle. This includes providing visitor services for UGC uploads of photos and videos plus reviews and ratings of itinerary activities. Visitors can use the vVIC blogs and wikis to create travel life cycle itinerary management resources and tools. The vVIC-provided collaboration spaces for registered community members can facilitate development of:

- Coordination of the organization for a group travel activity
- Destination insider travel guides and neighborhood tours
- Personalized vacation journals and trip albums
- Seasonal or special event tips or frequently asked questions

The vVIC services may be employed to privately share such resources with friends and family or to publicly publish them for like-minded travelers. This will enhance visitor experience before, during, and after the trip. Accordingly, the community knowledge associated with the destination becomes an explicit marketing asset, as well as generating increasing website online stickiness that is of value to the whole ecosystem.

The travel life cycle is intended to provide the foundation of a vVIC architectural concept for building a collaborative travel planning community as a social media network. This system architecture may be described in terms of the hardware, software, and Internet resources needed for implementing the distributed multiplatform portal as an ecosystem hub for a DMO ecosystem. It is recommended that development be performed in accordance with a DMO technology plan describing an iterative incremental implementation strategy expressed as a multiyear vVIC road map. Use scenarios are defined in eight steps as follows (Heisterberg 2008):

1. **Decide Travel:** Explore destination galleries to decide desired travel location.

   View SCT videos and other rich media on digital cable TV video on demand (VOD), and as streaming videos on commercial travel planning portals, or from vVIC to traveler devices, as appropriate based on platform capabilities and interactive digital advertising campaign objectives.

2. **Decide Destination:** Explore the destination gallery of the desired location for featured travel.

   View SCT attractions, hotels, restaurants, shopping, recreation, and other promotional videos and rich media on VOD, travel planning portals, or vVIC.

3. **Decide Itinerary:** View destination location travel guide for to-do list.

   View SCT venue videos (i.e., attractions, hotels, restaurants, shopping, recreation, etc.) and rich media on VOD, travel planning portals, or vVIC.

4. **Decide Booking:** Make travel reservations:
   ✓ Round-trip transportation
   ✓ Lodging
   ✓ Ground transportation
   ✓ Tours

   Use rich Internet applications on vVIC and affiliate partner network for in-depth research on options in accordance with personal traveler profile and expert concierge services in booking itinerary activities.

5. **Decide Plans:** Search travel tips library for trip issues and How2 interests.

   Build itinerary via rich Internet applications for viewing general trip and specific SCT How2 videos on vVIC.

6. **Decide Update:** Check travel guide when at destination hotel for itinerary update.

   View SCT venue videos on vVIC and interact with expert concierge via rich Internet applications to manage itinerary.

7. **Decide Change:** Check travel guide when on the move for itinerary change.

   Review SCT videos and interact with expert concierge via rich Internet applications for itinerary changes on vVIC.

8. **Decide Sharing:** Post travel guide feedback and UGC photos and/or videos on return home.

   Upload UGC to SCT travel guide space to share with members of registered community on vVIC.

Note that since a vVIC is both a technology platform and an advertising content library featuring rich media and rich Internet applications, content acquisition policies and practices need to be established in a modular manner so that they are aligned with the DMO marketing strategy, as well as keyed to the effectiveness of the associated digital media. Furthermore, content management processes and enabling systems must be implemented in an incremental manner in accordance with a comprehensive business case for development and operation of a vVIC that is integrated with interactive advertising campaign management systems. For example, content needs to be produced by the DMO ecosystem or sourced from digital media providers for destination galleries, travel guides, and travel tips as collections of rich Internet applications, which include:

- Integrated graphics, including interactive maps
- Animated graphics such as virtual reality scenes
- Audio files (i.e., MP3 for podcast guided tours)
- Video assets (i.e., prepurposed for multiplatform display)
- Collaborative processes for interactive synchronous and asynchronous communications between groups of visitors

They can be published for multiplatform display via VOD, web, and mobile devices. Rich media sourcing, publication, and placement priority is given to professionally produced video assets that tell a compelling story about "Why the destination is a great place to visit!" and that show "All the great things to do when you visit the destination!"

These professional video assets can also be syndicated on commercial travel planning portals as part of an affiliate marketing campaign that is targeted to the visitor experience context or behavioral interaction according to the travel life cycle. In such a manner, this video and rich media content can be produced once and published many times across the travel life cycle on multiple VOD, web, and mobile vVIC platforms for integrated to-destination and in-destination campaigns that are cooperatively funded.

Solution

Visitor Information Center as a Differentiator

So how can a DMO compete with travel planning portals that employ multimillion-dollar brand and product marketing campaigns to generate hundreds of millions of Internet visitors a year? Development of a vVIC can provide a DMO with a sustainable competitive advantage that is aligned with a collaborative marketing strategy for attracting prospective travelers.

This must be done as early as possible in the DMO's virtual customer decision journeys to find trustworthy destination information in order to develop the reputation as the preferred first stop in the travel-planning life cycle. Furthermore, this trusted insider relationship needs to be cultivated throughout the visitor's trip. The key is establishing the vVIC, via use of intelligent itinerary management tools and services, as the primary destination information hub before, during, and after the visitor's trip. This is enabled by interactive marketing technology for reusing the collection of rich Internet media and applications across all platforms that visitors employ in the scenarios of their travel life cycle experience.

Insights to the strategic concept of vVIC operations may be gained by reviewing a state-of-the-art visitor information center, as well as evaluating best practices for in-destination and to-destination marketing campaigns.

DMO Alternative: Distributed Virtual Center Concept

The strategic concept for a vVIC is described and being developed in the context as a generalized architecture suitable for implementation in accordance with the specification of a DMO's needs. DMOs can create a virtual tourism ecosystem by interconnecting stakeholder websites to form a coordinated service value network enabled by c-commerce technologies. As a leader of the business ecosystem, a DMO can both directly participate in as well as promote the value propositions of stakeholders in an economic community that is chartered with the mission to grow the business and leisure travel trade for the benefit of a regional location. This economic community produces travel and hospitality services of value to visitors throughout the region. Other regional DMOs, such as local chambers of commerce and convention and visitor bureaus (CVBs), may also be stakeholders in the greater DMO ecosystem.

The virtual enterprise of community members may evolve their ecosystem roles and responsibilities, as well as their capabilities and core competencies. In such a manner they will be dynamically aligned with one or more value chains operating in the ecosystem. Note that the role of the DMO as ecosystem leader is valued by the travel community because it enables business members to align their marketing operations with a collaborative destinational strategy.

The DMO ecosystems, illustrated in Figure E.3 and Figure E.4, are nested – with the SCT business ecosystem also shown as a regional DMO partner, being a member of the larger San Francisco Travel business ecosystem. Each ecosystem consists of two distinct networks with interdependent virtual enterprises cooperating to produce and deliver travel products that are of value to their mutual target customers, the destination visitors. The ecosystem service value networks operate as collaborative marketing campaign value chains. These networks provide travel services to promote to-destination visitor traffic into the destination location and to provide in-destination hospitality and tourism services to visitors during their stay. DMO community members include:

- Convention and visitor bureau organizations
- Travel planning and booking websites
- Travel agents
- Tour wholesalers

**Stakeholder Value Chain Business Rules Create Visitor
Experience Concept of Operation:
Who, What, When, Where, Why, and How**

*Ecosystem Hub Architecture Provides Shared Information Resources for
To-and In-Destination Collaborative Marketing Campaigns*

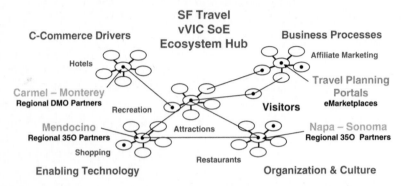

Figure E.3   San Francisco Travel Ecosystem as a Set of Virtual Enterprises

- Tour operators
- Tour managers
- Resorts
- Cruise lines
- Vacation properties
- Airlines
- Rental cars
- Merchandisers
- Attractions
- Hotels
- Restaurants
- Shopping
- Recreation
- Travel service affiliates

This collection of stakeholders will gain value by actively participating in the vVIC and engaging in a collaborative DMO strategy for cooperative marketing projects promoting integrated to-destination and in-destination digital advertising campaigns.

The process of creating a strategic vision for a vVIC concept of operation is governed by three design principles: *modularity, scalability,* and *incremental implementation.* The concept of operation for a vVIC

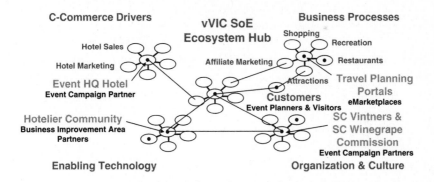

Figure E.4 Sonoma County Tourism Ecosystem as a Set of Virtual Enterprises

using the SCT as an example builds on technology transfer opportunities from the state-of-the-art virtual enterprise best practices.

Modularity. A vVIC will deliver video and other rich digital media assets in facilities and/or hardware platforms in order to support a ten-foot, three-foot, and one-foot viewing experience of visitor information. Viewing from these distances is associated with using a large-screen high-definition monitor, a flat screen on a PC or laptop computer, and a handheld mobile smartphone, respectively. All platforms will support reservations and/or ticketing services via Ares and OpenTable partnerships, as well as e-commerce applications for merchandising. With vVIC operations deployed in satellite locations, viewing stations may be either of a lounge design for use in SCT sites or stakeholder venues (i.e., hotel lobbies, attractions pavilions, shopping malls, etc.) or a self-service kiosk design for use in smaller venues and made rugged for outdoors.

Scalability. The vVIC will display the rich Internet applications with a consistent user interface, as well as software look and feel that optimizes the viewing experience across platforms. In addition to partnering with Google to implement its Earth, Maps, and Mobile products, the destination location software environment may employ virtual reality technology. A hybrid virtual reality experience for leisure and business meeting events may be created by also partnering with a leading hotel to offer the Cisco TelePresence system for videoconferencing.

Incremental Implementation.   The vVIC will be implemented and deployed in an incremental manner. The phased development process will be driven by an iterative business case methodology in order to assure the economic viability of each vVIC product release. Initial vVIC product releases will focus on the major sites, venues, and attractions within the central Sonoma County business ecosystem regional area, and then spiral outward in an iterative manner to incorporate other leading regional locations.

Virtual Visitor Information Center Solution

The ecosystem hub architecture provides the fundamental e-business platform to facilitate integrated to-destination and in-destination advertising value chain scenarios for the vVIC. Deployment as SaaS-hosted applications of virtual enterprise data management services can reliably deliver the c-commerce solution via safeguarding DMO ecosystem proprietary information as part of a SaaS service-level agreement. With the vVIC operating as the interactive marketing hub, the SOA enables the virtual enterprise data management model via web services that provide a standards-based, secure, shared data environment for a collaborative marketing campaign optimization.

Ecosystem Hub Content Management Services

Content management is a fundamental capability required by an EIP as a system of record (SOR) when it is deployed as an ecosystem hub, regardless of the industry or functional application. The generic integration services enable EIPs to act as virtual enterprise gateways providing semantic interoperability with diverse applications across multiple DMO hybrid cloud platforms and commercial travel portals. In general, an ecosystem hub contains a profile of every registered virtual enterprise member, including a catalog of the member's products, capabilities, and capacities, as well as trading partner agreements and communication system preferences. This profile provides data directory and dictionary services that describe all the sharable information at the data element level that is owned by a trading partner, including a security policy to permit the sharing of information with a virtual enterprise customer, but not with a potential competitor.

EIPs are made into products according to various industry needs. In this manner, virtual enterprise data management services include data format and communication translations as required for messaging services according to the required industry standards. Collaboration tools can also be provided to support both asynchronous groupware and synchronous real-time, multipoint data conferencing applications for both structured and unstructured data. In addition, an ecosystem hub can offer product data exchange translation in accordance with the governing industry standards, as well as a library of application software for a vertical industry where native data format exchange is considered to be mission critical, such as the aerospace industry.

Recall from Figure E.1 that core platform services, based on an SOA embracing open source software concepts, are hosted on a web server with firewalls and secure tunneling capable of handling public key encryption transactions. Layered web services extend outward to support directory and middleware, including interoperable object management services for enterprise content, including digital assets, product data managed as project portfolios, and business process management via a work flow engine; generic business collaboration tools and messaging services; trading partner profile and catalog services to facilitate virtual enterprise partnering; and customizable vertical industry specific tools and application services.

The messaging services provide the enabling technology that is fundamental for decision making in a real-time enterprise. For example, in manufacturing industries, such c-commerce messaging data provides the status of stock on hand that is stored at enterprise and trading partner locations, as well as stock in transit across the value chain for inventory visibility. Furthermore, supply chain management business activity monitoring solutions generate event notifications associated with the business rules that reflect the roles and responsibilities of each trading partner. Finally, operational metrics, such as supplier delivery history and status, are displayed as real-time dashboards for measurement of trading partner performance in accordance with their service-level agreements to support integrated value chain management decision making.

An EIP deployment, using the variety of ecosystem hub sourcing strategies currently available, may be developed by the internal IT organization or outsourced to a trading partner with an IT core competency in order to allow the enterprise to focus on executing its strategic business plan. These integration services offer virtual enterprise gateways providing semantic interoperability with diverse applications.

As a core service for EIP products, content management systems have become a primary application for DMOs—particularly solutions that have been designed specifically with destination marketing needs and processes in mind, such as the Simpleview content management system (CMS) and CRM platforms as an Ecosystem Hub. They enable staff members with moderate computer expertise to publish content without requiring technical knowledge of HTML or the uploading of complex files. The responsibilities can be dispersed across several departments as needed. The ultimate result of using content management systems is dynamic websites that will increase the time visitors spend on a vVIC interacting with the DMO and ecosystem stakeholders.

In the travel industry, for example, an ecosystem hub using CRM as a vVIC platform must interoperate with several intranets as part of the DMO enterprise information management system and with numerous business ecosystem stakeholder extranets as CRMs across multiple travel industry segments. Furthermore, the vVIC must interoperate with several commercial travel portals as part of affiliate marketing scenarios.

In general, enterprises need to build or acquire access to networks outside their four walls that will interoperate as a blend of extranets that consist of hybrid cloud platforms, as well as both public vertical industry and horizontal e-marketplaces. These ecosystem hubs also provide business process outsourcing and information integration services. Leading examples such as Exostar, primarily serving the aerospace and defense industry, and E2open, providing supplier on-boarding for diverse business networks, including industrial high-tech electronics and consumer packaged goods, demonstrate the broad applicability of the use of Ecosystem Hubs for virtual enterprise integration.

There are numerous EIP vendors featuring Web 2.0 technologies for DMOs to select as ecosystem hub software providers for building a vVIC using the DMO ecosystem business case for vVIC development, as well as an iterative incremental implementation road map.

vVIC Architecture as an Ecosystem Hub

Operation of a central ecosystem hub as a hybrid cloud with integrated private and community cloud platforms by a DMO will facilitate an SOA-based infrastructure for the virtual enterprise enabled as a network of ecosystem hubs providing collaborative marketing campaign management services for their business ecosystem. Such information system architecture is both robust and scalable, as well as extensible to a wide variety of travel industry scenarios.

The example is provided in the context of the incremental implementation model for a road map in terms of vVIC extranet integration to develop c-commerce competencies by investing in a portfolio of IT initiatives. It is focused on a strategy for a DMO to implement hybrid cloud platforms using an ecosystem hub architecture, as shown in Figure E.4, for interactive marketing campaigns. The DMO vVIC is the mission-critical part of a network of ecosystem hubs for creating a virtual enterprise with collaborative travel planning community services as part of a business ecosystem (Heisterberg 2008).

Note that such interactive marketing applications of knowledge management for the travel demand chain scenarios are fundamental for collaborative marketing success. Deciding what information is relevant for a marketing segmentation strategy depends on what needs to be achieved. Information can be gathered either explicitly, based on information that the customer has provided, or implicitly, gathered without the customer's direct knowledge (Heisterberg 2010). This knowledge capture is facilitated by the SOA for social networking as layers of travel destination community services reflecting increasing levels of customer intimacy:

Public portal services—the outermost layer of the DMO interactive marketing platform that provides general visitor destination information and travel services, such as:
- Travel planning and sample itinerary information
- Travel and tourism product catalog as rich media assets (attractions, lodging, dining, shopping, recreation, etc.)
- Community events calendar
- Mobile app gateway or responsive design website support

Private community services—the middle layer where returning visitor registration is required to become a DMO community member eligible to receive personalized customer services via traditional customer relationship management (CRM) or contemporary customer experience management (CEM) systems functionality, such as:

- Travel planning tools, including expert concierge itinerary builder
- Merchandising via e-commerce and booking engine services
- Rich media for social networking
- RSS feed for blogs and podcasts
- UGC functionality

Proprietary member services—the innermost layer is reserved for ecosystem stakeholders, as well as where VIP visitor entrée is provided to a customized travel itinerary management work space as a gated community on a subscription or fee-for-service basis:

- Expert concierge premium VIP membership
- Stakeholder membership partition with password-protected login
- Stakeholder collaboration spaces with password-protected login
- Interactive marketing campaign management suite, including:
  - Analytic tools
  - Creative library
  - Campaign ad unit performance dashboard

Since an ecosystem hub can provide a library of application software for a vertical industry, a vVIC can optimize the DMO ecosystem stakeholder collaboration in terms of economic impact via orchestrating integrated marketing campaigns by facilitating an interactive marketing campaign management system.

Such an online marketing suite, as defined by Forrester Research, consists of two key components, which describe the Ecosystem Hub architecture (Heisterberg 2010):

1. *Central Hub*—the core of the suite that enables marketers to manage and integrate online data as an ecosystem hub
2. *Network*—a thriving community of technology and service partners that delivers execution, targeting, and measurement services as a business ecosystem.

Four key architectural elements make the ecosystem hub the "design and decisioning engine of the online marketing suite":

1. A unified data model
2. Process tools and metadata repository
3. A centralized optimization engine
4. Standards-based architecture

This concept of the "central hub" as the "novel part of the suite" corresponds to the definition of an ecosystem hub in terms of the generic data management services of the SOA shown in Figure E.1, as well as the application-specific core Web 2.0 architecture in Figure E.5, including the adaptive strategic planning decision support system (DSS) services driven by big data analytics (BDA). Furthermore, the interactive marketing specialist vendors that make up the network layer correspond to the marketing-specific "digital media ad campaign

System of Engagement
Ecosystem Hub Architecture

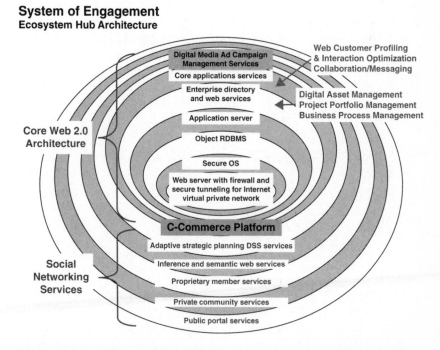

Figure E.5 Virtual Visitor Information Center Is SOE Ecosystem Hub

management services" representation of the generic "vertical industry applications libraries" layer of the ecosystem hub architecture. These interactive marketing tools may include:

- Web interaction optimization
- Behavioral targeting
- Multivariate testing
- E-mail campaigns
- Bid management
- Web analytics
- Ad serving

Developing and managing SOA-based business processes for marketing, advertising, sales, and customer support in aligned service value chains throughout the business ecosystem both require an architecture that provides a standards-based, secure, shared data environment. Such architecture for developing, monitoring, measuring, and optimizing SOA-enabled business processes in service networks may be exemplified as a suite of marketing campaign and performance management decision support system applications using Web 2.0 enabling technology to provide the functionality needed to implement c-commerce business models (Vittal, VanBoskirk, and Glass 2007):

> Today interactive marketing is a fragmented discipline in which marketers work with many different vendors to develop and execute marketing programs. But as the number of channels and programs grow, this situation becomes untenable. Today's interactive marketers have few options as neither enterprise marketing suites nor interactive specialists address their needs. Forrester believes that the time is right for the online marketing suite to emerge.

Such interactive marketing solutions are now widely available and may be deployed as an ecosystem hub enabled by SOA technology using an EIP platform; this "is the eventual destiny for all online marketing technology and will enable a single view of the customer across channels, provide process tools to support collaboration, centralize optimization, and support a partner ecosystem." The functional requirements for this marketing ecosystem hub may be summarized as:

enable efficient and effective collaboration, provide reliable perform-ance measurement, and optimize marketing spend.

Dynamic Itinerary Services for Travel Life Cycle Management

The key to the expert concierge strategic concept of c-commerce applications for interactive marketing in the travel industry is lever-aging the knowledge management contained within the DMO busi-ness ecosystem. This is accomplished by using an inferencing engine to manage graphical interface artifacts and relationship conventions according to their experience profiles. DMO community members can manipulate trip map objects representing itinerary icons such as events, places, and reservations as appropriate to their community member privileges. They can create and maintain dynamic itineraries that span many scenarios for trips, destinations, time lines past, present, future; store and edit travel information; and access it for use anytime—anywhere in the world.

Expert concierge employs proprietary semantic Web 3.0 technol-ogy for automatically creating itineraries from travel documentation. It extracts the travel data for the trip being planned to create and maintain an itinerary master file for each trip stored in the visitor's personal travel space on a vVIC. The intelligent agents work transpar-ently to aggregate all related travel data from trip-specific e-mails and travel planning portals, as well as other travel, tourism, and hospitality services, including:

- Travel schedule weather reports and forecasts
- Destination and tour maps with directions
- Location and event guides
- Transportation, lodging, and dining reservations
- Shopping lists and tips with recommended venues and deals
- Geo-synced rich media links for attractions and points of interest

Note that a vVIC supports standard web browsers, as well as mobile device interfaces using open source standards and responsive design principle, practices, and products to optimize diverse mobile platform functionality. According to the travel life cycle, the mobile capabilities may become the most valuable expert concierge services due to the portable and pervasive advantages of mobile computing. Beyond enabling DMO visitors to check their itinerary plans on the move, the expert system is capable of automatic or on-demand regeneration of itinerary recommendations when changes occur within the current trip-specific environment. This dynamic adaptation meets the expert concierge goal to most easily provide the most current travel information how, when, and where vVIC members want it.

Ecosystem Hub Via Simpleview Platform

Since 1991, the Simpleview vision has produced innovations in destination marketing for DMOs both large and small: the first company to create a web-based destination management system specifically to help DMOs manage relationships with industry partners and customer, as well as travelers; the first to integrate that system with an easy to use yet powerful web-based content management system; and also the first to extend that integrated CRM/CMS solution to sites optimized for mobile web.

The vision and mission for the social CRM platform in a DMO business ecosystem is described in Figure E.6 with highlights from the keynote presentation for the Simpleview Summit 2014 by CEO, Ryan George. He not only defines the digital business ecosystem hub

---

Since travel and tourism is big business, providing one out of every nine jobs in our country with annual economic impact of $2.1 trillion, the U.S. Travel Association performed a set of studies to support an awareness campaign around "the travel effect." That research has looked at what travel means to destination visitors and the implications on visitor experience management for DMOs. The bottomline is DMOs primary reason for existence is connecting people to partners in their business ecosystem.

Examples of the value of using the Simpleview platform for providing DMO membership services includes:

- Educate and coach on how to improve the visitor experience
- Show how to use new tools and understand technology
- Collaborate together in cooperative marketing and special events
- Connect with writers when they want a story
- Send business through visitor centers and phone calls and e-mail referrals
- Connect with meeting planners and group tours for diverse destination community services
- Help market with maps, special offers, tweets, pins, and posts, as well as by creating unique video content

Simpleview enables social CRM principles and practices for Partner Relationship Management.

Figure E.6   Social CRM Value Delivered in a Business Ecosystem

Source: Simpleview Inc.

Simpleview CRM offers a single, integrated system to replace legacy databases and accompanying technologies for lead-sharing, sales, industry partner management and more. While it streamlines work with industry partners, community stakeholders, prospective visitors, the media, meeting and event planners, and other key contacts, "customer relationship management" is just the beginning.

Simpleview CRM integrates all the features expected in an enterprise-grade relationship management with sales force automation, forecasting, reporting, and business analysis, combining all these functions with direct tie-ins to the Simpleview CMS content management system, and/or an available API for integration with a third-party website.

Mobile CRM is an extension of the Simpleview CRM system for use on mobile devices as a cloud-based, crossplatform service for virtually any mobile device. Access Simpleview CRM from a mobile phone to update leads, verify account information, call or e-mail a contact, and use more enterprise applications.

Figure E.7   Cloud-based Simpleview Platform Features

Source: Simpleview Inc.

solution value proposition in general, the partner extranet collaborative marketing campaign management use case benefits are specifically articulated to support the economic justification for virtual enterprise deployment. This strategic architecture is envisioned for the BAR CoE using the Ecosystem Hub via the cloud-based Simpleview CRM features summarized in Figure E.7. vVIC functionality is further delineated for Sneakaway campaigns with partner relationship management applications in the SCT ecosystem in Figure E.8. The bottom line is that the Simpleview platform enables successful execution of this Sonoma Sneakaway keystone scenario strategy and is a critical success factor for CIO-CMO alignment.

Lessons Learned

Collaborative Strategies for Cooperative Marketing

A c-commerce framework that facilitates the management of interactive marketing value chain system operations is presented to summarize the concept of adaptive strategic planning for demand chain optimization. An ecosystem hub architecture enabled by Web 2.0 services provides the foundation for a generic model of c-commerce applications for service value network management systems. This use case scenario is based on specific value propositions associated with deploying digital media ad campaign management applications in the travel and tourism industry.

Member/Partner Management Module

This module is the "hub" of the system, and is the central repository for all member/partner information. This module is integrated with all other modules in the system; any activity performed anywhere in the system which benefits a member is automatically recorded in the member account, and from throughout the system users may search member information. Module features provide support for digital marketing, data management, research analytics, and marketing partnerships. Examples include Simpleview data feeds for calendar of events submission are via a webform on the SCT website developed by Miles, providing responsive design for mobile users. Various RFP and request forms on the website are supported by either via built-in webforms or Wufoo forms. The data feeds between Simpleview and Miles website also enable collaboration using social media—Hootsuite for Twitter posts, as well as Facebook for Visitor Guide request tab that integrates a Wufoo form.

Member/Partner Extranet

Designated member/partner contacts can access their accounts via an online portal. Depending on permissions granted, partners can access a variety of functions that are used for collaborative Sneakaway marketing campaign management such as What's New submissions.

Figure E.8 Simpleview Extranet for Partner Relationship Management

Source: Simpleview Inc. and Sonoma County Tourism

The emerging term for this evolutionary approach is the *strategic conversation*. This is the ongoing "multilogue" around key issues, developments, trends, events, and possible options for coping with the rapidly changing business environment. In today's world, the strategic conversation must be almost continuous rather than annual; it must involve all functional areas and many levels of the organization; and it must incorporate the thinking of many contributors, not just the most senior leaders (DMAIF, 2008).

Collaborative marketing campaign management principles, practices, and processes have become mainstream in the travel, tourism, and hospitality industry. Such collaboration strategies leverage integrated marketing business processes enabled by SOA technology. The vVIC enables development of marketing plans for an interactive rich media advertising campaigns by stakeholders in the SCT business ecosystem that maximize economic impact by using collaborative marketing strategies for their inbound-destination and at-destination advertising campaigns. Using the vVIC as the ecosystem hub for a digital media ad content library facilitates collaborative DMO ecosystem campaigns that utilize:

- Multichannel campaign publication:
  - Digital cable TV with addressable ad units, including VOD
  - Internet ads on vVIC and affiliate marketing partner websites
  - Pervasive content served to mobile smartphones and tablets
- Contextual and behavioral messaging keyed to visitor experience in accordance to the travel life cycle and expert concierge itinerary management services
- Platform touch points and messaging mix optimized to achieve stakeholder to-destination and in-destination advertising objectives

In summary, the vVIC enables optimization of the DMO visitor experience across the travel life cycle by facilitating management of the visitor communication and stakeholder collaboration processes. This results in the ability to leverage cooperative marketing campaigns for integrated to-destination and in-destination advertising to maximize economic impact for the DMO ecosystem.

Sonoma County Tourism Sneakaway Marketing Campaign Leverages Hybrid Cloud Deployment as Platform for Ecosystem Hub

Operation of a central ecosystem hub as a hybrid cloud with integrated private and community cloud platforms by a DMO will facilitate a SOA-based infrastructure for the virtual enterprise enabled as a network of ecosystem hubs providing collaborative marketing campaign management services for their business ecosystem. Such an information system architecture is both robust and scalable, as well as extensible to a wide variety of travel industry scenarios (Heisterberg, 2010).

In an endeavor to build vVIC, Sonoma County Tourism evaluated various cloud deployment model and finally chose to deploy their various business applications, such as ecosystem stakeholders applications, on public cloud hosted and managed by while some of their back end applications such as financials and supply chain on private cloud.

The travel life cycle is intended to provide the foundation of a vVIC architectural concept for building a collaborative travel planning community as a social media network. This system architecture may be described in terms of the hardware, software, and Internet resources needed for implementing the distributed multiplatform portal as an ecosystem hub for a DMO ecosystem. Development is recommended to be performed in accordance with a DMO technology plan describing an iterative incremental implementation strategy expressed as a multiyear vVIC road map documenting the business ecosystem keystone scenarios (Heisterberg, 2008).

SCT has launched the winter/spring promotional campaign called "Sonoma Sneakaway," to encourage overnight visitation to Sonoma County during the slower months from January to May.

Sonoma Sneakaway campaign, hosted on public cloud with stakeholders and visitors engagement portal, allows tourism-related businesses to promote themselves, for free, to the millions of potential travelers they reach globally, breaking all geo location boundaries with access to pervasive devices.

Tourism businesses that were interested in participating in Sneakaway could submit their specials to Sonoma County Tourism through the partners section of the SCT website. The campaign, which is free for tourism-related businesses in Sonoma County, centered on the web microsite, www.SonomaSneakaway.com, which held all the offers.

Campaign Results

Summary of Sneakaway campaign results is contained in the following slide gallery, which depicts the broad range of business ecosystem value produced by Ecosystem Hub deployment.

Sneakaway: 2013

- **Priority geo markets:**
  - Sacramento, San Francisco, Los Angeles, San Diego, Seattle, Portland

- **Ad buys summary/highlights:**
  - Facebook – Ads/Sweepstakes
  - KCBS Radio – Jan 29 to March 10
  - Local Getaways – Feb 3 & March 3
  - SF Chronicle – Spring Sonoma Section
  - SFGate.com and Mobile

Sneakaway: 2013

- Ads in Cabs - video in 150 taxis and back of seat signage in at least 75 cabs as added value

- SF Weekly – Newspaper box window clings – 1000 locations (Feb. and Mar.)

- Spot Xchange – Video Ad Network
  - :15 and :30 pre-roll videos + companion banners
  - Targeted: geo, demo, behavioral, keywords and retargeting

- Wall Street Journal co-op –
  - National coverage – co-op with Vintners and Grapegrowers
  - March in WSJ Weekend Off Duty section, reaching 3.1 million people.

Sonoma County Tourism • SonomaCounty.com

Figure E.9   2013 Campaign Highlights

SF Weekly –
newspaper box
window clings

Sneak Away
to Sonoma

Text WINE to **41127**
for current deals or visit
www.sonomasneakaway.com

Message and data rates may apply.
Opt-in only, no spamming. Your info will never be shared.

Sonoma County Tourism • SonomaCounty.com

Figure E.10   SF Weekly Ad with Texting Call to Action

Sneakaway

Ads in cabs —
Seat-back signage

Sneak Away to Sonoma

Text WINE to **411247** for
current deals or visit **www.sonomasneakaway.com**

For more information: desk@sonomacountytourism.com / Message and data rates may apply. Opt-in only, no spamming. Your info will never be shared.

Sonoma County Tourism • SonomaCounty.com

Figure E.11   Ads in Cabs with Texting Call to Action

Sneakaway Feb.–May, 2013

101 Partners – 32 responded to survey (31.7% response rate).

41% received calls/inquiries

Majority would recommend to colleagues
Total Partners that report an ROI: 13 (11 hotels/inns/vacation rentals; 2 attractions)

The total reported increase in spending that surveyed businesses attributed to the Sonoma Sneakaway campaign is **$29,165.**

Registrants for trip giveaway:
• 2,172 resulting in more than 50 percent requesting for more information about Sonoma County.
• 520 people opting in for Alaska Air information

Web stats to promo: Feb.–May
14,400 visits
11,400 unique visitors
35,000 page views
2.43 pages/visit
79.38% new visits

Upcoming:
Fall Harvest Promotion:

Mid-Sept.—end of November
Target: West Coast cities

Submit your Fall Harvest deals now:
    www.sonomacounty.com/partners
Questions:
jillv@sonomacounty.com

Sonoma County Tourism • SonomaCounty.com

Figure E.12   Feb-May 2013 Results

SCT Sneakaway CMO-CIO Best Practices

Hospitality Sales and Marketing Association International (HSMAI) Adrian awards are given for excellence in travel industry marketing. Founded in 1957, the Adrian Awards embraces every segment of the industry, including hotels, airlines, cruise lines, car rental companies, destinations, credit card companies, and more. Winners are selected from a field of more than 1,200 entries by senior industry and media experts.

Sonoma Sneakaway, a seasonal marketing campaign that received the gold award, was recognized for innovations in destination marketing. The off-season campaign encourages travelers to come to Sonoma County for special deals. SCT featured creative advertising placements, including videos that ran in taxicabs in San Francisco and encouraged potential travelers to opt-in to receive more information as well as a partnership with Alaska Airlines to drive visitation from flight markets. During the campaign, which was in its second year, Sonoma County saw increases in lodging occupancy that surpassed pre-recession levels with occupancy in January and February hitting 56 percent and 61 percent, respectively.

A silver Adrian was awarded to the revamped SCT website, www.sonoma-county.com, which launched in February 2013. Traffic to the new website has increased 98 percent over the same period the previous year and has generated $11.1 million in additional spending in Sonoma County. The new website was also innovative in its use of "responsive design," which takes a mobile-first approach to websites. SCT worked with Miles Partnership, an industry leader in destination marketing, on the new website.

Figure E.13   Sneakaway Campaign and Mobile Responsive Website

Source: www.sonomacounty.com; "Sonoma County Tourism Sweeps Podium at Hospitality Marketing's Adrian Awards"

Next Steps

Business Agility Readiness Road Map

Business agility, defined as *innovation via collaboration to be able to anticipate challenges and opportunities before they occur,* produces a sustainable competitive advantage. The business value of IT is realized by creating business agility using a strategy of innovation for CIO-CMO alignment around big data analytics based on collaborative marketing best practices. This is made actionable as a decision framework by incorporating a holistic customer-centric performance management system using an IT balanced scorecard as the basis for a Business Agility Readiness (BAR) Road Map.

The BAR Road Map is defined in terms of an enterprise architecture that consists of the following three elements, integrated by data:

- People → Business architecture
- Process → Application architecture
- Tools → Technology architecture

BAR is actionable by means of using a gap analysis methodology to measure the change in business value associated with each of the four elements as scored in terms of a customer-centric model of business agility. The model is defined by four customer moments of engagement dimensions: profile, engagement, life cycle, and conscience. As the enterprise architecture evolves from the "as-is" state of the current system of record (SOR) to the "to-be" state of the envisioned system of engagement (SOE) supported with multi-dimensional scoring (MDS), the business is transformed in terms of its competitive position in the business ecosystem. This conceptual process is reflected in elements of the SCT "Strategic Thought Process."

The basis of the gap analysis is documented in the form of two social graphs reflecting both the current and the future states of the enterprise architecture. The social graph for the SOR is articulated by a concept of operation that describes how the product data is created, managed, and used by internal/external stakeholders in the context of their roles in the keystone use scenario. A corresponding social graph for the SOE depicts the concept of engagement for the shared customer data environment expressed as one of the following four levels of relationship:

1. From the initial state of *Communication* → exchange of information in a relationship
2. Through *Coordination* → communicating status while working separately
3. Then *Cooperation* → working separately together
4. To fully realize *Collaboration* → working separately together using intellectual capital for sharing risk and reward

Note that each higher level inherits the properties of the lower levels.

The change management rationale for evolving the enterprise IT systems is to transform the corresponding business model and its fundamental strategy from product-centered to customer-centered. This transformation drives data management practices that enable reengineering decision-making processes.

Elements of the BAR Road Map are represented using a balanced scorecard to describe and measure the CIO-CMO partnership alignment gap in the context of the moments of engagement that drive the transformation from a SOR to a SOE. An example of the balanced scorecard for the "as-is" SOR is shown in Figure E.14. Such a tool is used to assess how to best vet the internal/external collaboration activities associated with management of big data for driving advanced business analytics initiatives. This is accomplished by measuring the strategic readiness of the intangible assets

Sneakaway Campaign Alliance Strategy

This BSC is a work-in-process for evolving SCT BAR Roadmap for Digital Marketing and Data Management Partnerships

	Perspective	Objective	Measures	Target	Initiatives
	Financial	Economic impact	Visitor spending	$1.47 billion	Cultivate business improvement area community actions and business ecosystem partnerships
• Elements of BAR Gap Analysis for As-Is vs To-Be BSC Reflected in SCT "Strategic Thought Process"		Lodging occupancy	Yield, daily rates, and revenues	64% (2012), $114.5, and $73.99	
	Customer	Visitor experience management	Satisfaction and advocacy	Active monitoring & engagement on social media platforms	Build visitor and marketing partner relationships
• Use Innovation and Collaboration Best Practices		Sonoma County brand	Trio messaging	brand standards	
	Business Processes	Interactive marketing social media mobility	Web visitation Online visitor spend	Visits increase 90% $41 spend/web visitor	Research and analyze visitor behavior
• Gap Analysis via 8 Step Roadmap for vVIC SoEE Ecosystem Hub		Partner relationship management	Partner data management	1,900 business records updated or added	Use Simpleview CRM with partner extranet
	Learning & Growth	Human capital Information capital Organization capital	Ongoing training and professional development for SCT staff	Conference attendance Speaking engagements Workshop participation	Deploy certified tourism ambassador program

Source: Sonoma County Tourism Annual Report 2013

Figure E.14 Balanced Scorecard for the Sneakaway "As-Is" SOR

Strategic Center of Excellence Process Map

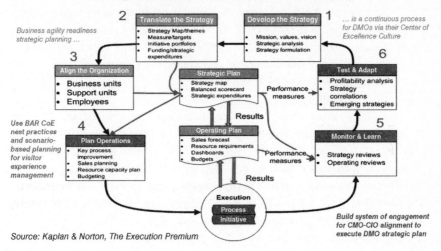

Source: Kaplan & Norton, The Execution Premium

Figure E.15   How the Business Agility Readiness Road Map Works
Source: Kaplan & Norton.

associated with human capital, information capital, and organizational capital, which describe the knowledge perspective of the balanced scorecard. The methodology for how the business agility readiness road map works is shown in Figure E.15 in terms of a gap analysis for a Sonoma Sneakaway scenario based on the *Selling Sonoma County Wine Country* case study.

Strategic visitor experience alignment may be expressed in terms of a vVIC road map for SOE implementation. The vVIC road map is a framework for a visitor experience management (VEM) solution that integrates DMO strategy with operational execution. This framework, built on enterprise performance management principles, consists of six interrelated elements:

1. DMOs develop the VEM strategy.
2. DMOs plan the strategy execution using the balanced scorecard, as well as vVIC concept of operation and architecture.
3. Use vVIC to align DMO operations and employees by means of formal organizational communications processes as well as human capital management practices, policies, and processes.
4. Plan operations using vVIC to design and deliver visitor experiences in accordance with the VEM Strategy.

5. DMOs monitor the performance of the ecosystem operations and evaluate the strategy via regular management review meetings facilitated by vVIC Business Intelligence tools.
6. Analyze internal DMO operational data and external destinational market environmental information in order to adapt the VEM Strategy via vVIC.

The analysis of vVIC touch points associated with the delivery of visitor services for the specific travel product content provides the context for optimization of travel life cycle decision making. That results in validation of performance criteria, and operational metrics described in the visitor experience Audit. This provides valuable insights for DMOs to evaluate their visitor experience strategy versus their capability to successfully deliver that experience. Such reengineering of the travel experience is referred to as "Strategic Visitor Experience Alignment" via center of excellence (CoE) for BAR.

Enterprises need to define the CoE in actionable terms. Gartner defines a CoE as "a physical or virtual center of knowledge concentrating existing expertise and resources in a discipline or capability to attain and sustain world-class performance and value across the supply chain" (Chadwick, 2014). Linking the CoE to tangible value in the value chain, either supply chain or demand chain, is achieved by focusing on the critical core competencies required to enable the Sonoma Sneakaway virtual enterprise strategy for collaborative marketing.

CoEs are critical enablers for the success of digital business value chains to facilitate business agility readiness in their business ecosystem. The dilemma of CIOs and CMOs in a digital business today is to know how to remain agile in execution while constantly looking ahead to future opportunities such as leveraging infonomics applications for BDA services. The CoE challenge is to avoid the "ivory tower" syndrome by maintaining the "silicon crystal ball" focus on the future while providing relevant insight to their virtual enterprise strategy execution challenges now.

Endnotes

Chadwick, K. (2014, April 21). *Centers of Excellence Are Critical Enablers of Success in Supply Chains.* Stamford, CT: Gartner Group.

(DMAIF, 2008). "The Future of Destination Marketing: Tradition, Transition, and Transformation." Destination Marketing Association International Foundation.

Heisterberg, R. 2003. "Collaborative Commerce (C-Commerce)." *The Internet Encyclopedia* (Vol. 1). John Wiley & Sons.

Heisterberg, R. 2009, November 22. "Strategic Architecture for a Virtual Visitor Information Center" (Strategy White Paper). Mountain View, CA: Rod Heisterberg Associates.

Heisterberg, R. 2001, February 22. "Data Ownership Extends Outside the Enterprise" (Research Note). Stamford, CT: Gartner Group.

Heisterberg, R. 2008, August 6. "Creating a Collaborative Travel Planning Community: Lessons Learned in Migrating to a Web 2.0 Experience" (Strategy White Paper). Mountain View, CA: Rod Heisterberg Associates.

Heisterberg, R. 2010. "Collaborative Commerce." *The Handbook of Technology Management* (Vol. III, Chapter 33). John Wiley & Sons, Inc.

Kaplan, R. and D. Norton 2008. *The Execution Premium: Linking Strategy to Operations for Competitive Advantage.* Boston: Harvard Business School Press.

Kaplan, R. and D. Norton 2010, January-February. "Managing Alliances with the Balanced Scorecard." *Harvard Business Review.*

Vittal, S., S. VanBoskirk, and S. Glass. 2007, October 17. *"Defining the Online Marketing Suite,"* Cambridge, MA: Forrester Research.

About the Authors

Alakh Verma is Director of Product Development (Platform Technology Solutions) at Oracle USA, headquarters at Redwood Shores, CA, USA. He has over 20 years of experience in the high technology industry blended with academia. Verma spearheads and evangelizes emerging-technologies-based solutions and services among global partner ecosystem and envisions major shifts in IT trends with cloud, social, mobile, big data, and predictive analytics.

Verma is engaged in Product Management of technology platforms (cloud, social, mobile, big data, and predictive analytics) at Oracle, and has traveled all across the U.S., Australia, Singapore, Hong Kong, Malaysia, Europe, Middle East, and African countries as a business and technology delegate in global forums and symposiums.

He is currently engaged in managing a wide range of technical and business responsibilities, including product management, marketing, evangelism, technical enablement, and global alliances and channel management.

He is distinguished speaker, author, and mentor in the area of business and technology. He has published several papers in journals and regularly writes blogs on the emerging technologies.

Verma is a postgraduate in management from Jamnalal Institute of Management Studies (JBIMS) in Mumbai, India, and has a Master of Science in Systems Management from Notre Dame de Namur University (NDNU) in Belmont, California. He is an adjunct faculty and advisor at the University of California, Berkeley, and University of California, Santa Cruz–Silicon Valley Extension, and offers lectures and thought leadership in the field of Cloud and Big Data.

Rodney Heisterberg serves as Professor in the School of Business and Management at Notre Dame de Namur University. He teaches courses on the application of information technology (IT) for enabling strategic management decision making in virtual enterprises for the Master of Business Administration and Master of Science in Systems Management degree programs. He applies the learnings of those principles and practices as Managing Partner of Rod Heisterberg Associates for clients who are IT users and vendors.

Dr. Heisterberg has over 25 years of experience in the field of IT. He holds BS, MS, and Ph.D. degrees from Purdue University, studying industrial engineering, computer science, and business administration. He has worked and consulted for numerous Global 500 companies, including British Aerospace, Eli Lilly, Ford, General Motors, Lockheed Martin, Mitsubishi, Procter & Gamble, Sunbeam, South African Breweries, and US Steel, as well as the U.S. Department of Defense at the Pentagon. Career highlights include serving as Program Director for a personal computer industry initiative sponsored by the U.S. Department of State to establish a PC manufacturing industrial base for economic development of the government of Iraq.

He was Director of Information Technology Management Consulting for Gartner in San Jose, where he performed technology product forecasting and led engagements for eBusiness transformation strategy and applications architecture development. His responsibilities focused on strategic planning for collaborative commerce, including formation, implementation, and operation of businesses as virtual enterprises.

This role leveraged his decade of experiences as a virtual enterprise architect for Lockheed Martin. This provided the credentials for him to be appointed as U.S. industry advisor to NATO, where he continued to work as virtual enterprise architect for a collaborative ecosystem of multinational government-industry programs. He is known as an international thought leader based on his early work in cloud computing serving as the co-chair of the joint government-industry group that authored the first U.S. standard for providing content management applications software-as-a-service.

Dr. Heisterberg is active in the travel industry as a destination and event marketing professional. He conducts research and develops products for delivering visitor experience management solutions, including social media and mobile technology featuring marketing apps integrated with streaming video. He serves the Destination Marketing Association International on the Technology Committee, where he is leading initiatives for integration of cloud computing with social, mobile, and video applications to produce big data analytics solutions for destinational ecosystem competiveness, as well as past chair of the Student Educator Advisory Council.

He is distinguished as an entrepreneur with active business and technology endeavors spanning the past three decades serving in the role of Chief Technology Officer. He performed market research and managed advisory programs that focused on collaborative commerce applications for building Internet communities using Web 2.0-enabling technologies incorporating cloud computing, social media, and mobile marketing technologies. He continues to be active as the graduate student faculty advisor at NDNU for mentoring prospective start-ups. In this role, he has also conducted workshops on developing business plans and investor presentations for undergraduate and graduate student entrepreneurs, as well as alumni start-ups.

As an internationally recognized speaker and writer, Dr. Heisterberg authored the collaborative commerce chapter of John Wiley & Sons' award winning *Internet Encyclopedia* in 2003. He contributed a chapter featuring interactive travel marketing solutions for *The Handbook for Technology Management* that was published by Wiley in 2010. His latest book, titled *Creating Business Agility: How Convergence of Cloud, Social, Mobile, Video, and Big Data Enables Competitive Advantage*, published by Wiley in 2014, provides a business case and game plan for integrating technology to build a smarter, more customer-centric digital business for a successful business ecosystem. The focus is on Business Agility Readiness (BAR) in terms of the five major developments transforming the IT environment. It describes how BAR is achieved by utilizing data-driven platforms enabling reengineered decision-making processes, which leverage digital relationships with a social business model to drive innovation and collaboration.

Interested in employing BAR strategies for implementing Systems of Engagement to sustain a competitive advantage for your digital business? Get started with the *Ecosystem Hub Roadmap for Virtual Enterprise Integration* so you can "raise the BAR" for business ecosystem leadership. To receive a copy email Rod@RodHeisterberg.com.

Acknowledgments

First, I acknowledge and thank my wife, Kavita, who seeded an idea of writing a book and kept energizing me with this noble thought. She was my buddy who always listened to my thoughts and gave me her honest and critical feedback on all aspects of this book. I thank my professor and co-author, Dr. Rod Heisterberg, who nurtured my ideas and moderated my plans in the most articulate and structured manner and finally wrote this book together.

I have to thank M. R. Rangaswami, founder of Sandhill group, who agreed to write the Foreword for this book. He brings enormous values to the book with his solid experience in the field of emerging technologies and its relevance to the business. I thank Jnan dash who has been advisors to many organizations such as Sonata Software, Solix Technologies, and now MongoDB, after spending long career with IBM and Oracle as senior executive. I appreciate his insights in the book that would be very relevant. I appreciate and thank Jeetu Patel, CTO and General Manger of EMC and now Syncplicity (sub-sidiary of EMC), for his thoughts and insights that surely enhances the value of this book. I appreciate Ramasubramanian Vaidyanathasw-amy, Senior Practice Director, Business Intelligence and Analytics at Wipro, for his invaluable contribution on Big Data processing and analytics. I thank my old-time friend Kalpesh Desai, who worked as COO at 3i Infotech and successfully founded crossroad, which got acquired by 3i Infotech, and now he established yet another successful venture, Agile Financial Technologies. His insights in the book truly reflect real-life illustrations and experiences. It will not be fair if I do not thank my friends Amit Srivastava, Solution Delivery Manger at NEC, and Devesh Srivastava, Android Architect at TCS, who con-tributed with their real-life industry experiences. I also thank and admire my friend Pankaj Jha, Architect at Brocade, who has many patents that were awarded with gold medals. We are privileged to have his insights in the book, which will surely add great values. I must thank Avanish Sahai, who is an industry veteran as VP of Salesforce.com for his immaculate thinking toward technology-led industry transformation. I have to also thank my business partners at Oracle, namely, Shashi Upadhyay, Founder and CEO of Lattice Engine, and Harbinder Khera, Founder and CEO of Mind Matrix, who have shared their relevant insights in the book.

I thank my ex-colleague and friend Markus Zirn, VP at Splunk, for his thoughts and insights. Last but not least I have to thank my colleagues at Oracle, who supported me directly by contributing their insights, namely, Javier Cabrerizo, VP, Big Data, Business Development; Christopher Sowa, VP, industry strategy and Insights; and Naeem Zafar, VP Mobility solutions. Their insights would definitely augment the theme and value of the book.

Also, I acknowledge and thank all faculty and staff at Notre Dame de Namur University, who directly and indirectly helped me to accomplish this milestone and I gratefully thank them for their support.

—Alakh Verma
San Jose, California

It takes a global village to write a twenty-first-century business technology book—and *Creating Business Agility* is no exception.

It all starts with the love of a good woman, my wife, Claire, that keeps me going. Then it builds on a foundation of intellectual curiosity from my father and mother and there is also the strong work ethic from both the Heisterberg and Karnosky clans. I especially want to recognize Denis Karnosky, who was my role model growing up and I find myself still growing with his inspiration. And of all my friends, the guy I go to for encouragement and advice due to his business savvy is my buddy for over fifty years, Dave Kossuth.

Colleagues with whom I have collaborated to develop, test, refine my ideas expressed in this book start with my mentors. First there was Dr. Ruddell Reed, the world-renowned Professor of Industrial Engineering, who served as the chair of my graduate committee for interdisciplinary programs at Purdue University. Next, Robert S. Kidwell, an information management pioneer, taught me how to have my head in the Cloud before the Cloud was cool. Then came Tom Hoobyar, an entrepreneur who challenged me to start sharing my ideas by writing for a business management audience. And most recently Dean Lane, who was my boss at Gartner, where I learned the principles and practices of information technology management consulting. He is also a contributor providing his CIO insights.

Correspondingly, in order to reinforce our strategic theme of CMO-CIO alignment, CMO insights are contributed by my longtime friend Ross Halleck, who is highly regarded in the world of digital marketing and is also founder of Halleck Vineyard, making the best Pinot Noir in Sonoma County and maybe the world. My new friends are also seasoned tech-savvy marketers, Blake Yeaman shows why he is regarded as a top marketing technology management consultant, and Ryan Bifulco, founder of Sensei Project, with his team of Sherry Heyl, Christopher Curley, and Lucie Hys demonstrate their expertise as a leader in social media marketing for travel and lifestyle brands.

Digital Business insights are contributed by Jon Stevenson, CEO of Mobotory, to provide an illustrative example of how mobility drives agility for competitive advantage in the global event management marketplace. The book features the "Selling Sonoma County Wine Country" story contributed by Ken Fischang, CEO of SCT, and his marketing team, led by CMO Tim Zahner and Jill Vanden Heuvel with Ariane Hiltebrand and Beth Snow, and was coordinated by Nicole Bradin. This case study provides insights as to how a digital business can make the Business Agility Readiness Roadmap work at the virtual enterprise level for the Sneakaway scenario within the SCT business ecosystem. Ryan George, CEO of Simpleview, contributes SCT Ecosystem Hub story elements that demonstrate best practices for how to build a Social CRM Partner Extranet for the Sneakaway campaign as an integrated system of customer engagement that delivers a sustainable competitive advantage. Business Ecosystem insights are contributed by Brad Snyder, General Manager, Kauai Marriott Resort and Beach Club, and coordinated by Sherri Holcomb, who highlight how they built their business ecosystem strategy based on a customer-centric business model.

I want to acknowledge all of the wonderful faculty and staff at Notre Dame de Namur University and particularly in the School of Business and Management that have made my teaching and research so enjoyable. It is important to note the generous intellectual support and encouragement that I have received from Dr. Barbara Caulley, former Dean, and Dr. Craig Brewer, current Dean, over the past several years while researching and writing this book. I especially recognize my colleague working in the Master of Science in Systems Management (MSSM) program: Dr. James Fogal is a brilliant professor who is also an outstanding teacher. I learn new things from him all the time. Also I would be remiss not to give a big thanks to Michele Yoskovich and Anne Gillan, our graduate student advisors, for the assistance they have provided in putting this book together.

I have been fortunate to have taught many wonderful students in the Master of Business Administration and MSSM programs, and I delight in learning something new from them. Several of my students have truly been exceptional. Jon Stevenson was one of the first students to receive a Master of e-Business Management and turned his thesis into a business plan to launch his start-up with venture capital funding. Of course by now you are familiar with Alakh Verma, a MSSM graduate. I am proud to count him as a colleague, as well as co-author. The third remarkable student is Delbar Yousefi, who demonstrated such an incredible thirst for knowledge that her life-long learning initiatives have become the target of our digital publishing project—to develop a Cloud-based product for a *Creating Business Agility* personal learning environment.

There are two other colleagues who deserve recognition for their contributions to the ideas in this book. Jamshid Lal was a consultant whom I mentored during my time at Gartner and I learned much from him concerning the use of the Balanced Scorecard of business case analysis of IT strategies. Likewise, Eric Lacy was instrumental in helping me develop the Business Agility Readiness Roadmap gap analysis models.

Finally, I want to acknowledge our John Wiley & Sons team for their patience and support in the publication of this book. We gratefully thank Jesse Wiley as our Executive Sponsor for green lighting this book project, and Sheck Cho, our Executive Editor, who deftly guided us along the path for this arduous yet exciting journey. We greatly appreciate the diligent and thoughtful collaboration with Jennifer MacDonald and Helen Cho as developmental editors and Chris Gage as our production editor. And now we are looking forward to working with Andrew Wheeler as Marketing Manager for Professional Development to spread the word about *Creating Business Agility*—Full Speed Ahead!!!

—Rodney Heisterberg
Mountain View, California

Index